GIS Methodologies for Developing Conservation Strategies

Biology and Resource Management Series
Michael J. Balick, Anthony B. Anderson, and Kent H. Redford, Editors

Biology and Resource Management Series

Edited by Michael J. Balick, Anthony B. Anderson, and Kent H. Redford

Alternatives to Deforestation: Steps Toward Sustainable Use of the Amazon Rain Forest,
  edited by Anthony B. Anderson

Useful Palms of the World: A Synoptic Bibliography,
  compiled and edited by Michael J. Balick and Hans T. Beck

The Subsidy from Nature: Palm Forests, Peasantry, and Development on an Amazon Frontier,
  by Anthony B. Anderson, Peter H. May, and Michael J. Balick

Contested Frontiers in Amazonia,
  by Marianne Schmink and Charles H. Wood

Conservation of Neotropical Forests: Working from Traditional Resource Use,
  edited by Kent H. Redford and Christine Padoch

The African Leopard: Ecology and Behavior of a Solitary Felid,
  by Theodore N. Bailey

Footprints of the Forest: Ka'apor Ethnobotany—the Historical Ecology of Plant Utilization by an Amazonian People,
  by William Balée

Medicinal Resources of the Tropical Forest: Biodiversity and Its Importance to Human Health,
  edited by Michael J. Balick, Elaine Elisabetsky, and Sarah A. Laird

The Catfish Connection: Ecology, Migration, and Conservation of Amazon Predators,
  Ronaldo Barthem and Michael Goulding

So Fruitful a Fish: Ecology, Conservation, and Aquaculture of the Amazon's Tambaqui,
  Carlos Araujo-Lima and Michael Goulding

GIS Methodologies
for Developing
Conservation Strategies

TROPICAL FOREST RECOVERY AND
WILDLIFE MANAGEMENT
IN COSTA RICA

Basil G. Savitsky and Thomas E. Lacher Jr., Editors

COLUMBIA UNIVERSITY PRESS
New York

Columbia University Press
Publishers Since 1893
New York   Chichester, West Sussex

Copyright © 1998 by Columbia University Press

Library of Congress Cataloging-in-Publication Data

GIS methodologies for developing conservation strategies : tropical
        forest recovery and wildlife management in Costa Rica   /   Basil G.
        Savitsky and Thomas E. Lacher Jr., editors.
            p.   cm.   —   (Biology and resource management
        series)
        Includes bibliographical references and index.
        ISBN 0–231–10026–4 (cloth   :   alk. paper)
            1. Wildlife conservation—Costa Rica—Remote sensing.   2. Forest
conservation—Costa Rica—Remote sensing.   3. Geographic information
systems—Costa Rica.   4. Digital mapping.   I. Savitsky, Basil G.
II. Lacher Jr., Thomas E.   III. Series.
QH77.C8G57   1998
333.95' 16'097286—dc21   97–38069

c 10 9 8 7 6 5 4 3 2 1

For
Ava, Lily, and Isabella
and
Iara and Laís

Contents

Foreword

James D. Nations

We shall not cease from exploration
And the end of all our exploring
Will be to arrive where we started
And know the place for the first time.

— T. S. Eliot, "Little Gidding" (1942)

Every sixteen days a Landsat satellite passes silently over the tropical landscape of Costa Rica, recording digital data on the rain forests, savannas, rivers, lakes, and mountains that lie 918 kilometers below. The recorded data are a worthless collection of zeros and ones until the scientific mind manipulates them and transforms them into images that have meaning for the future of human beings and the thousands of species that live in the habitats the images depict.

The analysis of remotely sensed images has come a long way from the biplane flights of World War I pilots, who brought back film that inadvertently showed traces of Roman-era ruins in British wheat fields. Seen from the air, the small rises and dips that farmers stepped across could be recognized as the foundations and walls of centuries-old Roman buildings. In the tropics today we find it easier to locate the ruins of ancient civilizations from hundreds of kilometers in space than from a hundred meters through the dense, green screen of the rain forest itself.

Combined with the seeming wizardry of digital mapping technologies, the applications of remote sensing have become enormous: mapping indigenous territories to monitor illegal encroachment, tracing national park boundaries across international boundaries and through unmarked wilderness, identifying wildlife habitat in regions where humans have no easy access, and so forth. The applications of digital images and digital mapping take us out of the realm of guesswork and into the world of the technological future. We are limited only by our own creativity.

In this volume editors Basil G. Savitsky and Thomas E. Lacher Jr. bring us new and novel applications for this future, including a gap analysis technique that allows researchers to superimpose the distribution of wildlife species on the boundaries of protected areas. This technique can show us where new work should be focused—where conservation is working and where it is not. In a series of case studies from Costa Rica, the authors point us toward new applications of digital mapping for the conservation of natural habitats and our work toward sustainable development.

These techniques and the visual images they create are becoming powerful tools in the hands of development specialists, financial decision-makers, and political leaders. We can no longer claim that we do not have the information we need to make sound decisions about the natural environment. The tools are ours, the data are real, and the future is literally in our hands.

James D. Nations, Ph.D.
Conservation International
Washington, D.C.

Preface

THIS book, and the research it is based upon, is the result of what makes most science happen today. An idea circulated among a network of individual acquaintances caught fire and stimulated the development of a proposal that was ultimately funded, leading to an outcome much larger and far-reaching than any one participant could have expected or produced. The seed was planted when then Ph.D. candidate Savitsky walked into the office of Clemson University faculty member (and director of the Archbold Tropical Research Center) Lacher and suggested doing a dissertation research project that would combine his interest in geographic information systems (GIS) and Central America. At the time, Lacher had worked mostly in the Caribbean and Brazil but knew Christopher Vaughan of the Universidad Nacional (UNA) from several conferences and workshops. We contacted Chris, who put us in touch with Jorge Fallas, and thus began the discussions of research ideas that, over time, developed into our research proposal and eventually this book.

The first concrete discussions occurred when Savitsky went to Costa Rica and met with the faculty and staff at UNA. The idea of a modified gap analysis began to develop about this time; the challenge was to develop an approach that had been applied with success in the United States but had yet to be utilized in a more data-poor country. The original idea was to do a regional project that would contrast countries with different levels of data availability, but this was soon discounted owing to logistical difficulties. We developed a proposal for Costa Rica together with our colleagues at UNA and were funded by the United States Agency for International Development (USAID) in a competitive grants competition.

Once we decided to focus on Costa Rica, we began to refine the approach. During a subsequent visit to Costa Rica by Savitsky, Lacher, and Wesley Burnett, we developed the idea of a three-sided decision matrix that would provide for multiple alternative management strategies for any given gap analysis. This seemed a particularly fruitful approach for developing countries with less data on wildlife distributions.

As we began to collect data for the project and to discuss our preliminary findings with colleagues, we were pleased with both the interest expressed and the suggestions we began to receive. One colleague, Kent Redford of the Nature Conservancy, suggested we contact Columbia University Press since our research seemed to be appropriate for several new series of books on the tropics that CUP had begun. We submitted a proposal to Ed Lugenbeel, which was accepted, and we have received excellent support from him, Alissa Bader, and Roy Thomas throughout the development of the manuscript.

A substantial proportion of the material in this volume is derived from Savitsky's Ph.D. dissertation, but much additional information has been added to round out and expand it. Chapter 14 ("Error and the Gap Analysis Model") is the result of an undergraduate honors research project by Clemson University student Jennifer Morgan. Chapter 6 ("GPS") was developed by Jeffery Allen to incorporate his experience in GPS training in Costa Rica. Christopher Vaughan, Jorge Fallas, and Michael McCoy have contributed their knowledge of Costa Rica to provide sufficient background for the reader. Finally, the section of five papers on the use of GIS in Costa Rica has been included to show the diversity of approaches and applications of GIS in the tropics.

The book is divided into four distinctly different parts. Part one provides an overview of the spatial nature of conservation and management activities and the current status of conservation mapping in Costa Rica. Part two offers a review of the basic principles behind GIS, the Global Positioning System (GPS), and image analysis. This section places a special emphasis on the application of these technologies in developing tropical countries. Part three presents a set of five research projects from Costa Rica that used digital mapping technologies at a variety of scales and for a variety of conservation and management purposes. The scales vary from local (La Selva Biological Station) to regional (the Paseo Pantera project), and activities include single-species management plans, ecosystem conservation, and the management of watersheds. The final section, part four, presents the results of the Costa Rican gap analysis project. The layout of the book will allow even readers with no previous exposure to digital mapping technologies to gain a sufficient understanding of the techniques to be able to follow the research results.

We have many people we wish to acknowledge. It is impossible to conduct international research without colleagues in-country, and in our case we were fortunate to have the strong support of professors Jorge Fallas and Christopher

Vaughan at the Programa Regional en Manejo de Vida Silvestre para Mesoamerica y el Caribe (PRMVS), Universidad Nacional, Heredia. We wish to thank the staff of Professor Fallas's Laboratorio de Teledetección y Sistemas de Información Geográfica in Costa Rica for their assistance throughout the project, and other staff of the PRMVS which assisted with various aspects of the research.

We acknowledge the work of David Tarbox on this project; he could well be listed as an author for his work on data entry and analysis and for the production of many of the maps. We also thank Craig Campbell and Jeannine Maldonado for data entry and Donald Van Blaricom for technical guidance in ARC/INFO. Dr. Hoke Hill provided valuable advice concerning statistics, and Robert Sandev was instrumental in creating several of the figures.

We thank all the staff of the Strom Thurmond Institute and the Archbold Tropical Research Center who contributed to this project while both of us were at Clemson University. In addition to writing a chapter for the book, Jeffery Allen provided encouragement and support throughout the project. Patrick Harris helped with data transfers and provided software support. Jean Martin provided secretarial support and helped with presentation materials, and Diane Moore and Janice Rogers kept track of finances and purchasing. Martha Morris and Kathy Skinner assisted with word processing on earlier drafts.

Basil Savitsky especially thanks Dr. Robert H. Becker for his mentorship while completing his Ph.D., for backing all of his work, and for cochairing his doctoral committee; his coeditor and cochair (Thomas E. Lacher Jr.) and the rest of his committee (Dr. G. Wesley Burnett, Dr. Kerry R. Brooks, and Dr. James B. London) for their support and guidance; and Jackie, Ava, and Lily Savitsky for their help in the preparation of his dissertation, much of which came to be included in his chapters in this volume.

This research was supported under Grant No. HRN-5600-G-002008-00, Program in Science and Technology Cooperation, Office of the Science Advisor, United States Agency for International Development.

Basil G. Savitsky
Worcester, Massachusetts

Thomas E. Lacher Jr.
College Station, Texas

Abbreviations

ACCVC	Area de Conservación Cordillera Volcanica Central (Central Volcanic Cordillera Conservation Area)
AVHRR	Advanced Very High Resolution Radiometer
CAMS	Calibrated Airborne Multispectral Scanner
CATIE	Centro Agronómico Tropical deInvestigación y Ensenanza
CIES	Council for International Exchange of Scholars
DBMS	Database Management Systems
ECODES	National Conservation Strategy for Sustainable Development
EOS	Earth Observing System
EOSAT	Earth Observation Satellite Company
EROS	Earth Resources Observation System Data Center

FUNDECOR	Fundación para el Desarrollo de la Cordillera Volcanica Central (Foundation for the Development of the Central Cordillera)
GIS	Geographic Information System(s)
GPS	Global Positioning System
IUCN	International Union for Conservation of Nature and Natural Resources (*aka* World Conservation Union)
IDA	Instituto de Desarrollo Agrario (Institute of Agrarian Reform)
IGN	Instituto Geográfico Nacional de Costa Rica (National Geographic Institute of Costa Rica)
IICA	Instituto Interamericano de Ciencias Agrícolas
INBIO	Instituto Nacional de Biodiversidad (National Institute of Biodiversity)
MIRENEM	Ministerio de Recursos Naturales, Energía, y Minas (Ministry of Natural Resources, Energy, and Mines)
MNCR	Museo Nacional de Costa Rica (National Museum of Costa Rica)
MODIS	Moderate-Resolution Imaging Spectrometer
MSS	Landsat Multispectral Scanner
NASA	National Aeronautics and Space Administration
NPS	National Parks Service of Costa Rica
NAVSTAR	Navigation Satellite Timing and Ranging
NOAA	National Oceanic and Atmospheric Administration
NSCA	National System of Conservation Areas
NSLRSDA	National Satellite Land Remote Sensing Data Archive

OTS	Organization for Tropical Studies
PRMVS	Programa Regional en Manejo de Vida Silvestre para Mesoamerica y el Caribe (Regional Wildlife Management Program for Mesoamerica and the Caribbean)
RENARM	Regional Environmental and Natural Resources Management Project
SPOT	Satellite pour l'Observation de la Terre
TIGER	Topologically Integrated Geographic Encoding and Referencing system
TIMS	Thermal Infrared Multispectral Scanner
TM	Landsat Thematic Mapper
UNA	Universidad Nacional
UNEP	United Nations Environment Programme
UNFAO	United Nations Food and Agricultural Organization
USAID	United States Agency for International Development
USGAU	United States Government and Affiliate Users
WRI	World Resources Institute
WWF	World Wildlife Fund

GIS Methodologies
for Developing
Conservation Strategies

PART ONE

Overview

1

The Spatial Nature of Conservation and Development

Thomas E. Lacher Jr.

ABOUT 2,200 years ago a scholarly librarian in charge of the prestigious collections of the museum at Alexandria conducted an elegant exercise in logic and experimentation. Using seemingly unrelated bits of information such as the observation of the penetration of sunlight into a well in the city of Syene, the speed of a camel caravan, and the shadow cast by an obelisk in Alexandria, Eratosthenes calculated a remarkably accurate estimate of the circumference of the earth (Wilford 1981). This was a profound observation; the limits of a planet as yet unexplored had been defined. As the human population of Earth continues to grow, these limits become increasingly more constraining. How we use and conserve space becomes more important every day.

The making of maps was one of the earliest of human activities. The Chinese were making accurate maps with legends in the second century B.C., and clay maps with cardinal directions present (that is, east—toward the rising sun— appeared at the top of the maps) have been recovered in Iraq which date to 2300 B.C. These maps might have been used to map and tax real estate. The Egyptians produced maps of gold mines, complete with roads. The spatial representation of development is an ancient craft, and contemporary research on conservation and development is heavily reliant upon spatial analyses.

Virtually all aspects of land use revolve around issues of area and geometry. Agriculture, forestry, urban and regional planning, and the design of parks and protected areas all address the size of the area under consideration as well as its shape and location relative to other elements on the landscape. Agriculturists deal with the area under cultivation, the placement of fields in relation to wind breaks and shelter belts, the location and timing of crop rotations, and the proximity of areas of crop production to roads and distribution centers. Foresters must manage harvests so that economically viable blocks of trees will be available for cultivation under cycles of long-term rotation. They must also address the management of no-cut zones along streams, rivers, and roads, and must increasingly integrate protected reserves into a mosaic of mixed-age stands.

Much of the tone of contemporary ecology was set by the late Robert MacArthur in his book *Geographical Ecology* (MacArthur 1972), and he had an equally great influence on the development of conservation biology through his work on island biogeography (MacArthur and Wilson 1967). The size and shape of protected areas is a primary focus of conservation biology, and the principles of island biogeography have been incorporated into the design of parks and reserves (Diamond 1975; Harris 1984; Shafer 1991). The relationship of protected areas to one another is paramount in the design of wildlife corridors (Noss and Harris 1986; Fahrig and Merriam 1985). The space needs of species of concern are an integral component of the development of a population viability analysis (Soulé 1987; Boyce 1992). The field of metapopulation dynamics addresses systems of local populations connected by flows of dispersing individuals and is essentially a geometric tool (Hanski and Gilpin 1991). The metapopulation paradigm is well suited to a number of different analyses used in the study of fragmented ecosystems, such as source-sink metapopulations (Pulliam 1988; Dunning et al. 1995), patchy populations, and non-equilibrial populations (figure 1.1). Finally, the study of the distributions of species over large geographic areas, facilitated by geographic information systems (GIS) and mapping software, has become a promising new area of research (Rapoport 1982; Brown 1995).

The complex geometry of land use patterns has necessitated the development of new tools for spatial analysis. The introduction of powerful computer software for the analysis of spatial patterns and processes such as GIS and image analysis has allowed for major advances in the study and modeling of the dynamics of land use (Jensen 1995; Goodchild, Parks, and Steyaert 1993). Abstract mathematical procedures such as fractal geometry have become increasingly common in the analysis of landscapes (Lam and DeCola 1993).

Concurrent with developments in quantitative geography, ecology has progressed through a hierarchy of complexity of study, from the natural history of individual organisms, through population and community ecology, to systems ecology. The focus of ecological research in the 1990s has been on landscape-level processes. Part of the reason is the realization that one of the goals of applied ecology is conservation, and this cannot be achieved without the explicit recognition of the primacy of spatial relations in both conservation and development.

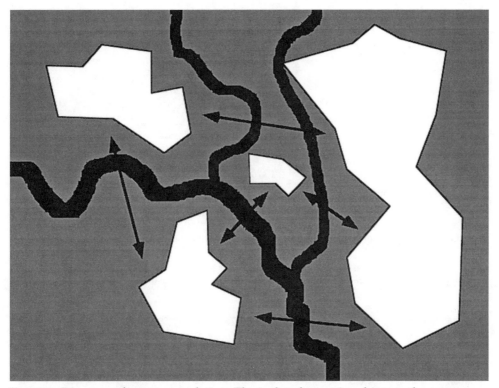

FIG. 1.1 Diagram of a metapopulation. The isolated areas in white are those occupied by individuals of the species in question. The metapopulation is connected to varying degrees by migration (arrows). Some subpopulations will function as sources (births exceeding deaths), while others will function as sinks (deaths exceeding births). The fate of the population as a whole depends upon the structure and dynamics of the metapopulation.

Humans, Economy, Ecology, and the Need to Consider Resource Management in Land Use Planning

Humans rely on the landscape for most of their economic activities. These activities include mining, agriculture, forestry, livestock, and urbanization. The extent of the surface of the planet under some form of development is substantial (table 1.1). Land use categories are cropland, rangeland, and forests or woodland. The other major land use category, mining, is not included. Mining is of great economic importance, but the amount of land altered by mining activities is generally very small, amounting to only about 0.25 percent of the land area in the United States, for example (Hodges 1995). Estimates for the period 1989–1991 are that 37 percent of the total land area of the planet is either in cropland or permanent pasture (WRI 1994). Europe is the most extensively altered geographi-

TABLE 1.1 *Land Use Activities by Region for 1983, in Millions of Hectares (modified from Wolf 1986)*

Region	Cropland	Rangeland	Forests and Woodland
North America	236	265	591
Central America / South America	175	550	999
Europe / Soviet Union[a]	373	459	1,075
Africa	183	778	688
Oceania	47	459	116
Asia / Mideast	456	645	561
TOTAL	1,470	3,156	4,030

[a] Includes all of the former Soviet Union.

TABLE 1.2 *Percents of Total Areas Under Various Land Use Activities*

Country	Total Area	% Domesticated	Crops	% Crops	Pasture	% Pasture	Forest	% Forest
Developed countries								
United States	916,660	47	187,776	20	239,172	26	287,400	31
Canada	922,097	8	45,947	5	28,100	3	359,000	39
Germany	34,931	50	12,002	34	5,329	15	10,403	30
France	55,010	56	19,187	35	11,381	21	14,817	27
United Kingdom	24,160	74	6,665	28	11,186	46	2,391	10
Japan	37,652	14	4,595	12	647	2	25,105	67
Australia	764,444	61	48,267	6	417,264	55	106,000	14
AVERAGE[a]		44		20		24		31
Developing Countries								
Ivory Coast	31,800	52	3,680	12	13,000	41	7,330	23
Zaire	226,760	10	7,863	3	15,000	7	174,310	77
Malaysia	32,855	15	4,880	15	27	0	19,361	59
Thailand	51,089	47	23,042	45	830	2	14,113	28
Indonesia	181,157	19	21,967	12	11,800	7	109,800	61
Colombia	103,870	44	5,410	5	40,400	39	50,300	48
Brazil	845,651	29	59,933	7	184,200	22	493,030	58
AVERAGE[a]		31		14		17		51

[a] Averages are the unweighted means of the column values (WRI 1994).

cal region, with 47 percent of the land under some form of domestication; North America and Central America together are the least disturbed at 30 percent, largely because of Canada (WRI 1994).

There is a sharp contrast between developed countries and developing countries in the relative dependence on intensive land use. A comparison of seven different developed and developing countries demonstrates some counterintuitive results (table 1.2). The developed countries appear to have much larger percentages of land under some form of domestic use and substantially lower percentages of forest cover, as compared to the seven selected developing coun-

TABLE 1.3 *Percent Change in Land Use Activities Between 1979–1981 and 1989–1991 (WRI 1994)*

| | % Change | | |
Country	Crops	Pasture	Forest
Developed countries			
United States	−1.5	0.7	−2.5
Canada	0.5	0.9	5.4
Germany	−4.2	−11.1	1.2
France	1.5	−11.4	1.6
United Kingdom	−4.3	−2.3	13.8
Japan	5.8	11.8	−0.1
Australia	10.2	−4.8	−0.2
Developing countries			
Ivory Coast	19.0	0.0	−25.8
Zaire	3.5	0.0	−1.9
Malaysia	1.5	0.0	−8.8
Thailand	25.5	29.7	−14.3
Indonesia	12.3	−1.5	−6.6
Colombia	4.1	5.8	−5.6
Brazil	23.1	7.5	−4.9

tries. Static figures can be misleading, however, because the dynamic trends in land use change are hidden.

A comparison of the percent change in land use practices over a ten-year period is more revealing (table 1.3). In general, the amount of cropland and pasture in the developed countries has declined or remained stable, and forested areas have remained constant or increased. The amount of land dedicated to cultivation has increased dramatically in developing countries, primarily at the costs of forests and woodlands. In addition, many tropical countries rely heavily on agricultural activities, and development is often haphazard or uncontrolled (figure 1.2).

There is a double concern in the developing world. The amount of land being converted to natural resources exploitation and other economic activities is on the increase, and there is little evidence of land use planning. The amount of area that is suitable for conservation is on the decline as a result of expanding development. Resource managers and land use planners need to realize that space is a finite resource; the ultimate balance between conservation and development must take into consideration not just the area under development but also the spatial relationships between developed and protected zones. Regional and national initiatives which develop computer-based mapping capabilities that can present current patterns of land use and model the impacts of future changes will be imperative in order to avoid conflicts and optimize the economic benefits of resource utilization at the minimal environmental cost. Sustainable development and the use of GIS are interwoven.

FIG. 1.2 Aerial view of heavily fragmented rain forest along the Pacific slope of the Talamanca Mountains in Costa Rica.

Technology and the Interface Between Science and Politics

The rapid development of major technological advances has taken place almost exclusively in the developed world. Computers, satellite technology, the Global Positioning System (GPS), and sophisticated software for spatial analyses and visualization have all been developed in the Northern Hemisphere, and many have been the result of research and development in the defense industries. The transfer of these technologies to the developing world has been slow. This advanced technology and the science that it supports therefore has a political tone; technology is power and the control of this technology is in the hands of few. It is important to disengage scientific research that addresses conservation and sustainable development from international politics. This is difficult when international aid programs are politicized, an understandable consequence of furnishing aid to political allies.

Academic exchanges can assist in facilitating this transfer. The United States has a history of openly sharing the intellectual capabilities of its professoriat with the rest of the world. The Council for International Exchange of Scholars (CIES), sponsor of the Fulbright Scholars Program, has effectively showcased the best of American academia throughout the world for decades. Since 1946 the program has sponsored the teaching and research of over 31,000 Americans overseas

(CIES 1995). Cooperative endeavors sponsored by the United States Agency for International Development (USAID), the U.S. Fish and Wildlife Service, and the U.S. Environmental Protection Agency (USEPA) have enhanced environmental research capabilities in developing nations and have benefited the careers of many North American scientists by exposing them to new cultures and novel approaches to resolving problems. United States federal agencies have also helped to finance the development of new graduate programs in conservation and wildlife management in Latin America (Lacher et al. 1991; Vaughan and McCoy 1995). The participants from both sides of these exchanges attest to their mutual benefit.

Academic research scientists are predisposed to being good ambassadors because they are well educated and have the tradition of teaching and sharing information. This mind-set should be the rule rather than the exception, especially when dealing with developing countries, because the so-called First World has much to gain by preventing environmental crises in the Southern Hemisphere. International projects which entail the collaboration of university researchers with government scientists and international financial support are among the most successful projects involving technology transfer because the participants tend to be driven by intellectual curiosity and a quest for knowledge. This results in the more open exchange of ideas and concerns and generates more trust. Projects that call for the collaboration between academia and government are important and are a valuable component of U.S. foreign policy.

Science and Decision Making and the Special Problems of Tropical Nations

Several decades ago science was related to decision making only through the application of the scientific method to the testing of specific hypotheses. Now most congressmen have science advisers and the White House has an Office of Science and Technology Policy, primarily to provide guidance to the executive branch on the political implications of scientific discoveries and technological advances. Science has assumed an ever more important role in decision making. This is true for development, environmental protection, human health care, social programs, and conservation. Science continues to play an ever-increasing role in the courtroom, so that today, for example, scientific testimony on DNA evidence can sway the decision of a jury. Risk assessment is an integral component of the new environmental decision-making paradigm and is heavily dependent upon the input of scientific information of high quality (USEPA 1992).

There is a new twist on science. Science influences policy, and access to scientific information is essential to the ability of politicians to make wise policy decisions. Restricting the access of developing countries to science and technology can be counterproductive to the United States over the long term because poor political decisions made in the so-called Third World can develop into expensive international crises. Much of the criticism levied at the World Bank over environmentally destructive development in the Brazilian state of Rondonia came not from environmental groups, but from U.S. senator Robert Kasten (R-Wis.) because of concern over the use of U.S. taxpayer's money for environmentally and economically unsustainable projects. This clear recognition of the high cost of environmental problems led to demands that the World Bank be more accountable to the wealthy nations that supply the bulk of the funding to the bank (Walsh 1986).

Problems like the poorly designed development scheme for Rondonia can be expected to arise again with development in the tropics. Countries like Brazil require environmental impact assessments prior to the initiation of internationally funded development projects. However, many tropical nations are at a special disadvantage when making policy decisions concerning land use practices. Most have restricted access to environmental technology, and many are poor and underdeveloped. Their ecosystems and landscapes are more poorly studied than any in the world. It has been estimated that tropical habitats might contain over 67 percent of the world's species (Raven 1988). Clearly, no one knows if this is true; however, the tropics without question harbor a very high proportion of the global biodiversity (Wilson 1988). This means that the land use decisions made in the tropics can have a per hectare impact on diversity of up to ten times a similar decision made in the North Temperate zone.

The long-term costs of environmental degradation are well recognized in the United States. The Comprehensive Environmental Response, Compensation, and Liability Act (Superfund) was originally passed in 1980 and created a $1.6 billion fund for the cleanup and remediation of hazardous waste sites. The 1986 Superfund Amendments and Reauthorization Act increased the scope of the legislation and allocated an additional $8.5 billion to the fund. The Office of Technology Assessment has estimated that there might be as many as ten thousand hazardous waste sites in the United States eligible for Superfund. The total cost to remediate the environmental damage could exceed $300 billion over the next fifty years (Miller 1990). A retrenchment of international support for the transfer of environmentally useful technologies to the developing world will be equally costly in long-term remediation. The cost to restore the degraded savannas, forests, and rivers of the tropics will likely be far greater than Superfund, and the transfer and application of digital mapping technologies can be useful in facilitating economic planning and the mitigation of environmental degradation.

The earth is a sphere, and the continents and waterways are complex polygons and vectors lain upon the surface. These polygons and vectors contain populations of species, and the presence of these species form ecosystems. The ecosystems generate energy fluxes and material cycles which result from the processes caused by the interactions of the species with themselves and the abiotic components of the landscape. The sum total of these processes across all landscapes is the biosphere. Each polygon on the surface of the earth therefore has both shape and function.

Human activities, whether to conserve or develop, alter not only the geometry of the earth but the functional processes as well. As the extent and magnitude of human activities increase, it becomes increasingly more important to monitor Earth's changing geometry. Twenty years ago this was not possible. Now the technology needed to monitor the spatial nature of conservation and development is accessible throughout the world. Our ability to integrate conservation and development on the landscape so that appropriate policy can be formed will be crucial for the protection of global biodiversity. This is especially true for the tropics.

This book presents a variety of case studies which apply digital mapping technology to conservation and development in Costa Rica. An important component of these case studies is the development of a visual policy-making paradigm that brings together very large amounts of digital data in maps that allow nontechnical policymakers to clearly and quickly perceive conservation and development options on the large scale. We believe that this digital mapping model for decision making can be successfully applied in other regions of the tropics.

References

Boyce, M. S. 1992. Population viability analysis. *Annual Review of Ecology and Systematics* 23: 481–506.

Brown, J. H. 1995. *Macroecology.* Chicago: University of Chicago Press.

Council for International Exchange of Scholars (CIES). 1995. *1996–1997 Fulbright scholar program: Grants for faculty and professionals.* Washington, D.C.: CIES.

Diamond, J. M. 1975. The island dilemma: Lessons of modern biogeographic studies for the design of natural preserves. *Biological Conservation* 7: 129–46.

Dunning, J. B. Jr., D. J. Stewart, B. J. Danielson, B. R. Noon, T, L, Root, R. H. Lamberson, and E. E. Stevens. 1995. Spatially explicit populations models: Current forms and future uses. *Ecological Applications* 5: 3–11.

Fahrig, L. and G. Merriam. 1985. Habitat patch connectivity and population survival. *Ecology* 66: 1762–68.

Goodchild, M. F., B. O. Parks, and L. T. Steyaert, eds. 1993. *Environmental modeling with GIS.* New York: Oxford University Press.

Hanski, I. and M. Gilpin. 1991. Metapopulation dynamics: Brief history and conceptual domain. *Biological Journal of the Linnean Society* 42: 3–16.

Harris, L. D. 1984. *The fragmented forest.* Chicago: University of Chicago Press.

Hodges, C. A. 1995. Mineral resources, environmental issues, and land use. *Science* 268: 1305–12.

Jensen, J. R. 1995 (2d ed.). *Introductory digital image processing: A remote sensing perspective.* Englewood Cliffs, N.J.: Prentice-Hall.

Lacher, T. E. Jr., G. A. B. da Fonseca, C. Valle, and A. M. P. B. da Fonseca. 1991. National and international cooperation in wildlife management and conservation at a Brazilian university. In M. A. Mares and D. J. Schmidly, eds., *Latin American mammalogy: History, biodiversity, and conservation,* 368–80. Norman: University of Oklahoma Press.

Lam, N. S. and L. DeCola. 1993. *Fractals in geography.* Englewood Cliffs, N.J.: PTR Prentice-Hall.

MacArthur, R. H. 1972. *Geographical ecology.* New York: Harper and Row.

MacArthur, R. H. and E. O. Wilson. 1967. *The theory of island biogeography.* Princeton: Princeton University Press.

Miller, G. T. Jr. 1990. *Resource conservation and management.* Belmont, Calif.: Wadsworth.

Noss, R. F. and L. D. Harris. 1986. Nodes, networks, and MUMs: Preserving diversity at all scales. *Environmental Management* 10: 299–309.

Pulliam, H. R. 1988. Sources, sinks, and population regulation. *American Naturalist* 132: 652–61.

Rapoport, E. H. 1982. *Areogeography: Geographical strategies of species.* Oxford: Pergamon.

Raven, P. H. 1988. Our diminishing tropical forests. In E. O. Wilson, ed., *Biodiversity,* 119–22. Washington, D.C.: National Academy Press.

Shafer, C. L. 1991. *Nature reserves: Island theory and conservation practice.* Washington, D.C.: Smithsonian Institution Press.

Soulé, M. E., ed. 1987. *Viable populations for conservation.* Cambridge: Cambridge University Press.

USEPA. 1992. *Framework for ecological risk assessment.* EPA/630/R-92/001. Washington, D.C.: Environmental Protection Agency.

Vaughan, C. and M. McCoy. 1995. Graduate training in wildlife ecology and conservation biology in Latin America. In J. A. Bissonette and P. R. Krausman, eds., *Integrating people and wildlife for a sustainable future: Proceedings of the first international wildlife management congress,* 147–51. Bethesda, Md.: The Wildlife Society.

Walsh, J. 1986. World Bank pressed on environmental reforms. *Science* 234: 813–15.

Wilford, J. N. 1981. *The mapmakers.* New York: Knopf.

Wilson, E. O. 1988. The current state of biological diversity. In E. O. Wilson, ed., *Biodiversity,* 3–18. Washington, D.C.: National Academy Press.

Wolf, E. C. 1986. Managing rangelands. In L. R. Brown, W. V. Chandler, C. Flavin, C. Pollock, S. Postel, L. Starke, and E. C. Wolf, eds., *State of the world—1986,* 62–77. New York: Norton.

World Resources Institute (WRI). 1994. *World Resources: 1994–1995.* New York: Oxford University Press.

2

Conservation Mapping in Costa Rica

Christopher Vaughan, Jorge Fallas, and Michael McCoy

Historical Perspective on Costa Rica

Costa Rica is one of Latin America's smallest countries (51,100 km^2), with a human population of about three million people (or fifty-seven people per square kilometer). Its Gross Domestic Product (GDP) is equivalent to U.S.$6.4 billion and its per capita income is $2,200. The industry sector contributes 26.1 percent, and the primary sector contributes 19.6 percent. By 1994 tourism, especially ecotourism, had become the primary source of foreign currency income, replacing the traditional three major products of coffee, bananas, and cattle meat. Much of this ecotourism has arrived to observe the country's biodiversity (Damon and Vaughan 1995).

Covering only 0.04 percent of the world's terrestrial area, Costa Rica has extremely high biodiversity, with an estimated 500,000 biotic species, or 4 percent, of the world's total (Jiménez 1995). This includes 208 mammal species, 850 bird species, 160 amphibian species, 200 reptile species, 130 freshwater fish species, and 225,000 insect species (Umaña and Brandon 1992). Over 95 percent of the biodiversity is thought to be protected in a world-class wildlands system. One can travel in 100 kilometers from a mangrove estuary, through a tropical rain forest, a montane cloud forest and a *páramo* (subalpine scrub). The extreme biodiversity in Costa Rica is a result of a land bridge formed between two continents (figure 2.1) with their migrating biota, a tropical setting between two oceans, and wide variations in climate, slopes, and soil formations (Vaughan 1990a).

Twenty years ago Costa Rica shared many of neighboring Central America's socioeconomic-ecological problems, and its immense biodiversity treasures were threatened (Anis 1992; Leonard 1987). It had one of the world's highest deforesta-

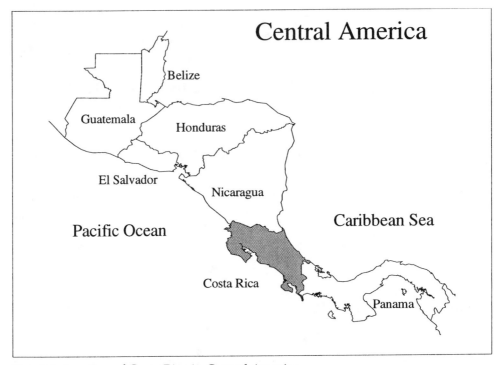

FIG. 2.1 Location of Costa Rica in Central America

tion rates, one of the world's highest population growth rates, a legal system that promoted deforestation, a huge international debt, and land-hungry rich and poor (Vaughan 1990b). However, it also had less poverty, a better educational system, no military, a better health record than the rest of the region, an active democracy, and an active and outspoken conservation community.

Through an interesting combination of ecological, sociopolitical, and economic influences, Costa Rica channeled its own energies and limited financial resources with those of outside donors into important conservation programs. Perhaps the most well-known example was the development of a national system of protected areas which began in the 1970s and today protects almost 27 percent of the national territory (Vaughan 1994).

Institutional Framework for Natural Resource Management in Costa Rica

Costa Rica created over seventy-eight federally protected wildland areas in only twenty-four years, between 1970 and 1994 (Boza 1993). The national parks and biological reserves were most effective wildlands in offering absolute protection of the country's biodiversity and encompassed over 6,000 km^2, or 12 percent, of the country (Boza 1993). The remaining 15 percent (7,500 km^2) of the protected areas consisted of privately and publicly owned, human populated, and partially protected multiuse areas such as wildlife refuges, indigenous peoples reservations, protected zones, and forest reserves. These wildland areas were located in each of the twelve major lifezones found in Costa Rica on both the Atlantic and Pacific slopes from sea level to the highest mountaintops at 3,820 m (Holdridge 1967; Boza 1993). Until 1990, four government agencies—the Forestry Service, the National Indian Affairs Commission, the Wildlife Service, and the National Parks Service—managed most of these wildlands. Several private conservation organizations also owned and managed reserves.

Independently, these four agencies and private organizations achieved partial ecosystem biodiversity conservation, established some institutional mechanisms for cooperation and consolidation of economic and financial systems, and developed several wildland management projects (Vaughan 1994). However, the four agencies had insufficient human and economic resources as well as limited knowledge on social issues; they further experienced tremendous pressures for short-term exploitation and thus did not coordinate activities together or with surrounding human communities. Traditional management strategies isolated protected areas from neighboring local rural peoples, causing noticeable environmental deterioration (MacKinnon et al. 1986; Boo 1990; Wells and Brandon 1992).

By the middle 1980s it became obvious that the objectives for creating the wildlands system were not being carried out and that their long-term survival was at stake (Vaughan and Flormoe 1994). These objectives were: (1) preservation of biological diversity; (2) maintenance of ecological processes and essential natural systems in undisturbed ecosystems; (3) restoration of natural processes in disturbed ecosystems; and (4) provision for sustainable utilization of species and ecosystems (Vaughan 1990a). The system was threatened by rural communities, other sectors of society, and transnationals, all wishing to utilize wildland natural resources to improve their standard of living and economic base. Many past biodiversity conservation efforts have alienated local human communities by removing them from their land and/or changing resource use laws so that economic and cultural survival was no longer feasible (Wells and Brandon 1992). Misunderstandings and hostility toward conservation efforts resulted because of a lack of dialogue with neighboring communities. Direct economic incentives and involvement in wildland projects are needed for local communities to support conservation efforts. For Costa Rican wildlands to survive, it was imperative to create management and development strategies that complemented the general landscape of protected wildlands and surrounding local human communities.

In 1986 the wildlands system was partially revitalized when Oscar Arias Sanchéz became the country's president. One month after Arias took office, the Ministry of Natural Resources, Energy, and Mines (MIRENEM) was created. Thus for the first time in Costa Rican history, natural resource management was given legal equality with other economic and social governmental sectors. The Arias administration had three key objectives in natural resource management: (1) define and carry out a national strategy for sustainable development; (2) promote the understanding of Costa Rica's rich biodiversity and its use by society; and (3) encourage the integrated approach to wildland and buffer zone management (Umaña and Brandon 1992). To fulfill the first objective, the first National Conservation Strategy for Sustainable Development (ECODES), containing nineteen sector reports (including health, energy, biodiversity, wildlands, and culture, among others), was written during 1987–88 and was considered the blueprint for future sustainable conservation efforts in Costa Rica (Quesada and Solís 1990).

National System of Conservation Areas (NSCA)

The second and third objectives of the Arias administration were served by an integrated approach to wildland management. This was recommended by the wildlands, forestry, and biodiversity sectors of ECODES to overcome current and future limitations. Therefore, Costa Rica created the National System of Conservation Areas (NSCA) in June 1991 (Garcia 1992; Vaughan 1994), based largely on the experience of the Guanacaste Conservation Area (Janzen 1988). The "biosphere" reserve concept, consisting of a multiple use conservation area with a manipulative (buffer) and natural (core) zones, was chosen as the new system's model. NSCA unites seventy-three of the seventy-eight wildland areas within eight Regional Conservation Areas (RCA): La Amistad, Arenal, Cordillera Volcanica, Lower Tempisque, Guanacaste, Tortuguero, Osa, and Central Pacific. Figure 2.2 shows four of the RCAs which are referenced in other chapters of the text. For instance, La Amistad RCA united fourteen formally disjunct wildland areas and also shares with Panama a binational "peace park" (Arias and Nations 1992).

NSCA's mission is to regionally consolidate protected area conservation and management, paying special attention to minimum population sizes, biodiversity inventories, restoration ecology, and long-term monitoring, while satisfying the socioeconomic needs of surrounding communities and accounting for other national and international interests (MIRENEM 1991). Specifically, communities in the buffer zones are to receive benefits from the system through their participation in specific biodiversity related projects, such as wildlife and wilderness management, tourism, and related services (MIRENEM 1991). A 1993 decree (22 481-MIRENEM, 24 AUG 93, Gaceta 173 9 SET 93) legally ensured seats for local community representatives on the RCA committees. In general, the new laws incorporating surrounding communities into the NSCA system are presently

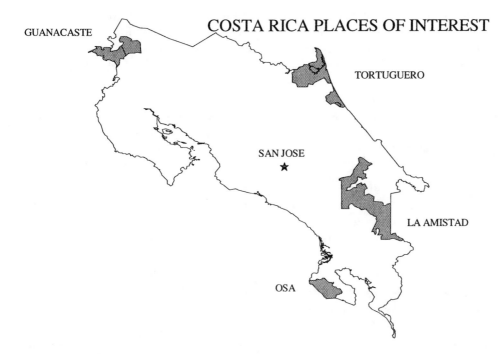

FIG. 2.2 Place names frequently referred to throughout the text

largely policy, and implementation is still in the early stages (per. com.: Rafael Gutierrez and Yadira Mena, National Parks System—NSCA).

Costa Rican Field Biology

The early transformation of the environment and the social structure of Costa Rica was produced by the cultivation of coffee (Hall 1978). The use of monocultures with their dependent economies characterizes underdevelopment and leads to poor use of human and physical resources. However, the coffee cultivation in ninteenth-century Costa Rica facilitated a social climate which promoted a strong development of the natural sciences (Goméz and Savage 1983).

Immigration of Europeans to Latin America in the nineteenth century was a result of the apparent utopian conditions of the New World and the difficult sociopolitical situation in the Old World. Foreign entrepreneurs and scholars came to carve their niches in commerce, crafts, and various professions in the relatively stable Central American countries. The Gold Rush of 1848 also fueled a demographic explosion because the route to California across southern

Nicaragua provided a safer alternative route to Cape Horn (Folkman 1970). The traveler-naturalists were intrigued by the romance of exploration, discovery, and travel in the unexplored American continent. Some of these traveler-naturalists included Moritz Wagner and Karl Scherzer, who published *Die Republik Costa Rica*; Anders Sandoe Orsted, who published *L'Amerique Centrale: Rescherches sur sa géographie politique, sa faune et sa flora*; William More Gabb, who worked in geology, paleontology, and zoology; and F. Duncane Godman and Osbert Salvin, who between 1879 and 1915 published the most comprehensive work on Central American biology, *Centrali-Americana* (Goméz and Savage 1983).

The emergence of Costa Rican biologists began in 1853 with the arrival in Costa Rica of two German physicians, Carl Hoffman and Alexander von Frantzius. Both collected botanical specimens and von Frantzius's faunal collections provided the basis for the first list of mammals and birds. José Zeledón, von Frantzius's apprentice, became a world-famous ornithologist, and collaborators Anastasio Alfaro and J. F. Tristán became well-known local naturalists. Their natural science was truly Victorian, and these men—known as the "drugstore gang" (called so because Franzius opened a drugstore)—and their collaborators were seen throughout the country with nets, plant presses, and other collecting equipment.

When public schooling became government-sponsored and compulsory until the seventh grade, and high schools were opened for men and women, European teachers were hired to staff the high schools. One of the hired teachers was Henri Pittier, who soon became in charge of all scientific activity in Costa Rica in its golden age of natural history. Henri Pittier began a multidisciplinary approach to field biology, started the national herbarium, and published the Primitiae Florae Costaricensis in 1891, which was the first Costa Rican systematic flora. Pittier and his collaborators amassed a body of natural history information which has never been surpassed. When Pittier left Costa Rica in 1904, science was flourishing throughout the country.

After Pittier's departure, and for political and economic reasons, science didn't keep up the pace begun twenty years before. However, Costa Rica's first academic biologist, Clodomiro Picado Twight, graduated doctor of science at the Sorbonne in 1913 and returned to study natural history in Costa Rica, where he organized a clinical laboratory. Picado published over 131 scientific articles on tropical medicine, microbiology, and natural research. His doctoral thesis was on the ecology of tank bromeliads. His death in 1944 deprived the country of a great thinker and scientist.

The University of Costa Rica's biology program was officially opened in 1955, designed with the thoughts of Dr. Rafael Lucas Rodríguez and Dr. Archie F. Carr, a famous North American natural historian. Dr. Rodríguez inspired many young students to carry out research projects. Soon the School of Biology was staffed with fifteen Ph.D.s, several of whom were interested in field biology. Then during the early 1970s, the National Museum was reformed under the guidance of Luis Diego Goméz with a focus on field biology.

Another institution that contributed to the increase in field studies was the Centro Agronómico Tropical de Investigación y Ensenanza (CATIE), founded by the Organization of American States as the Instituto Interamericano de Ciencias Agrícolas (IICA). In 1972 CATIE became independent but continued applied teaching and research in wildland, forestry, agriculture, and animal husbandry. The Tropical Science Center (Centro Científico Tropical) is a private consulting firm organized in 1962 which has carried out substantial field biology studies throughout Costa Rica.

The Regional Wildlife Management Program for Mesoamerica and the Caribbean (PRMVS) of the Universidad Nacional was established in 1987 with three objectives: (1) train Latin American students at the graduate and short-course levels in neotropical conservation biology and wildlife management; (2) promote and manage model wildlife managment projects throughout the Mesoamerican region; and (3) promote an information and technological transfer in the wildlife field. Over 40 percent of the twenty-seven months of the graduate program is spent under field conditions. To date, the PRMVS has graduated more than fifty students from over fifteen Latin American countries. The field biology approach promoted by the PRMVS has resulted in more than two hundred scientific articles and reports to date based on field research, many representing the first detailed studies on neotropical vertebrate species.

The Organization for Tropical Studies (OTS) was established in 1963 as a consortium of seven North American universities and the University of Costa Rica (Wilson 1991). Its primary objective then as now was to develop a center for research in neotropical science and advanced graduate education centered on basic knowledge of tropical environments (Goméz and Savage 1983). Today OTS has grown to include forty-seven institutions of higher education in the United States, five institutions of higher education from Costa Rica, the USDA Forest Service research branch, and the national museums of the United States and Costa Rica. There is a central office in Costa Rica, an administrative center at Duke University, and three field stations (San Vito—botantical garden in a reforested region; Palo Verde—tropical dry forest and coastal marine; and La Selva—tropical rain forest) owned by OTS in different habitats. With more than two thousand graduates of OTS courses, OTS is a principal developer of a new generation of tropical biologists with knowledge based on field experience. On a long-term basis, Costa Rica can expect a tremendous amount of scientific information based on research carried out by OTS. Most publications from Costa Rica on tropical biology have been done by OTS-related projects. In 1983–84 more articles published in the journals *Ecology* and *Biotropica* were from Costa Rica than any other country in the world (Clark 1985).

Published information is very important as background material for management efforts. The publication of *Costa Rican Natural History* in 1983, edited by

Dan Janzen with 174 contributors, was a milestone in the state of the art (Janzen 1983). The above-mentioned organizations contributed to the book and yearly are carrying out research and publishing results. These organizations will contribute greatly in this effort, and governmental institutions in Costa Rica charged with management of natural and wildlife resources can utilize this information for management purposes.

Potential Studies of Habitat

The destruction of tropical forests is the most important factor affecting the survival of wildlife species on a global level. Some 76,000 to 92,000 km^2 of tropical forests are being totally cleared yearly, and 100,000 km^2 are being severely altered (Myers 1986; WRI 1992). If this deforestation rate continues unabated, an estimated 50 percent of the world's tropical forests will be eliminated by the year 2000 (USDS 1981).

At the time of the Spanish conquest (around 1500), Costa Rica had primary forests which covered an estimated 49,000 km^2, or 96 percent, of the national territory; the rest was made up of mangrove, swamp forest, and subalpine *páramo* (Vaughan 1983). The extent of indigenous deforestation is unknown but was significant in some regions. Up to 1940 some 15,000 km^2 of the forested habitat had been altered, but by 1977 more than 18,000 km^2 had been deforested—indeed, more dense forest was altered in these thirty-seven years than in the four hundred and forty years between 1500 and 1940 (figure 2.3).

The distribution of a wildlife species depends on several factors, including habitat needs, past human interference, and zoogeography. Many wildlife species need primary forests and their edges. For instance, the jaguar, *Panthera onca* (Vaughan 1993), and tapir, *Tapirus bairdii* (Naranjo 1995), are found from sea level to 3,820 m in Costa Rica and are usually restricted to unaltered environments because of human predators. However, the squirrel monkey (*Saimiri oerstedii*) prefers secondary forests (Boinski 1986) and is found in southwest Costa Rica from sea level to about 500 m elevation. The resplendent quetzal (*Pharomachrus mocinno*) is both a dense forest and edge inhabitant, found between 1000 and 3000 m elevation (Powell and Bjork 1994).

Based on aerial photographs, remote sensing, and more than six hundred interviews carried out with local people and scientists throughout Costa Rica, Vaughan (1983) calculated that, between 1940 and 1982, forested habitat for twenty-eight endangered wildlife species in Costa Rica was reduced by an average 40 percent. As of 1982 these twenty-eight wildlife species had an average 28 percent of their original forest cover remaining. In 1982 the giant anteater (*Myrmecophaga tridactyla*) had the least amount (20 percent) of its original habitat remaining, and the quetzal had the most amount (55 percent) of its original

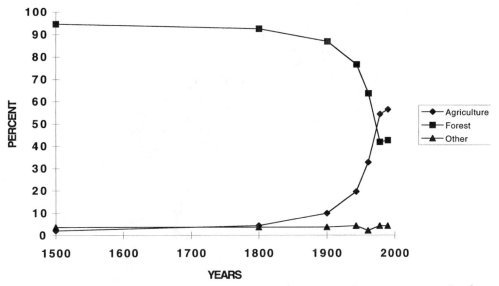

LAND USE IN COSTA RICA

FIG. 2.3 Trends in land use in Costa Rica since colonization. Forest cover remained relatively stable until this century.

habitat remaining (Vaughan 1983). Most forested habitat for these species was found in protected wildland areas.

Of more importance than total available forest for a species is the size and distribution of islands of suitable habitat which partially determines population size (figure 2.4). A minimum population is needed for long-term survival and five hundred reproducing individuals are given as the minimum effective population (Franklin 1980; Soulé 1980). In Costa Rica individual or complexes of protected wildland areas are found up to 5,900 km^2 in size but usually are much smaller. Some of the most important areas include Braulio Carrillo National Park–Cordillera Central Forest Reserve (833 km^2), Corcovado National Park–Golfo Dulce Forest Reserve (1,011 km^2), and a complex of thirteen wildland areas (5,900 km^2) found in the Talamanca mountain range which also take in Chirripo National Park–La Amistad International Park (Vaughan 1983).

The Role of Digital Data in Costa Rican Conservation

Vaughan's 1983 study was never stored in digital format and thus the mapping and analytical capabilities of GIS were never applied. Several Costa Rican agencies have begun to use digital mapping technology since 1983, however. The lack

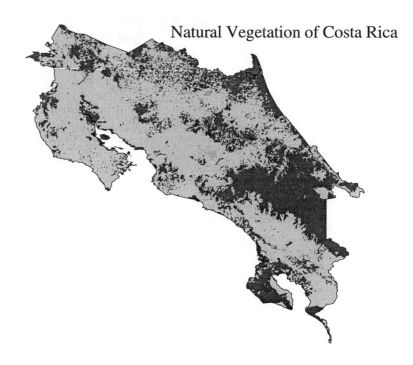

Natural Vegetation of Costa Rica

FIG. 2.4 Current status of natural vegetation in Costa Rica. Areas in black are under some form of natural (pre-Columbian) vegetation. Map is derived from 1992 data.

of digital information in Costa Rica in a form that was accessible to the general public and decision-makers was first noted by the Nature Conservancy in the 1980s. The Nature Conservancy had previously promoted the development of conservation data centers in the United States and was expanding this program into Latin America. The Costa Rican conservation data center originally functioned as a part of the Fundación de Parques Nacionales but was later moved to INBIO (Instituto Nacional de Biodiversidad). The conservation data center began the compilation of information on the distribution, abundance, and status of the conservation of the flora and fauna of Costa Rica. The objective of the center was to maintain up-to-date information on diverse aspects such as land use, the distribution of wildlife species, and technical information on natural resources. This information on biodiversity and land use could then be utilized to evaluate the environmental impact of development activities or to plan the creation of new parks and reserves. The data base currently has information on the habitat requirements, ecology, and distribution of many species of the flora and fauna; some of this information is geo-referenced. Most of the data do not have precise information on locality. Another limiting factor in this data is that many records are historic and therefore the information on distribution might not reflect current status.

The National Museum of Costa Rica (MNCR, Museo Nacional de Costa Rica) maintains collections of plants and wildlife. Most of the specimens date from the 1950s, 1960s, and 1970s. The collections have several limitations for the construction of current distribution maps.

1. The number of localities per species is very small and most specimens were collected near population centers.
2. Most specimens were collected many years ago and the habitat indicated on the tags usually has changed dramatically.
3. Most specimens are insects and birds; mammals are poorly represented.
4. Most of the specimens lack exact information on locality of collection.
5. The collections were not part of a plan to maximize the coverage in the country and therefore the sampling pattern is heterogeneous.

All of these facts suggested that it was necessary to conduct another countrywide study like that of Vaughan (1983), but that this time the study should incorporate digital mapping technology. This would allow for the continual upgrading of the information in the database, and the maps generated could be used for change detection, conservation planning, and in the implementation of sustainable development activities. A study performed from 1992 to 1995 is highlighted in part four of this text.

References

Anis, S. 1992. Overview: Poverty, natural resources, and public policy in Central America. In S. Anis, ed., *Poverty, natural resources, and public policy in Central America*, 3–27. New Brunswick, N.J.: Transaction.

Arias, O. and J. Nations. 1992. *A call for Central American peace parks.* In S. Anis, ed., *Poverty, natural resources, and public policy in Central America*, 43–58. New Brunswick, N.J.: Transaction.

Boinski, S. 1986. The ecology of squirrel monkeys in Costa Rica. Ph.D. diss., University of Texas, Austin.

Boo, 1990. *Ecotourism: The potentials and pitfalls.* Vol. 1. Washington, D.C.: World Wildlife Fund.

Boza, M. 1993. Conservation in action: Past, present, and future of the national park system of Costa Rica. *Conservation Biology* 7: 239–47.

Clark, D. 1985. Ecological field studies in the tropics: Geographical origin of reports. *Bulletin of the Ecological Society* 66(1): 6–9.

Damon, T. and C. Vaughan. 1995. Ecotourism and wildlife conservation in Costa Rica: Potential for a sustainable relationship. In J. A. Bissonette and P. R. Krausman, eds., *Integrating people and wildlife for a sustainable future: Proceedings of the first international wildlife management congress*, 211–16. Bethesda, Md.: The Wildlife Society.

Folkman, D. I. 1970. *The Nicaragua Route.* Salt Lake City: University of Utah Press.

Franklin, F. 1980. Evolutionary change in small populations. In M. E. Soulé and B. Wilcox, eds., *Conservation biology: An evolutionary-ecological perspective*, 135–49. Sunderland, Mass.: Sinauer Press.

Garcia, R. 1992. El sistema nacional de areas silvestres protegidas de Costa Rica: Hacia un nuevo enfoque. *Flora, Fauna y Areas Silvestres* 6: 14–18.

Goméz, L. D. and J. Savage. 1983. Searchers on that rich coast: Costa Rican field biology, 1940–1980. In D. Janzen, ed., *Costa Rican Natural History*, 1–11. Chicago: University of Chicago Press.

Hall, C. 1978. *El café y el desarrollo histórico-geográfico de Costa Rica.* San José, C.R.: Editorial Costa Rica-EUNA.

Holdridge, L. R. 1967. *Life zone ecology.* San José, C.R.: Tropical Science Center.

Janzen, D. 1988. Guanacaste National Park: Tropical ecological and biocultural restoration. In J. Cairns Jr., ed., *Rehabilitating damaged ecosystems* 2: 143–92. Boca Raton, Fla.: CRC Press.

—, ed. 1983. *Costa Rican Natural History.* Chicago: University of Chicago Press.

Jiménez, J. 1995. Training parataxonomists and curators to help conservation: The biodiversity inventory. In J. A. Bissonette and P. R. Krausman, eds., *Integrating people and wildlife for a sustainable future*, 165–67. Bethesda, Md.: The Wildlife Society.

Leonard, H. J. 1987. *Natural resources and economic development in Central America: A regional environmental profile: Executive Summary.* New Brunswick, N.J.: Transaction Books.

MacKinnon, J., K. MacKinnon, G. Child, and J. Thorsell (compilers). 1986. *Managing protected areas in the tropics.* Gland, Switzerland: International Union for Conservation of Nature and Natural Resources.

Ministry of Natural Resources, Energy, and Mines (MIRENEM). 1991. *The Costa Rican national system of conservation areas and its role in sustainable development: A position paper.* San José, C.R.: MIRENEM.

Myers, N. 1986. Tropical deforestation and mega-extinction spasm. In M. E. Soulé, ed., *Conservation biology: The science of scarcity and diversity*, 394–409. Mass.: Sinauer Press.

Naranjo, E. 1995. Abundancia y uso de habitat del tapir (*Tapirus bairdii*) en un bosque tropical humedo de Costa Rica. *Vida Silvestre Neotropical* 4: 20–31.

Powell, G. and R. Bjork. 1994. Implications of altitudinal migration for conservation strategies to protect tropical biodiversity: A case study of the resplendent quetzal, *Pharomachrus mocinno*, at Monteverde, Costa Rica. *Bird Conservation International* 4: 161–74.

Quesada, C. and V. Solís, eds. 1990. *Memoria Primer Congreso Estrategía de Conservación para el Desarrollo Sostenible de Costan Rica.* San José, C.R.: Ministerio de Recursos Naturales, Energía y Minas.

Soulé, M. E. 1980. Thresholds for survival: Maintaining fitness and evolutionary potential. In M. E. Soulé and B. Wilcox, eds., *Conservation biology: An evolutionary-ecological perspective*, 151–69. Sunderland Mass.: Sinauer Press.

Umaña, A. and K. Brandon. 1992. Inventing institutions for conservation: Lessons from Costa Rica. In S. Anis, ed., *Poverty, natural resources, and public policy in Central America*, 85–107. New Brunswick, N.J.: Transaction.

United States Department of State (USDS). 1981. *The world's tropical forests: A United States policy, strategy, and program.* Washington, D.C.: USDS.

Vaughan, C. 1983. *A report on dense forest habitat for endangered wildlife species in Costa Rica.* Heredia: Universidad Nacional.

Vaughan, C. 1990a. Biodiversidad. In C. Quesada and V. Solís, eds., *Memoria Primer Congreso Estrategía de Conservación para el Desarrollo Sostenible de Costan Rica*, 59–69. San José, C.R.: Ministerio de Recursos Naturales, Energía y Minas.

Vaughan, C. 1990b. Patterns in natural resource destruction and conservation in Central America: A case for optimism? *Transactions of the North American Wildlife and Natural Resources Conference* 55: 409–22.

Vaughan, C. 1993. Human population and wildlife: A Central American focus. *Transactions of the North American Wildlife and Natural Resources Conference* 58: 129–36.

Vaughan, C. 1994. Management of conservation units: The Costa Rican national system of conservation. In G. Meffe and C. R. Carroll, eds., *Principles of conservation biology*, 395–404. Sunderland, Mass.: Sinauer Press.

Vaughan, C. and L. Flormoe. 1994. Integrating resource use and biodiversity in neotropical ecosystems: The Costa Rican example. In I. D. Thompson, ed., *Proceedings of the International Union of Game Biologists XXI Congress*, 91–102. Halifax, N.S., Can.: IUGB.

Wells, M. and K. Brandon. 1992. *People and parks: Linking protected area management with local communities*. Washington, D.C.: The World Bank.

Wilson, D. E. 1991. OTS: A paradigm for tropical ecology and conservation education programs. In M. A. Mares and D. J. Schmidly, eds., *Latin American mammology: History, biodiversity, and conservation*, 357–67. Norman: University of Oklahoma Press.

World Resources Institute (WRI). 1992. *World Resources, 1992–1993*. Washington, D.C.: WRI.

PART TWO

Digital Mapping Technologies

3

Digital Mapping Technologies

Basil G. Savitsky

DIGITAL mapping technologies include computer-assisted mapping tools such as GIS, satellite image-processing software, and Global Positioning System (GPS) field collection devices. Each of these three technologies is covered individually in chapters 4, 5, and 6. This chapter contrasts digital mapping technologies with traditional cartography and addresses issues that are common to all three tools, particularly in the implementation of these technologies for conservation mapping in tropical developing countries.

A Comparison of Traditional Cartography and Digital Mapping Techniques

Cartography is the "art, science and technology of making maps, together with their study as scientific documents and works of art" (Robinson, Sale, and Morris. 1978:3). A comparison of digital cartography with traditional cartography reveals the benefits available through computer mapping. A case will be made that digital cartography is faster, more efficient, and more powerful and versatile than analog cartography. This comparison will be discussed regarding data sources, process, and products.

DATA SOURCES

Traditional, manual, or analog cartography is typically dependent upon data sources such as previously published maps, aerial photography, or some form of annotated geographic data, such as field notes or surveyed sample points (Star and Estes 1990). These data sources are expensive as well as voluminous, so they tend to be stored in specific isolated locations. The isolation of the data reduces access by data users to what is perceived by the owner of the data as a fixed asset.

Digital cartography utilizes the same types of data sources as analog cartography but has access to a wider pool of digital data sources from previously performed digital projects. Traditional cartography is constrained to the use of a published map or set of maps and often requires redrafting of information from the old maps to the new map. In contrast, digital cartography makes immediate use of existing digital data to update or create a published map.

Another component of the wider data pool is a growing set of products which were designed for use in a digital format and which are distributed via the Internet or CD-ROM. Internet users are able to identify new sources of information and retrieve data almost instantaneously (Thoen 1994; Sieber and Wiggins 1995). The CD-ROM hardware is inexpensive and provides easier access to larger digital data files (600 megabytes) than was practical with the floppy disk drives associated with personal computers (1 megabyte) or with the tape drives associated with mainframe computers (50 to 100 megabytes). One example of the type of data that is being widely distributed by CD-ROM is the 1:1,000,000 scale *Digital Chart of the World* (ESRI 1993).

The entire set of satellite imagery also must be considered in the growing library of digital data, particularly with the advent of the Earth Observing System (EOS) planned under the National Aeronautics and Space Administration's (NASA) Mission to Planet Earth (Lillesand and Kiefer 1994). EOS sensor systems are being designed to provide a wide array of data sources for global and, in particular, tropical assessments.

Developers of digital databases are still susceptible to the institutional forces which tend to support division and isolation and to the political forces which tend to reduce access to data (Hassan and Hutchinson 1992). However, it is the experience of the author that digital cartographers are aware of their reliance on widely disseminated data sources and tend to add their data to the wider pool.

PROCESS

Analog cartography produces a map as its final product. The map is a static object which provides a snapshot of some set of spatial phenomena at a set time. Digital geographic analysis offers the ability to process data in a variety of ways. The process of analysis is interactive and is usually iterative—built layer by layer. Digital analysis of geographic data allows several maps to be treated concurrently, thus building an understanding of relationships between the various mapped phenomena. This capacity has led to the development of numerous geographic models (Fedra 1993).

A geographic model represents spatial and temporal aspects of reality in digital terms. For example, a model that estimates soil loss may use rainfall, land cover, soil, and slope data to identify areas with the highest erosion potential. The ability to represent complex processes in a way that is easy to interpret has created a high demand for GIS technologies by decision-makers and policy analysts (Goodchild 1993; Steyaert 1993).

Digital processing also is conducive to combining geographic data from a variety of scales. For example, it is difficult to interpret simultaneously information from a soil map at a scale of 1:200,000 and an elevation map at 1:50,000 scale using traditional cartographic map sheets. However, GIS allows the user to generate slope and aspect maps from the elevation data and to change the scale of the new data to 1:200,000 for direct overlay with the soil data. Thus, trends can be identified using digital analysis that would not be obvious through visual interpretation of the two map sources.

One noteworthy feature of the storage structure of digital data is that some information is carried inherently in the system. For example, area totals for the various classes in a GIS map do not need to be estimated using laborious techniques as in traditional cartography since they can be reported instantaneously on the computer. The storage of data in a format conducive to statistical analysis is the foundation for the entire discipline of image analysis as it has developed (Jensen 1995). Quantitative techniques in geography have revolutionized both the research time frame and the types of questions that can be posed (James and Martin 1981).

Digital cartography often stops at the same point as traditional cartography, providing a similar product whose only difference is in the form of generation or the medium of delivery. However, GIS differs from computer mapping of a static map in that GIS generates new information through geographic analysis (Cowen 1988).

PRODUCTS

Digital mapping technologies and analog cartography also can be compared in terms of the quality of their products. One of the most cost-effective benefits associated with digital cartographic products is that they can be updated efficiently. For example, incorporation of changes in traditional cartography typically requires redrafting, but digital cartography requires that only the changed features be updated.

Many digital products were designed to define baseline conditions in order to detect and monitor future change (Jensen 1995). For example, a land cover map indicating forested vegetation in 1975 can be superimposed on a 1995 land cover map to measure forest loss and to identify the locations of greatest loss.

Automation is the process of computerizing. The operation of automating geographic analysis is itself a product independent of the set of maps produced, particularly in technology transfer. Automation requires a standardization of procedures and a degree of centralization of data. When a resource agency is able to bring its data to a standard of quality sufficient to release to other agencies, then that agency benefits from having more usable data. Likewise, the evolution of data exchange mechanisms between agencies has direct benefit to all agencies and to the management of the public resource (Hassan and Hutchinson 1992). Conservation and resource management is increasingly interdisciplinary and interdepartmental in nature. Building the capacity to contribute to and receive from the rapidly growing body of data is a valuable product.

Implementation of Digital Mapping Technologies in Tropical Developing Countries

It is useful to evaluate the costs and constraints in implementing digital mapping technologies. Successful applications have been demonstrated in the utilization of image analysis, GIS, and GPS (table 3.1). The three technologies have been applied in measurement of deforestation, identification of suitable habitat for various species, and a variety of protected area wildlife management issues. However, the initial investment in advanced mapping technologies is high, and many remote sensing technology transfers have failed to address the unique

TABLE 3.1 *Examples from the Literature Demonstrating Applications in Image Analysis, GIS, and GPS*

Technology	Application	Citation
Image analysis	Measure deforestation	Fearnside (1993)
		Tucker, Holben, and Goff (1984)
	Identify habitat	
	Crane	Herr and Queen (1993)
	Sage grouse	Homer et al. (1993)
	Snow leopard	Prasad et al. (1991)
GIS	Protected areas	Campbell (1991)
		McKay and Kaminski (1991)
		Parker et al. (1991)
		Pearsall (1991)
		Riebau et al. (1991)
	Wildlife management	
	Bear	Clark, Dunn, and Smith (1993)
		Holt (1991)
	Elephant	Falconer (1992)
	Cougar	Gagliuso (1991)
	Ecosystem modeling	Curran (1994)
		Johnson (1993)
	Deforestation trends	Ludeke, Maggio, and Reid (1990)
GPS	Rainforest populations	Wilkie (1989)
	Forest management	Gerlach (1992)
		Thee (1992)
		Bergstrom (1990)
	Park resource inventory	Lev (1992)
		Fletcher and Sanchez (1994)
	Habitat mapping	Wurz (1991)

conditions of the recipient country (Forster 1990). The reasons for failure in technology transfer within developed countries are similar to the causes of failure of technology transfer in tropical developing countries, but the quality of conditions in tropical developing countries makes technology implementation more difficult.

The implementation of an information technology such as GIS or image analysis can be evaluated along the three major components of the information system—hardware and software, data, and staff (figure 3.1). The concept of the GIS as a triangle was developed by the author to stress the balance required in investments and activities in each of the three components in a well-functioning information system. A successful implementation plan should address all three components. Excessive focus often is placed upon hardware and software considerations, particularly if competing vendors are involved. Often, agencies are

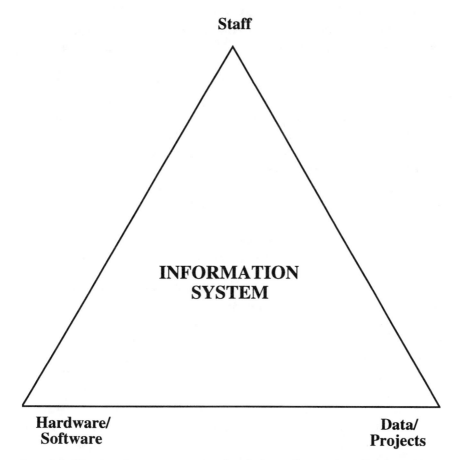

FIG. 3.1 Three major components of an information system. Implementation of an information system should be balanced along each component. The presence of any two components should produce the third component.

eager to acquire the hardware and software, and vendors are eager to close the sale. If the other two system components are not realistically evaluated at this stage, it is possible that an agency will be left with a powerful computer-processing capability and insufficient funds to hire skilled staff or to run projects.

The third component will naturally evolve in a system where two of the components are well-managed and appropriately funded. For example, an agency can make an investment in hardware and software and then make a parallel investment in trained staff. Staff who are given a designated time period to provide a return on the investment of the initial purchase and to cover a specified percentage of their salaries should be able to leverage their available hardware and their free time to start profitable projects.

There are alternative combinations of the presence of only two positive components in the system triangle. Talented staff who have a project or are handling data which would benefit from the acquisition of hardware and software will either purchase additional resources through the project or utilize existing capabilities under entry-level conditions. Successful project performance will provide justification for advances in hardware and software in future activities.

Also, consider the presence of sufficient equipment and a project that needs to be performed. An agency will be forced to allocate staff for the project if it is to be completed. The level of importance of the project will determine the level of staff commitment. It is impossible to achieve successful project implementation without appropriate staff commitment. If full-time staff cannot be assigned to the project, then at least 50 percent of a staff person's time should be designated for handling all of the issues associated with data manipulation and system maintenance. Part-time staff cannot devote sufficient attention to the complexities of managing an information system or to the data requirements of a successful project. An agency that cannot assign someone at least half-time to the system should contract the work to an outside party in order to accomplish the objectives of the project.

When systems only exhibit one strong component, then it is unlikely that they will succeed. An example of this condition resides in an administrative unit which invests in the hardware and software or receives a grant that provides the same. Insufficient allocation of trained staff to use the system will result in poor quality of data or inferior project performance. Typically, a project that includes a set of application objectives in addition to system implementation does not allocate sufficient time for the system implementation. It is unrealistic to expect even a trained staff to garner funds for the start-up costs of hardware and software as well as salary costs. If it were necessary to invest initially in only one of the three system components, then an investment in the best available staff would have the most probable success.

The balance of this section will address current trends and developments in each of the system components and particular conditions of the three components in relation to tropical developing countries.

HARDWARE AND SOFTWARE

Hardware costs for both personal computers and workstations have been declining steadily during recent years. This trend, combined with the rapid increases in computer processing speed, has dramatically benefited the GIS market. Geographic data are voluminous and require several unique hardware and software adaptations for data entry, processing, and output. These adaptations are referred to as hardware peripherals and include digitizers, scanners, and plotters. With a healthy GIS market, these peripherals have become more sophisticated, easier to use, and less expensive. The GIS market also has supplied a variety of hardware and software configurations from which to choose. Although increased choices provide more opportunities for the end user, the choices are often overwhelming for those entering the digital mapping arena.

Three guidelines facilitate the decision processes associated with selecting hardware and software. First, a low-cost information system, such as one based upon a personal computer (PC), has low risk in terms of investment and high returns in staff training. Software such as IDRISI is PC-based and has a short learning curve which enables the generation of faster output from a project. Networked and stand-alone workstations have more sophisticated requirements for implementation than PCs. Software such as ARC/INFO which operates on the more advanced hardware systems tends to have a steep and long learning curve. A successful PC implementation may develop into needing more advanced hardware, but the growth should be balanced along the three system components.

The second guideline in the selection of hardware and software is to evaluate the quality of support. If a hardware or software company is a leader in its field, then its technical support infrastructure is likely to be more accessible and informative than that of a small company. This consideration is particularly significant if the unit is geographically remote. Hardware support and maintenance are critical. One dysfunctional element in the system can severely impair the entire system. If assurance cannot be obtained that hardware will be serviced or replaced rapidly, then an alternative hardware selection should be considered.

Third, a wide variety of peripheral hardware devices should be considered with full awareness of the temporal limitations of all the devices. Whichever data entry, storage, display, or output device is selected, it is likely to become outdated technology or insufficient for growing needs in a short period of time. It is advisable for management staff to accept this fact at the outset and solicit the recommendations of staff rather than limiting the ability of the technical staff to keep the system current. One benefit of this phenomenon in information systems is that a unit can start out small, knowing that it will be upgrading almost continuously. Another benefit is that outgrown technology can be maintained as backup equipment or it can be used by entry-level personnel or students.

DATA

GIS databases are increasing in availability. The United States has benefited from the government publication of 1990 census data which have been distributed along with 1:100,000 scale road and stream data for the continental United States (Sobel 1990). The provision of a consistent national digital framework has allowed GIS users to have a readily available base map upon which to build. Numerous digital geographic databases have been published in recent years and are available over the Internet. The availability of high-quality satellite data also has facilitated numerous environmental mapping applications. Satellite imagery is a particularly rich data source because the availability of historic data from the 1970s enables the creation of a consistent baseline from which to perform change detection.

Although there are more data available in the public domain or at a nominal cost, satellite data prices have increased over the last twenty years. Further, the need to add specific information layers to existing data sources adds to the data costs of a given project in salary time for data entry. Also, field efforts are typically required in conjunction with digital mapping applications. Walklet (1991) suggests that data costs can account for as much as 80 percent of total information system costs over the life of the system.

Collection of traditional and digital data in the tropics has been constrained by the number of scientists working there, the economic realities associated with the fact that many tropical countries are developing countries and thus less equipped to fund database construction, and the physical difficulty of collecting data for remote areas. The first two constraints are beyond the arena of digital mapping technologies, but the third constraint has been addressed by the utilization of satellite data in mapping remote areas (Sader, Stone, and Joyce 1990; Malingreau 1994).

Satellite image processing or remote sensing has provided the capability to map some areas of the world that were difficult and more expensive to chart using traditional techniques. Unfortunately, there is not as much satellite imagery available for the tropical regions of the world as is available for the temperate zones because there is more cloud cover present in the tropics. In most cases, cloud-free images can be pieced together, but the process requires use of multiple images often temporally distinct by as much as two to three years. Even if the cost of data acquisition can be reduced through data grants or data-sharing mechanisms, the processing time remains high because of the need to handle more images. In many final image analysis products, areas under cloud cover remain unmapped, and reliance is placed upon combining aerial photographic data sources or other previously mapped data with the output from the image analysis to map these areas.

The use of radar imagery has long held promise for use in the tropics since it can be collected day or night and has the ability to penetrate cloud cover (Lillesand and Kiefer 1994). However, radar data are less readily available than other satellite data sources. Further, radar has unique processing requirements for which many image analysts are not trained. The advent of radar sensors in the planned EOS platforms should alleviate the data availability and cost constraints, but the international community must allocate resources to training in radar data processing.

STAFF

The high demand for professionals trained in GIS and image analysis has been constant as the digital mapping industries have grown. The supply of skilled analysts is more acute in the tropical developing countries. The phenomenon of "brain drain," where individuals who gain advanced training pursue opportunities outside their home countries, often limits the ability of a country to increase its technical capacity. In a GIS workshop held in San José, Costa Rica, for natural resource managers (March 6–7, 1995), the most commonly listed weakness in current GIS operations were staff shortages and inadequacies in training programs.

The issue of staff may be better understood in the tropics as an issue of training because it is likely that a resource professional already on staff will be given additional digital mapping responsibilities. In this case it is important to realize that in order for the individual to perform digital mapping functions well, several conditions should be met. The percentage of time allocated for digital mapping functions should be clearly specified if it is necessary for it to be less than 100 percent. The tasks associated with mapping technologies are so varied that it is difficult for an individual to be productive if he or she also is assigned a variety of unrelated functions.

The digital mapping staff should not be perceived as the hardware experts for the agency simply because they are proficient in hardware concerns. The digital mapping staff should have expertise in hardware, software, and the specific set of applications (forestry, soils, etc.). It is rare that one individual is skilled in all three areas. The software expertise may reside with a hardware expert or with an applications expert or be shared by both. It is difficult for an applications professional to remain current in a suite of hardware concerns, and it is unrealistic to expect a hardware professional to be skilled in an applications area. If possible, two people should fill complementary roles.

Ample support should be provided to the staff. The support may be in the form of additional compensation, discretionary budget to acquire the resources they deem necessary to perform their job, or in permission to travel to attend conferences or training courses. The frustration level of digital mapping staff can be high, and any effort directed to making their job easier will increase the chance of retaining valuable staff. The significance of the role of the staff component in computer systems should not be underestimated, particularly in computer mapping where the demand for trained professionals exceeds the supply.

One approach to maximizing investment in training the applications staff in digital mapping technologies is to select a familiar development path and build around that technology. For example, staff who are already performing aerial photo interpretation may be able to gain the necessary skills in image analysis in a time period shorter than the two semesters which would normally be required. Likewise, staff who are already collecting field data will be able to be trained in the use of GPS receivers more effectively than office staff. GPS training can be obtained in less than a week. An agency that develops either image analysis or GPS capability can then invest in building GIS capacity. Also, it is possible for an agency to contribute to collaborative project efforts between agencies and allow other parties to address the more complex issues associated with GIS. The collaborative approach allows staff in the agency developing GIS capacity to gain exposure to issues of database design, data integration and analysis, and cartographic output. Development of staff abilities through partnerships with other agencies will enable those staff to make recommendations on GIS development based upon their direct experience.

If agencies are able to accept their constraints and to identify where areas of interagency cooperation could help all parties to maximize limited resources, then there is a possibility that data sharing and collaborative training programs will enable those agencies to balance their investments along all three components of information systems.

References

Bergstrom, G. C. 1990. GPS in forest management. *GPS World* 1(5): 46–49.

Campbell, K. L. I. 1991. Using GIS for wildlife conservation in Tanzania: Prospects and possibilities. *Proceedings, Resource Technology '90, 2nd International Symposium on Advanced Technology in Natural Resource Management,* 265–74. Washington, D.C.: American Society for Photogrammetry and Remote Sensing.

Clark, J. D., J. E. Dunn, and K. G. Smith. 1993. A multivariate model of female black bear habitat at use for a GIS. *Journal of Wildlife Management* 57: 519–26.

Cowen, D. J. 1988. GIS versus CAD versus DBMS: What are the differences? *Photogrammetric Engineering and Remote Sensing* 54: 1551–54.

Curran, P. J. 1994. Attempts to drive ecosystem simulation models at local to regional scales. In G. Foody and P. Curran, eds., *Environmental remote sensing from regional to global scales,* 149–66. Chichester, Eng.: Wiley.

Environmental Systems Research Institute (ESRI). 1993. *Digital chart of the world* (CD-ROM Cartographic Database). Redlands, Calif.: ESRI.

Falconer, A. 1992. Geographic information technology fulfills need for timely data. *GIS World* 5(7): 37–41.

Fearnside, P. M. 1993. Deforestation in Brazilian Amazonia: The effect of population and land tenure. *Ambio* 22: 537–45.

Fedra, K. 1993. GIS and environmental modeling. In M. F. Goodchild, B. O. Parks, and L. T. Steyaert, eds., *Environmental modeling with GIS*, 35–50. New York: Oxford University Press.

Fletcher, M. and D. Sanchez. 1994. Etched in stone: Recovering Native American rock art. *GPS World* 5(10): 20–29.

Forster, B. 1990. Remote sensing technology transfer: Problems and solutions. *Proceedings of the Twenty-third International Symposium on Remote Sensing of the Environment* 1:209–17. Ann Arbor, Mich.: Environmental Research Institute of Michigan.

Gagliuso, R. A. 1991. Remote sensing and GIS technologies—an example of integration in the analysis of cougar habitat utilization in Southwest Oregon. In M. Heit and A. Shortreid, eds., *GIS applications in natural resources*, 323–30. Fort Collins, Colo.: GIS World.

Gerlach, F. L. 1992. "GPS/GIS in forestry." Paper presented at the Second International Conference on GPS/GIS. Newport Beach, Calif.

Goodchild, M. F. 1993. The state of GIS for environmental problem-solving. In M. F. Goodchild, B. O. Parks, and L. T. Steyaert, eds., *Environmental modeling with GIS*, 8–15. New York: Oxford University Press.

Hassan, H. M. and C. Hutchinson. 1992. *Natural resource and environmental information for decisionmaking*. Washington, D.C.: The World Bank.

Herr, A. M. and L. P. Queen. 1993. Crane habitat evaluation using GIS and remote sensing. *Photogrammetric Engineering and Remote Sensing* 29(10): 1531–38.

Holt, S. 1991. Human encroachment on bear habitat. In M. Heit and A. Shortreid, eds., *GIS applications in natural resources*, 319–22. Fort Collins, Colo.: GIS World.

Homer, C. G., T. C. Edwards Jr., R. D. Ramsey, and K. P. Price. 1993. Use of remote sensing methods in modelling sage grouse winter habitat. *Journal of Wildlife Management* 57: 78–84.

James, P. E. and G. J. Martin. 1981. *All possible worlds: A history of geographical ideas.* New York: Wiley.

Jensen, J. R. 1995 (2d ed.). *Introductory digital image processing: A remote sensing perspective.* Englewood Cliffs, N.J.: Prentice-Hall.

Johnson, L. 1993. Ecological analyses using GIS. In S. B. McLaren and J. K. Braun, eds., *GIS applications in mammalogy*, 27–38. Norman: Oklahoma Museum of Natural History.

Lev, D. 1992. Park management and GPS. *GPS World* 3(5): 35.

Lillesand, T. M. and R. W. Kiefer. 1994. *Remote sensing and image interpretation.* New York: Wiley.

Ludeke, A. K., R. C. Maggio, and L. M. Reid. 1990. An analysis of anthropogenic deforestation using logistic regression and GIS. *Journal of Environmental Management* 31: 247–59.

Malingreau, J. P. 1994. Satellite-based forest monitoring: A review of current issues. In *Tropical forest mapping and monitoring through satellite imagery: The status of current international efforts.* Arlington, Va.: USAID Environment and Natural Resources Information Center.

McKay, G. W. and E. Kaminski. 1991. The GIS at Yellowstone National Park—development, acquisition, and applications for resource management. *Proceedings, Resource Technology '90, 2nd International Symposium on Advanced Technology in Natural Resource Management*, 400–407. Bethesda, Md.: American Society for Photogrammetry and Remote Sensing.

Parker, C. R., K. Langdon, J. Carter, S. Nodvin, and H. Barrett. 1991. Natural resources management and research in Great Smoky Mountains National Park. *Proceedings, Resource Technology '90, 2nd International Symposium on Advanced Technology in Natural Resource Management*, 254–64. Bethesda, Md.: American Society for Photogrammetry and Remote Sensing.

Pearsall, S. 1991. Advanced technologies and nature reserves in western Samoa. *Proceedings, Resource Technology '90, 2nd International Symposium on Advanced Technology in Natural Resource Management*, 221–30. Bethesda, Md.: American Society for Photogrammetry and Remote Sensing.

Prasad, S. N., R. S. Chundawat, D. O. Hunter, H. S. Panwar, and G. S. Rawat. 1991. Remote sensing snow leopard habitat in the trans-Himalaya of India using spatial models and satellite imagery—preliminary results. *Proceedings, Resource Technology '90, 2nd International Symposium on Advanced Technology in Natural Resources Management*, 519–23. Bethesda, Md.: American Society for Photogrammetry and Remote Sensing.

Riebau, A. R., W. E. Marlatt, S. Coloff, M. L. Sestak. 1991. Using microcomputers for wilderness management: The wildland resources information data system (WRIDS). *Proceedings, Resource Technology '90, 2nd International Symposium on Advanced Technology in Natural Resource Management*, 231–43. Bethesda, Md.: American Society for Photogrammetry and Remote Sensing.

Robinson, A., R. Sale, and J. Morris. 1978. *Elements of cartography.* New York: Wiley.

Sader, S. A., T. A. Stone, and A. T. Joyce. 1990. Remote sensing of tropical forests: An overview of research and applications using non-photographic sensors. *Photogrammetric Engineering and Remote Sensing* 56: 1343–51.

Sieber, R. and L. L. Wiggins. 1995. Tour the World Wide Web: A look at three GIS sites. *GIS World* 8(6): 70–75.

Sobel, J. 1990. Principal components of the Census Bureau's TIGER file. In D. J. Peuquet and D. F. Marble, eds., *Introductory readings in geographic information systems*, 112–19. Bristol, Penn.: Taylor and Francis.

Star, J. and J. Estes. 1990. *Geographic information systems: An introduction.* Englewood Cliffs, N.J.: Prentice-Hall.

Steyaert, L. T. 1993. A perspective on the state of environmental simulation modeling. In M. F. Goodchild, B. O. Parks, and L. T. Steyaert, eds., *Environmental modeling with GIS*, 16–30. New York: Oxford University Press.

Thee, J. R. 1992. GPS tames the jungle. *GPS World* 3(5): 34.

Thoen, B. 1994. Access the electronic highway for a world of data. *GIS World* 7(2): 46–49.

Tucker, C. J., B. N. Holben, and T. E. Goff. 1984. Intensive forest clearing in Rondonia, Brazil, as detected by satellite remote sensing. *Remote Sensing of Environment* 15: 255–61.

Walklet, D. C. 1991. The economics of GIS: Understanding the economic motivation and requirements which justify the use of GIS as a practical solution for environmental and resource planners. *Proceedings, GIS/LIS*, 643–47. Atlanta, Ga.

Wilkie, D. S. 1989. Performance of a backpack GPS in a tropical rain forest. *Photogrammetric Engineering and Remote Sensing* 55: 1747–49.

Wurz, B. E. 1991. National treasures: GPS helps preserve a bald eagle habitat. *GPS World* 2(3): 28–33.

4

GIS

Basil G. Savitsky

THERE are numerous definitions of GIS. Maguire (1991) lists eleven different definitions. Some place emphasis on the computer processing or analytical procedures, such as Burrough (1986:6), who defines GIS as a "set of tools for collecting, storing, retrieving at will, transforming, and displaying spatial data from the real world for a particular set of purposes." Other definitions emphasize the institutional and project context in which the GIS hardware and software reside (Dickinson and Calkins 1988). The discussion in chapter 3 revolving around the information system triangle (figure 3.1) uses this broader approach to defining GIS.

As sufficient attention has been allocated to the system components of GIS in the previous chapter, this chapter will focus on the extraction of information from geographic data. Emphasis is given to the type of information produced through GIS and to the types of data stuctures which are commonly employed.

Information Extraction and Synthesis

There is a decision-making continuum which ranges from data to information to knowledge (figure 4.1). The policy community is dependent upon the scientific community to provide meaningful information so that those in power can make intelligent decisions. The ability of the decision-maker to link various pieces of information with his or her own personal and political experience regarding an issue defines the level of knowledge achieved about the issue. There is often frustration on the part of scientists who feel that they have successfully provided a governing body with information only to see that information mixed with political pressures, media presentation of anecdotal cases, and the opinions of

SCIENCE ------------ POLICY

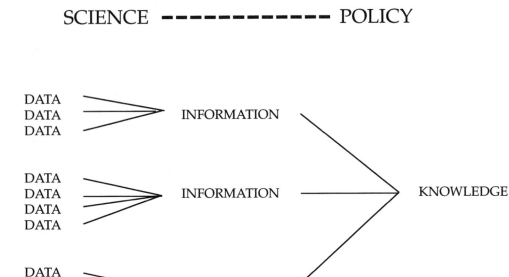

FIG. 4.1 A decision-making continuum

"uninformed" individuals. Nevertheless, underpinning the motivation of scientists in conservation, resource management, and environmental protection disciplines is the belief that the provision of information to the policy community is critical to the future of our natural resources.

There are numerous types of information used in bridging science and policy, such as statistics and tabular or graphic presentations of data, but the utility of the map is particularly powerful in its ability to convey concurrently a variety of spatial relationships. The spatial nature of information required to make decisions in resource management makes GIS a tool that is commonly utilized. It should be noted that just as policymakers synthesize a variety of information sources to develop knowledge, information is based upon the synthesis of data. In fact, one distinction between data and information is the role that communication plays. Data need to be interpreted before they can be made useful. Once a pattern within the data is identified and summarized, then information is extracted from the data, and that information can be conveyed.

It also should be noted that the scientific community is often unable to supply the policy community with information because critical data are missing or of insufficient quality. Often data collection programs are funded as a result of this recognition. One current example is the advent of increased satellite monitoring programs to supply researchers with data on global environmental changes such as biodiversity loss and global warming.

The manner in which GIS has been used in support of natural resource management and other spatial applications has evolved over three phases (Maguire 1991, citing Crain and MacDonald 1984). The primary focus in the first phase is inventory, and spatial query typically is limited to simple operations, mainly retrieval. Complex analytical operations, such as suitability analyses, develop during the second phase. The hallmark of the third phase is the capability to perform decision support. Maguire (1991) suggests that new GIS implementations should allow three to five years for each of the first two phases before expecting an institutional system to have the GIS experience necessary to fully utilize the management potential of GIS. Eastman et al. (1995) describe a series of tools which have been developed to enhance the decision-making role of GIS, thus, holding potential to shorten the length of the GIS implementation cycle.

It is useful to distinguish between the various levels of analytical capacity in the constantly growing body of GIS and related software packages. The simplest packages in the family of GIS software perform computer mapping. At this level, maps are entered, stored, retrieved, displayed, and output, but they are not used analytically. An example of the computer mapping level is the digital atlas or the electronic map file. A more sophisticated level of mapping is achieved when a linkage is present in the software between the geographic data elements and a separate database. At this level, specific points, lines, or polygons can be selected according to criteria defined in the database. Demographic analysis and tax parcel mapping can be done with this level of software. The industry of facilities management (e.g., telephone, cable, electric, and gas) realizes significant savings by using computer-assisted drafting / computer-assisted mapping (CAD /CAM) software. However, because they are not used to create new information, none of these digital mapping software packages can be said to be a GIS. A GIS is able to perform a variety of spatial operations that are useful to identify relationships between the geographic elements within the computer map. Likewise, a GIS can be used to combine data from two or more maps to generate a new map or set of maps. The types of spatial modeling or decision support functions included varies from one GIS software package to another. Some GIS packages include image processing capability, just as some image analysis packages include various GIS functions. Careful examination of the functions present in a suite of software packages is recommended prior to selecting a specific package. This process is greatly facilitated by a clear definition of the user's needs. The more effort that is placed in the design of a GIS, the greater the probability of a successful implementation.

The growing popularity of GIS in recent years is due to the numerous benefits that it offers. Even at the simplest level of computer mapping implementation, mapped data are archived and retrieved more efficiently than their paper counterparts. Paper maps are subject to damage and wear, and digital storage offers historic data virtually eternal life. A digital map can be updated by changing only the features that have changed.

The more sophisticated levels of GIS software offer additional benefits. At a very basic level, tabulation by area of individual classes within a file is inherent to the data structure and thus can be performed almost instantaneously. Likewise, the ability to integrate data from variable source scales is not a trivial contribution. GIS has been used as a tool to facilitate interdisciplinary research because various types of maps from disparate disciplines can be synthesized through map overlay. The superimposition of map files from two or more dates for the same area can be used to identify and quantify change. Numerous geographic models have been developed to forecast demands, project change, identify optimal locations, and otherwise enhance planning and management activities.

Data Structures

The major categorization of GIS software is in the data structure utilized by the software for spatial analysis. Raster data are stored in an array of rows and columns of cells with each cell holding a single value characterizing all of the area within that cell. Image data collected by satellites are a special type of raster data. Vector data are stored as a series of points, lines, and polygons with each element having unique identifiers that serve to link the geographic elements to attribute data.

In a raster database the geographic coordinate of every cell is inherently stored as a distance function, calculated by multiplying the spatial resolution of the cell (e.g., 100 meters) by the x and y distance between the origin (1,1) and the row and column position of the cell (e.g., 2003,45). By storing only the coordinate of position 1,1, the position of 2003,45 is known to be 200,300 meters east of 1,1 and 4,500 meters south of 1,1. In a vector database, x,y geographic coordinates are stored for every point element, for every point in a line segment where direction changes, and for a labeling point within every polygon.

Data entry techniques for vector-based GIS include drafting maps electronically on digitizing tablets and the collection of field coordinates using a GPS receiver. Data entry techniques for raster-based systems include scanners (of which facsimile machines and satellites are both a type) and transfer of vector data to a raster format. The output of both raster and vector maps can be sent to most devices including laser writers, ink-jet printers, sublimation dye printers, and electrostatic plotters. Pen plotters are conducive for use with vector data.

Eastman (1995) contrasts the strengths and weaknesses of vector and raster structures along six factors. These are summarized in table 4.1. Users requiring maplike output, network analysis, or repeated database query will be inclined to utilize a GIS with a vector data structure. Users who utilize continuous data sources such as elevation data or satellite imagery or users who regularly perform context analysis will require a GIS with a raster data structure. Most users need to utilize vector-based systems at some times and raster-based systems in other instances. Many software packages offer a blend of capabilities, but the

TABLE 4.1 *Strengths and Weaknesses of Vector and Raster Data Structures*

Vector	Raster
Feature-oriented	Space-oriented
Efficient storage of boundaries only	Data-intensive
"Maplike"	"Image-like"
Geometry of spatial relationships is complex	Simple relational geometry
Network analysis	Numerous spatial analyses
Strong in database query	Strong in analysis of continuous data

(SOURCE: *Eastman 1995*)

data strucure and analytical capabilities are either raster or vector. A GIS that includes both raster and vector capabilities usually maintains its secondary capability in the display mode as opposed to the analytical mode.

GIS as a Decision-making Tool in Developing Countries

Regardless of the data structure employed, GIS offers the resource manager the ability to bring together a variety of types of maps into one system to facilitate the processes of decision making about the resource base. The logic present in almost all GIS analyses is the logic of map overlay. New information, such as suitability ranking, is created through the intersection of certain features when two or more maps that are geographically referenced are digitally superimposed. It also is possible to weigh more heavily the factors associated with some map layers than others, thus creating different outcomes based upon the selection of the weighting scheme. The objectivity associated with the GIS instrument has potential in providing rational information to the often politicized arena of planning, but caution needs to be exercised in documenting the subjective decisions made in selecting the weights. An example of a weighted GIS analysis is provided in chapter 9 of this text.

Examples of such weighted linear combinations abound in the GIS literature. However, research on the selection and effectiveness of various weighting schemes is young. Eastman et al. (1993) describe several cases and a variety of decision operations using a raster GIS. They contrast the simple process of identifying geographic areas having the highest suitability to maximize a single objective (conservation as an example) with the more complex process of allocating spatial resources to meet multiple objectives (i.e., forest reserve use for conservation, recreation, and timber harvesting). When multiple objectives are in conflict with each other rather than complementary (i.e., conservation and development), then four possible outcomes are possible: areas of high suitability to both objectives, areas of low suitability for both objectives, and areas of high suitability for only one of the objectives (Eastman et al. 1993). The conflict areas when spatially indicated on a map depicting areas of all four decision outcomes can be helpful in informing what must ultimately be a political decision. Knowing the contextual information, specifically where the conflict areas are in relation to both of the regions of high suitability, is a first step in providing an objective and consistent framework for communication toward compromise or conflict resolution. Additionally, specific data regarding the number of hectares in each of the four categories may facilitate determination of areal thresholds to be attained in the division of the conflict areas.

Another area of GIS research which requires attention is the feasibility of the technology in international development. Toledano (1997) and Auble (1994) demonstrate some of the complexities in such development issues as local (community) participation, translation of community knowledge into a GIS, and building GIS capacity from the bottom up. Taylor (1991) provides a review and critique of GIS technology transfer from developed to developing countries. Although GIS is perceived as having potential in being successfully employed in resolving development issues, too much of the international GIS work is being done by North American and European professionals rather than by the nationals in the developing countries.

> It is argued that current developments in GIS are primarily technology-driven and that such an approach has limited relevance to the problems of development in the countries of Africa, Asia, and Latin America. GIS technology is not scientifically objective and value free. It is an artifact of industrial and post-industrial society. Its structures, technologies and applications are products of the needs of these societies. If it is to be used in the context of development then it must be introduced, developed, modified and controlled by indigenous people who understand the social, economic and political context of the situation as well as the technical capabilities of GIS. This may involve some quite different GIS configurations and solutions from those already successful in the developed nations. It poses special problems of technology transfer and education and training.   (Taylor 1991:71)

Although development problems are different in many ways from conservation issues, most of the issues related to technology transfer remain the same. Further, it is becoming more and more difficult to deal with environmental and development issues independently. The extent to which the potential of GIS is actualized by the scientific communities in developing tropical nations may very well be an indicator of the extent to which those nations are able to conserve their environmental resources and manage their economic development.

References

Auble, J. 1994. Leveling the GIS playing field: Plugging in non-governmental organizations. *Proceedings, AURISA*, Sydney, Australia.

Burrough, P. A. 1986. *Principles of geographical information systems for land resources assessment.* Oxford: Clarendon Press.

Crain, I. K. and C. L. MacDonald. 1984. From land inventory to land management. *Cartographica* 21: 40–46.

Dickinson, H. and H. W. Calkins. 1988. The economic evaluation of implementing a GIS. *International Journal of Geographical Information Systems* 2: 307–27.

Eastman, J. R. 1995. *IDRISI for Windows student manual.* Clark Labs for Cartographic Technology and Geographic Analysis. Worcester, Mass.: Clark University.

Eastman, J. R., J. P. Weigen, A. K. Kyem, and J. Toledano. 1995. Raster procedures for multi-criteria / multi-objective decisions. *Photogrammetric Engineering and Remote Sensing* 41: 539–47.

Eastman, J. R., P. A. K. Kyem, J. Toledano, and W. Jin. 1993. *GIS and decision making.* Vol. 4, *UNITAR explorations in GIS technology.* Geneva, Switzerland: UN Institute for Training and Research.

Maguire, D. J. 1991. An overview and definition of GIS. In D. J. Maguire, M. F. Goodchild, and D. W. Rhind, eds., *Geographical information systems: Principles and applications,* 9–20. New York: Longman Scientific and Technical.

Taylor, D. R. F. 1991. GIS and developing nations. In D. J. Maguire, M. F. Goodchild, and D. W. Rhind, eds., *Geographical information systems: Principles and applications,* 71–84. New York: Longman Scientific and Technical.

Toledano, J. 1997. The ecological approach: An alternative strategy for GIS implementation. Ph.D. diss., Clark University, Worcester, Mass.

5

Image Analysis

Basil G. Savitsky

THIS chapter provides a general background on the utilization of satellite imagery in tropical habitat mapping. The introductory section covers basic concepts in image analysis that are prerequisite to the content covered in the balance of the chapter. The second section provides a review of the literature on the habitat mapping capability of a variety of sensor systems. The third section covers the utility of satellite imagery in national and regional conservation mapping efforts in the tropics.

Basic Concepts in Image Analysis

Remotely sensed data include a variety of data sources that are defined from the range of the spectrum of electromagnetic radiation. Aerial photography is used to capture reflective signals from the visible and near-infrared portion of the spectrum. Most digital scanners operate in similar portions of the spectrum. Thermal and radar sensor systems are sensitive to a different portion of the energy spectrum.

Remotely sensed data provide an operational GIS with timely and synoptic data. Image analysis techniques are commonly utilized to perform regional vegetation mapping and to update existing vegetation maps.

The utility of a sensor system for the detection of surface phenomena must be assessed along four dimensions: spatial resolution (area or size of feature that can be identified), spectral resolution (number and width of electromagnetic bands for which data are collected), radiometric resolution (detector sensitivity to various levels of incoming energy), and temporal resolution (frequency of satellite overpass) (Jensen 1995). The four satellite sensors that are addressed in this chapter are (in decreasing order of spatial resolution) Advanced Very High Resolution Radiometer (AVHRR), Landsat Multispectral Scanner (MSS), Landsat Thematic Mapper (TM), and Satellite pour l'Observation de la Terre (SPOT). The spatial, spectral, temporal, and radiometric resolution of each sensor are listed in table 5.1.

Airborne and satellite digital sensors collect and store data values for discrete units of the surface of the earth. A scene is composed of a large matrix of these cells. Each cell is referred to as a picture element, or pixel, and may correspond to a square meter, hectare, or square kilometer, depending on the sensor. The spatial resolution of the sensor is usually expressed as the length of one side of the cell. AVHRR has a spatial resolution of 1.1 kilometer (Kidwell 1988); MSS resolution is 79 meters; TM is 30 meters; and multispectral SPOT is 20 meters (Jensen 1995).

The spectral resolution of a sensor refers to its ability to capture data in a certain portion or band of the electromagnetic spectrum. The spectral resolution of AVHRR is five bands; MSS has four bands; SPOT has three bands; and TM has

TABLE 5.1 *Spatial, Spectral, Temporal, and Radiometric Resolution of Four Sensors*

		Resolution		
Sensor System	Spatial	Spectral (bandwidth in micrometers)	Temporal	Radiometric (brightness values)
SPOT				
Panchromatic	10 m	0.51–0.73	11–26 days	0–255
Multispectral	20 m	Three bands		
		0.50–0.59		
		0.61–0.68		
		0.79–0.89		
TM	30 m	Seven bands	16 days	0–255
		0.45–0.52		
		0.52–0.60		
		0.63–0.69		
		0.76–0.90		
		1.55–1.75		
		2.08–2.35		
	120 m	10.4–12.5		
MSS	79 m	Four bands	16–18 days	0–63
		0.5–0.6		
		0.6–0.7		
		0.7–0.8		
		0.8–1.1		
AVHRR	1.1 km	Five bands	daily	0–255
		0.58–0.68		
		0.725–1.10		
		3.55–3.93		
		10.5–11.3		
		11.5–12.5		

SOURCES: Kidwell (1988) for AVHRR; Jensen (1995) for SPOT, TM, and MSS.

seven bands. Sensor bandwidth refers to the range of energy units recorded by a sensor. Most sensor systems have several sensors on board, which results in concurrent data collection across multiple bands. For example, all Landsat sensors have had a green and a red band and at least two infrared bands. The Landsat TM sensors have a blue band and infrared bands additional to the MSS sensors. Visible energy has wavelengths of 0.4 to 0.7 micrometers, near-infrared energy has wavelengths of 0.7 to 1.3 micrometers, mid-infrared energy has wavelengths of 1.3 to 3.0 micrometers, and thermal infrared energy has wavelengths of 3 to 14 micrometers.

False color composite prints that are similar to color infrared photographs can be generated from these satellite data, but the true power of the digital data lies in the ability to statistically assess each band of the spectrum independently or in combination with any or all of the other bands. For example, a body of water and a patch of forest may both have high brightness values in the green band, but the forest emits infrared energy in contrast to the water, which absorbs infrared energy. Thus, water and forest are readily discriminated using only one band of data. It may be necessary to use several bands of data to classify different types of forest, in which case probabilities are assigned to each pixel as to its membership within a given cluster of spectrally similar pixels. Digital image analysis is a process that was built around the statistical techniques of such information extraction (Jensen 1995). Land use and land cover maps are one type of map generated from the image analysis process.

The radiometric resolution of the MSS sensor is lower than the other three sensors. The MSS sensor records brightness values between 0 and 63 for a given pixel in each of its bands. The other sensors are sensitive to a range of 0 to 255. Thus very subtle differences in the spectral properties of a material may not be discriminated as well using MSS data. For example, if the brightness values associated with a material were exactly 50 percent of the maximum reflectance in all bands, then MSS would record 32 and TM would record 127 for each band. A difference in a TM band for two materials might result in brightness values of 126 and 129, but the MSS sensor could only record a value of 32 for both materials.

The temporal resolution of the sensor refers to the frequency with which imagery is obtained for the same geographic area. AVHRR provides daily coverage of the earth (Kidwell 1988), whereas TM collects at most twenty-three images of an area per year. MSS temporal resolution is eighteen days for Landsat 3 data and sixteen days for Landsat 4 and 5 data (Jensen 1995). The temporal resolution of SPOT data is variable, eleven to twenty-six days, depending on whether side-look data are desired. The SPOT satellite has the capability of collecting side-look imagery at an angle of up to 27 degrees, thus improving the probability of collecting cloud-free data.

The two major classification techniques in image analysis are unsupervised and supervised (Lillesand and Kiefer 1994). The unsupervised classification approach statistically assigns each pixel to a cluster or class based upon the probability distance of the pixel to similar clusters when considering all the various bands of data. The unsupervised approach requires the user to label the classes according to the best understanding of the spatial distribution of all the members of a given class after the processing is complete. A supervised approach is different from the unsupervised technique in that it requires "training" data upon which to initiate the statistical classification program. The algorithms assign each pixel in the remainder of the image to a class based upon the statistics associated with the training data. Both approaches require ground truth data from other maps, aerial photography, or from field observation. In the supervised approach the ground truth data are used first, and in the unsupervised approach they are used last.

Although the use of remotely sensed data is becoming common, it is an expensive technique because of the cost of satellite imagery acquisition and processing. Staff specialists and image interpretation software and hardware are required. As a result, few areas within Central America have existing satellite classification maps. AVHRR analysis of all of Mexico has been completed (Evans et al. 1992b), Landsat scenes have been analyzed in the Yucatán (Green et al. 1987), and NASA airborne sensors have been utilized in Belize (O'Neill 1993). Extensive analysis has been performed in Costa Rica (Sader and Joyce 1988; Powell et al. 1989; and Mulders et al. 1992).

Review of Habitat-Mapping Capability of Four Sensors

The four sensors have been assessed for the purpose of mapping habitat as an input to gap analysis (Scott et al. 1993). AVHRR has utility in monitoring greenness, but has limited utility in mapping vegetation types because of its coarse spatial resolution. SPOT has several advantages over other sensors, but it is limited by its spectral resolution, notably missing the mid-infrared band. Sensors with bandwidths recording mid-infrared energy are useful in vegetation analysis because of the water absorption characteristics of leaves, which are spectrally detectable.

The tendency to misclassify areas because of too fine a spatial resolution is another weakness of SPOT (also present in TM but to a lesser degree). For example, patches of trees within a pasture can be classified accurately as isolated pixels of the forest land cover. However, the land use of the area is pasture, so the ability to convert land cover data to land use data must be considered in the image analysis process.

TM is the sensor of choice for gap analysis, primarily because of its high spectral resolution and its adequate spatial resolution (Scott et al. 1993). MSS is a second choice to TM, primarily because of its reduced spectral resolution. MSS has only four bands with the two infrared bands in the near-infrared rather than the mid-infrared.

The conclusions of Scott et al. (1993) are valid, but cost considerations require an evaluation of MSS and AVHRR in addition to TM. International conservation mapping should utilize satellite data that cost the least and are able to be integrated meaningfully with wildlife and protected area data sets. It is useful to distinguish between three levels of vegetation mapping and the satellite systems that can support each level: AVHRR for global surveys with scale ranging around 1:2,000,000 and with discrimination between forest and nonforest; MSS for national surveys with scale ranging from 1:250,000 to 1:1,000,000; and TM or SPOT for local surveys with scale ranging from 1:50,000 to 1:100,000 (Blasco and Achard 1990).

Successes and limitations of the various sensors utilized in tropical forestry applications have been reviewed (Sader, Stone, and Joyce 1990). It was found that AVHRR has its highest value as a tool for identifying the geographic areas most suitable for more detailed imagery analysis. Various biophysical parameters such as net primary productivity have been generated for global studies using AVHRR, but they are least accurate in the complex ecosystems of the tropics. MSS has proven successful in numerous cases of change detection, particularly in the identification of areas of deforestation (Sader, Stone, and Joyce 1990). However, MSS studies have had mixed results in identifying secondary growth other than young secondary growth and in discriminating forest species consistently. Published results of TM analyses are relatively few, and very little has been published on SPOT investigations in the tropics (Sader, Stone, and Joyce 1990). TM has been utilized successfully in the identification of relatively undisturbed primary forest. However, old secondary forest and disturbed primary forest were indistinguishable, and confusion occurred between secondary forest and regions of mixed crops (Sader, Stone, and Joyce 1990). The four sensors clearly vary in their utility in habitat mapping applications.

AVHRR

AVHRR applications have been reviewed by Hastings and Emery (1992). Most of the examples of terrestrial surface mapping address general trends associated with vegetation indices or thermal aspects of the sensor such as snow cover mapping or forest fire monitoring. In terms of change detection, AVHRR has been shown to have utility in detecting forest clearing in Amazonia (Tucker, Holben, and Goff 1984). Early work done in Africa with AVHRR by Townshend and Justice (1986) and by Justice, Holben, and Gwynne (1986) indicated that vegetation indices had potential in vegetation monitoring, particularly if a strong seasonal component can be measured.

More recent efforts in North America indicate the utility of AVHRR in producing regional vegetation maps. A multitemporal analysis made use of various ancillary databases to produce a land cover characteristics database for the conterminous United States (Loveland et al. 1991). A similar project was performed for Mexico (Evans et al. 1992b). The level of detail associated with Mexico's classes of natural vegetation are temperate forest, tropical dry forest, tropical high and medium forest, and scrub vegetation.

A combination of the thermal data of AVHRR with the visible data may prove useful in discriminating finer levels of vegetation information than has been achieved previously using AVHRR (Achard and Blasco 1990; Li et al. 1992). Because of the strong commitment to global change programs and the growing attempts to more fully exploit AVHRR data as a regional mapping tool, it is likely that further advances in its application will be achieved in the near future. The level of vegetation mapping done for North America and Mexico using AVHRR is currently being extended to Central America.

MSS

MSS data have been utilized in assessing deforestation trends in Costa Rica (Sader and Joyce 1988). The study targeted identification of primary forest, disturbed forest, and cleared lands, but relied on several ancillary data sources to accomplish its objectives. These data sources included digitized versions of previously prepared forest inventories, life zone maps, and elevation data.

MSS was utilized also in a deforestation study in Guinea, West Africa (Gilruth, Hutchinson, and Berry 1990). This study was similar in approach to the Costa Rican MSS analysis in that a variety of additional data sources were utilized in conjunction with MSS. The Guinea study produced more detailed information about patterns of shifting agriculture and degradation by erosion because it utilized aerial photography and videography.

In both studies MSS was found to be useful, but only because it was able to be utilized with other previously existing data sources or more powerful sensor data. The level of vegetation mapping that was expected from the MSS data was also relatively low. In an ongoing attempt to monitor regional trends of global change, MSS is being used as a historical baseline data source (Chomentowski, Salas, and Skole 1994). The Landsat Pathfinder project is comparing historical MSS data to recent TM data, but the resulting change detection classes are constrained to the level which MSS can consistently produce: forest, deforestation, regrowing forest, water, grasslands, and clouds/cloud shadows (Chomentowski, Salas, and Skole 1994).

TM

The increased information content associated with TM imagery was demonstrated in a project in which six forest and five nonforest classes were mapped in Minnesota (Bauer at al. 1994). The level of analysis that can be achieved using TM data is supported further by the work of Moran et al. (1994) in the Amazon.

The classes produced in their vegetation maps included not only forest, pasture, crop, bare, wetland, and water but also various stages of secondary growth: initial, intermediate, and advanced. A two-pass image analysis was performed that combined unsupervised and supervised classification techniques (Moran et al. 1994).

Evans, Schoelerman, and Melvin (1992a) also report advances in level of information extraction utilizing similar logic in the design of a TM analysis in Louisiana. A supervised classification was made of the TM image producing a six-class map of open/harvest areas, pine regeneration, pine, hardwoods, mixed, and water. A second pass was made over the pine class to break out low- and high-crown density subclasses. Congalton, Green, and Teply (1993) describe an elaborate methodology to map the distribution of old growth forests in the Pacific Northwest using TM imagery. Both supervised and unsupervised classification methods were employed. Extensive field data were available, and ancillary data were often used to differentiate vegetation classes that were spectrally indistinguishable but were located at distinct positions of elevation. Remote sensing was utilized to identify crown closure, size class, and structure to build species-level identification.

Each of these projects utilized detailed data for training statistics and applied a second or third level of analysis to achieve higher information content. Such effort is necessary to link local change detection analyses with regional and global mapping efforts. A similar theme is evidenced at an institutional level in the call by Justice (1994) to increase partnerships between international agencies and local experts. The question of scale is applicable both in bridging global and national inventories and in creating more collaboration between international and national scientists and resource managers.

SPOT

Very little has been published on the efficacy of SPOT data in habitat mapping, particularly in the tropics. A five-class habitat map was successfully produced using SPOT data in India (Prasad et al. 1991). Rasch (1994) describes a project in the Philippines that produced twenty-two habitat classes, comparable to the level achieved with TM (previously described). The unique benefit of SPOT in the Philippines project was the ability to produce cloud-free imagery in a shorter time span than could have been generated through TM data acquisition because SPOT has a market-driven schedule for data acquisition. Pohl (1995) describes an Indonesian mapping project that merged SPOT wth ERS radar. The combined strength of the SPOT sensor in spectral and spatial resolution with the cloud-penetrating capability of radar resulted in the production of a 1:100,000 scale image useful for updating existing maps.

The trade-off between the increased spatial resolution offered by SPOT and the lower spectral content has not been fully evaluated, in particular regarding forestry applications. A comparison of SPOT and TM in detection of gypsy moth defoliation in Michigan indicated that the performance of SPOT was 4 to 8 percent worse than TM in generating maps of defoliation and nondefoliation (Joria, Ahearn, and Connor 1991).

Most of the identified literature on SPOT is similar to Ehlers et al. (1990) and Johnson (1994)—emphasis is on the advanced spatial resolution and the associated ability of performing more effective urban mapping. Additional information on SPOT applications in the tropics could probably be obtained in the French remote-sensing literature. Further, because of the commercial interests of many of the SPOT users, fewer results might get published in the technical literature (personal communication, C. Hanley, marketing and communication specialist, SPOT Image Corp., Reston, Va., 1996). A recent SPOT newsletter indicated that SPOT data are being utilized extensively in Brazil and Bolivia, but the level of success of projects on the mapping of tropical habitats in these countries has not been assessed.

The Utility of Satellite Imagery in National and Regional Conservation Mapping Efforts

Other variables must be considered in planning the image analysis component of conservation mapping efforts in addition to an assessment of the efficacy of a given sensor in habitat mapping. Data costs, data volume, data availability, and the probability of alternative sensor solutions all have advantages and disadvantages which need to be evaluated independently for each country or region where habitat is mapped.

Data Costs

The most obvious factor in weighing the trade-offs between high spatial resolution sensors such as TM and SPOT and the lower spatial resolution sensors such as MSS and AVHRR data is cost. The higher spatial resolution data are much more expensive and cost $4,400 per TM scene and $2,600 per SPOT scene (1995 prices). Historical MSS scenes (older than two years) are available for $200, and AVHRR data costs $80 per scene. It also requires more SPOT scenes than Landsat and more Landsat scenes than AVHRR to cover the same geographic region. Thus, coverage for Costa Rica using one AVHRR scene costs $80, while five MSS scenes cost $1,000, five TM scenes cost $22,000, and twenty-two SPOT scenes cost $57,200. There are numerous cooperative data acquisition programs in place which help to defray the costs of national or regional mapping programs. The existence of such cooperative agreements is variable geographically, depending upon the initiative of the natural resource agencies in a state or country to pool their investments in data.

DATA VOLUME

Differences in the spatial resolution of various sensors can translate to considerable differences in data volume, especially if compounded by a greater frequency of bands. For example, a geographic area measuring 240 meters on each of four sides would require a three-by-three array of MSS data, or nine pixels. Each pixel has four bands; thus the image would require 36 data values. The same geographic area covered by TM (which has 30-meter spatial resolution rather than the 80-meter resolution of MSS) would require an eight-by-eight array, or sixty-four pixels. Six of the seven bands of TM data are typically used, thus there is a total of 384 data values. The TM data have over ten times the volume as the MSS, and this has repercussions in terms of the time required to process data as well as in the requirements for data storage.

The size of an AVHRR dataset is approximately 1 percent of the size of an MSS dataset for the same area (Hastings, Matson, and Horbitz 1989). A country the size of Costa Rica (51,100 square kilometers) generates a habitat database with approximately 50,000 points if the 1-kilometer AVHRR sensor is employed. AVHRR may provide a good data volume alternative to both Landsat systems, particularly if the region being mapped is as large as the entirety of Central America.

There are advantages to using general sensor systems such as AVHRR. In assessing the utility of coarse resolution satellite data, Roller and Colwell (1986) list several benefits of synoptic sensors such as AVHRR. These benefits have immediate savings if certain compromises in spatial resolution can be accepted. The acquisition of a single database obtained at a single time eliminates the need to merge numerous adjacent images. It may be easier to acquire cloud-free or cloud-reduced imagery in certain areas with the higher temporal repetition (daily) available with coarse resolution sensors. It is possible that multitemporal analysis might compensate for some of the information loss associated with decreased spatial resolution.

DATA AVAILABILITY

Most imagery of the tropics has limited data availability due to extensive cloud cover. For many areas, a computer search of all available imagery may result in only one or two dates of imagery having less than 20 percent cloud cover. One can acquire multiple dates and use the cloud-free areas in both images, but this is expensive and may not solve the problem. Further, there are possible temporal complications which could affect classification results. For example, it may be difficult to discriminate between different vegetation classes unless imagery is collected during an optimal season of the year. Analysis of imagery from two distinct seasons of the year may result in different classification results.

If cloud cover is a severely limiting constraint, it may be necessary to employ a multiple-sensor approach. The additional platform could be any of the higher-cost systems to ensure better data for those areas. The other data sources may include aerial photography or airborne videography, depending upon the information needed and the budget of the project. Videography and other sensors are covered in the following section.

There are plans to complete regional AVHRR mapping of Central America (Eggen-McIntosh, Lannom, and Zhu 1993). However, it is not yet certain that national composite maps of Costa Rica and the southernmost countries can be generated using AVHRR, due to the high cloud cover at the time of day of satellite overpass. The extent of the cloud cover may limit the utility of the map or database for the entire country of Costa Rica, but the data for the majority of the Central American region may remain viable.

ALTERNATIVE SENSOR SOLUTIONS

The focus of this chapter has been on four satellite platforms. Although these systems have been the most commonly used in habitat mapping, there are numerous other systems becoming operational or being planned for the near future. The most significant for tropical applications is radar imaging. Radar has had appeal for tropical habitat mapping for some time because it has the ability to provide data in spite of cloud cover (Ringrose and Large 1983; Churchill and Sieber 1991). However, airborne radar data have been expensive and difficult for many image analysts to interpret. With the advent of spaceborne radar systems on recent Canadian, European, and Japanese satellites, and on the planned American EOS and the Russian Almaz-2, a more consistent data source is anticipated than the early short-lived satellite radar systems. An evaluation of the utility of current spaceborne radar systems for mapping in the tropics found that the multiple radar bands in the EOS configuration holds the greatest potential for vegetation mapping in the tropics (Pope et al. 1994).

It is possible that the Moderate-Resolution Imaging Spectrometer (MODIS) sensor planned as part of the EOS program may provide a database that is neither as general as AVHRR nor as voluminous as Landsat. MODIS will collect data at three spatial resolutions—250, 500, and 1,000 meters—and will collect thirty-six bands of data, including spectral data similar to the TM sensor (Lillesand and Kiefer 1994).

Airborne videography also is a cost-effective data collection technique, particularly if used in conjunction with other sensor systems (Graham 1993). A multisensor approach on board a single aircraft was used to map vegetation in the Arizona gap analysis project (Graham 1993). Continuous video was captured in conjunction with regular acquisitions of photography taken at two different scales, in order to compare samples of the video with higher resolution data. The airplane also was collecting positional data with a GPS receiver; thus all the airborne imagery could be combined with other geo-referenced data such as Landsat TM.

Forthcoming Databases

There are several efforts to construct regional databases. Justice (1994) documents two major international tropical mapping programs. The first is the forest assessment being done by the United Nations Food and Agricultural Organization (UNFAO). UNFAO forest assessments conducted for 1980 and 1990 utilized Landsat and AVHRR data for select regions of the world with a goal of continuous coverage. The NASA Landsat Land Cover Change Pathfinder Tropical Deforestation Project is analyzing three image dates between the mid-1970s and 1989 for approximately one thousand MSS scenes in large tropical regions such as Amazonia, Southeast Asia, and Central Africa. The geographic and temporal status of these programs and the quality of their results should be evaluated in relation to specific project needs when designing any national or regional conservation mapping programs.

The disadvantage of waiting for any database is that it may be delayed or canceled. Further, the data quality for a particular region may be lower than that required by the user. There are serious cost advantages to waiting, not only in data acquisition but also in staff time allocated to processing the data. One might identify avenues of collaboration and cooperation in ongoing projects that are helpful to both the local and the international mapping efforts by investigating the prospects of waiting or advancing independently.

References

Achard, F. and F. Blasco. 1990. Analysis of vegetation seasonal evolution and mapping of forest cover in West Africa with the use of NOAA AVHRR HRPT data. *Photogrammetric Engineering and Remote Sensing* 56: 1359–65.

Bauer, M. E., T. E. Burk, A. R. Ek, P. R. Coppin, S. D. Lime, T. A. Walsh, D. K. Walters, W. Befort, and D. F. Heinzen. 1994. Satellite inventory of Minnesota forest resources. *Photogrammetric Engineering and Remote Sensing* 60: 287–98.

Blasco, F. and F. Achard. 1990. Analysis of vegetation changes using satellite data. In A. F. Bouwman, ed., *Soils and the greenhouse effect*. New York: Wiley.

Chomentowski, W., B. Salas, and D. Skole. 1994. Landsat pathfinder project advances deforestation mapping. *GIS World* (April): 34–8.

Churchill, P. N. and A. J. Sieber. 1991. The current status of ERS-1 and the role of radar remote sensing for the management of natural resources in developing countries. In A. S. Belward and C. R. Valenzuela, eds., *Remote sensing and geographical information systems for resource managment in developing countries*, 111–44. Boston: Kluwer Academic.

Congalton, R. G., K. Green, and J. Teply. 1993. Mapping old growth forests on national forest and park lands in the Pacific Northwest from remotely sensed data. *Photogrammetric Engineering and Remote Sensing* 59: 529–35.

Eggen-McIntosh, S., K. B. Lannom, and Z. Zhu. 1993. Study plan: Development of forest distribution maps of Central America and Mexico from AVHRR data. Starkville, Miss.: U.S. Forest Service.

Ehlers, M., M. A. Jadkowski, R. R. Howard, and D. E. Brostuen. 1990. Application of SPOT data for regional growth analysis and local planning. *Photogrammetric Engineering and Remote Sensing* 56: 175–80.

Evans, D. L., L. Schoelerman, and T. Melvin. 1992a. Integration of information on vegetation derived from Landsat Thematic Mapper data into a national forest geographic information system. *Proceedings, Resource Technology '92, 3rd International Symposium on Advanced Technology in Natural Resources Management*, 517–22. Bethesda, Md.: American Society for Photogrammetry and Remote Sensing.

Evans, D. L., Z. Zhu, S. Eggen-McIntosh, P. G. Mayoral, and J. L. O. de Anda. 1992b. *Mapping Mexico's forest lands with advanced very high resolution radiometer.* Washington, D.C.: U.S. Forest Service Research Note, SO-367.

Gilruth, P. T., C. F. Hutchinson, and B. Berry. 1990. Assessing deforestation in the Guinea highlands of West Africa using remote sensing. *Photogrammetric Engineering and Remote Sensing* 56: 1375–82.

Graham, L. 1993. Airborne video for near-real-time vegetation mapping. *Journal of Forestry* 91(8): 28–32.

Green, K. M., J. F. Lynch, J. Sircar, and L. S. Z. Greenberg. 1987. Landsat remote sensing to assess habitat for migratory birds in the Yucatan Peninsula, Mexico. *Vida Silvestre Neotropical* 1(2): 27–38.

Hastings, D. A., M. Matson, and A. H. Horbitz. 1989. AVHRR. *Photogrammetric Engineering and Remote Sensing* 55(2): 168–69.

Hastings, D. A. and W. J. Emery. 1992. The advanced very high resolution radiometer (AVHRR): A brief reference guide. *Photogrammetric Engineering and Remote Sensing* 58: 1183–88.

Jensen, J. R. 1995. *Introductory digital image processing: A remote sensing perspective.* 2d ed. Englewood Cliffs, N.J.: Prentice-Hall.

Johnson, K. 1994. Segment-based land-use classification from SPOT satellite data. *Photogrammetric Engineering and Remote Sensing* 60: 47–53.

Joria, P. E., S. C. Ahearn, and M. Connor. 1991. A comparison of the SPOT and Landsat Thematic Mapper satellite systems for detecting gypsy moth defoliation in Michigan. *Photogrammetric Engineering and Remote Sensing* 57: 1605–12.

Justice, C. 1994. Satellite monitoring of tropical forests: A commentary on current status and international roles. In *Tropical forest mapping and monitoring through satellite imagery: The status of current international efforts.* Arlington, Va.: USAID Environment and Natural Resources Information Center.

Justice, C. O., B. N. Holben, and M. D. Gwynne. 1986. Monitoring East African vegetation using AVHRR data. *International Journal of Remote Sensing* 7: 1453–74.

Kidwell, K. B. 1988. *NOAA polar orbiter data (TIROS-N, NOAA-7, NOAA-8, NOAA-9, NOAA-10, and NOAA-11) users guide.* Washington, D.C.: National Oceanic and Atmospheric Administration.

Li, J., S. E. Marsh, P. T. Gilruth, and C. F. Hutchinson. 1992. Improved vegetation mapping at a regional scale by integrating remotely sensed data in a GIS. *Proceedings, Resource Technology '92, 3rd International Symposium on Advanced Technology in Natural Resource Management*, 358–67. Bethesda, Md.: American Society for Photogrammetry and Remote Sensing.

Lillesand, T. M. and R. W. Kiefer. 1994. *Remote sensing and image interpretation.* New York: Wiley.

Loveland, T. R., J. W. Merchant, D. O. Ohlen, and J. F. Brown. 1991. Development of a land-cover characteristics database for the conterminous U.S. *Photogrammetric Engineering and Remote Sensing* 57: 1453–63.

Moran, E. F., E. Brondizio, P. Mausel, and Y. Wu. 1994. Integrating Amazonian vegetation, land-use, and satellite data. *BioScience* 44: 329–38.

Mulders, M. A., S. De Bruin, and B. P. Schuiling. 1992. Structured approach to land cover mapping of the Atlantic zone of Costa Rica using single date TM data. *International Journal of Remote Sensing* 13: 3017–33.

O'Neill, T. 1993. New sensors eye the rain forest. *National Geographic* (September): 118–24.

Pohl, C. 1995. Updating Indonesian maps using SPOT/ERS image maps. *SPOT Magazine* 24: 17–19.

Pope, K. O., J. M. Rey-Benayas, and J. F. Paris. 1994. Radar remote sensing of forest and wetland ecosystems in the Central American tropics. *Remote Sensing of Environment* 48: 205–19.

Powell, G. V. N., J. H. Rappole, and S. A. Sader. 1989. Neotropical migrant landbird use of lowland Atlantic habitats in Costa Rica: A test of remote sensing for identification of habitat. In *Manomet Symposium,* 287–98. Washington, D.C.: Smithsonian Institution Press.

Prasad, S. N., R. S. Chundawat, D. O. Hunter, H. S. Panwar, and G. S. Rawat. 1991. Remote sensing snow leopard habitat in the trans-Himalaya of India using spatial models and satellite imagery—preliminary results. *Proceedings, Resource Technology '90, 2nd International Symposium on Advanced Technology in Natural Resources Management,* 519–23. Bethesda, Md.: American Society for Photogrammetry and Remote Sensing.

Rasch, H. 1994. Mapping of vegetation, land cover, and land use by satellite—experience and conclusions for future project applications. *Photogrammetric Engineering and Remote Sensing* 60: 265–71.

Ringrose, S. M. and P. Large. 1983. The comparative value of Landsat print and digitized data and radar imagery for ecological land classification in the humid tropics. *Canadian Journal of Remote Sensing* 9: 435–60.

Roller, N. E. G. and J. E. Colwell. 1986. Coarse-resolution satellite data for ecological surveys. *BioScience* 36: 468–75.

Sader, S. A. and A. T. Joyce. 1988. Deforestation rates and trends in Costa Rica, 1940 to 1983. *Biotropica* 20: 11–19.

Sader, S. A., T. A. Stone, and A. T. Joyce. 1990. Remote sensing of tropical forests: An overview of research and applications using non-photographic sensors. *Photogrammetric Engineering and Remote Sensing* 56: 1343–51.

Scott, J. M., F. Davis, B. Csuti, R. Noss, B. Butterfield, C. Groves, H. Anderson, S. Caicco, F. D'Erchia, T. C. Edwards Jr., J. Ulliman, and R. G. Wright. 1993. *Gap analysis: A geographical approach to protection of biological diversity.* Wildlife Monograph no. 123 (41 pp.). Bethesda, Md.: The Wildlife Society.

Townshend, J. R. G. and C. O. Justice. 1986. Analysis of the dynamics of African vegetation using the normalized difference vegetation index. *International Journal of Remote Sensing* 7: 1435–45.

Tucker, C. J., B. N. Holben, and T. E. Goff. 1984. Intensive forest clearing in Rondonia, Brazil, as detected by satellite remote sensing. *Remote Sensing of Environment* 15: 255–61.

6

GPS

Jeffery S. Allen

General Overview of GPS

The Global Positioning System (GPS) is a new tool recently added to the growing hardware and software utilities which comprise computer mapping. This chapter will include an explanation of GPS, how it is currently being used, some examples of use in Central America, and suggestions for training and implementation for natural resource management in developing tropical countries.

Accuracy of positional information for navigation and positioning has been something that mappers have persistently pursued over the ages. Some historical maps are almost comical in their presentation and oversimplification of spatial details. However, many historical maps are amazing works of cartography and impressive in their relative accuracy. Previous chapters have compared and contrasted traditional cartography and the use of GIS. One of the issues discussed related to adding information into a digital cartographic database. The most common avenue of entering this data has been the digitizer tablet or table. While entering data in this fashion has improved the efficiency of mapmaking enormously, the utilization of GPS takes digitizing to a new level.

The GPS technology which has emerged recently in the digital mapping community uses satellites for navigation and location finding. It is revolutionizing spatial data capture and could potentially be the most important remote sensing tool since the aerial photograph. This technology has been developed by the Department of Defense (DOD) to support military navigation and timing needs at a cost of approximately $8–10 billion (Leick 1995). The GPS is a constellation of twenty-four satellites (named Navigation Satellite Timing and Ranging, or NAVSTAR) orbiting the earth which became fully operational on December 8, 1993. Each satellite continuously transmits precise time and position (latitude, longitude, and altitude) information. It was initially implemented to give the

DOD a more reliable navigational system than LORAN and other systems and to offer worldwide coverage for navigation on land, sea, or air. The system was designed to be operational twenty-four hours a day and is free of the flaws of most land-based systems (i.e., going out of range of the signal) as well as being impervious to jamming by those other than the DOD. GPS is predicted to be the major tool for positioning points worldwide and under all weather conditions for all computer mapping systems (Leick 1987).

With a GPS receiver, information transmitted by the satellite is used to determine the geographic position of the receiver. Data can be collected anywhere on the earth's surface, recorded in the GPS unit, and then transferred into a computer. These location files can then be either displayed on the computer or incorporated into various types of mapping or GIS software. Ultimately, processes such as updating old maps or digital files, establishing control points for maps and images, and mapping new routes or areas has become faster and easier.

The GPS is comprised of three segments: space, control and user. The space segment consists of the constellation of satellites, originally planned as twenty-one operational *space* or *satellite vehicles* (SVs) and three spares, but currently operating as twenty-four operational SVs. Four SVs orbit in each of six orbital planes at an altitude of about 20,200 km in a twelve-hour period (Wells et al. 1987). Each satellite is equipped with four high-precision atomic clocks and continuously transmits a unique code which can readily be identified for that particular satellite. The control segment is comprised of five monitor stations, three ground antennas or upload stations, and one master control station located at Falcon Air Force Base in Colorado. The monitor stations track the satellites, accumulating ranging data and passing the data along to the master control station. The information is processed at the control station to determine satellite orbits and to update each SV's navigational message and clock. Updated information is forwarded to the upload station and transmitted to each SV using the ground antennas. The user segment consists of antennas and receiver-processors that provide positioning, velocity, and timing information on land, sea, or air for various civilian and military users.

Each of the GPS satellites transmits signals on two L-band radio frequencies: L1 at 1575.42 MHz and L2 at 1227.6 MHz. Each of the L-band transmissions is modulated with what are called pseudorandom noise codes. There are two types of digital codes—coarse/acquisition (C/A) code and precision (P) code. The C/A code is sometimes referred to as civilian code, and the P code is sometimes referred to as military code. The C/A code is assigned to the L1 frequency only whereas the P code is assigned to both the L1 and L2 frequencies. Each of the satellites transmits on the same frequencies, L1 and L2, but have individual code assignments.

The satellite and the GPS receiver have clocks that are synchronized; the GPS works by comparing the time of reception of the signal on earth to the time of transmission of the signal by the satellite. The GPS measures how long it took the receiver to get the code that was emitted from the satellite, using the formula of distance = velocity × time. In other words, the GPS can calculate the distance between the user with the receiver and the satellite because it calculates how fast the code is traveling (radio waves travel at the speed of light or about 186,000 miles per second) and how long it took the signal to get to the receiver. By using measurements from three or more satellites, the GPS receiver can then triangulate a precise position of the user anywhere on the face of the earth. Through the ground control stations, deviations in satellite orbit can be detected and these changes (ephemeris errors) can also be broadcast down to the GPS receiver (Trimble Navigation 1989). Therefore the receiver is continually updated on relative satellite positions with respect to one another and can use that information for calculating GPS fixes or positions on the earth.

When the receiver calculates a position using three satellites, it relates the position in two dimensions (latitude and longitude) and is called a *2D measurement*. When the receiver uses at least four satellites to calculate a position, it relates the position in three dimensions (latitude, longitude, and altitude) and is called a *3D measurement*. Using four or more satellites and measuring along the third dimension helps to improve the accuracies of positions. Most receiver manufacturers recommend using only the 3D measurements because of their higher accuracies. If 2D measurements are used, the positions may be off by a factor of one half to two or more (Trimble Navigation 1992). In areas where the view of the receiver to the satellites is obstructed (e.g., under dense canopy or adjacent to steep slopes), the user may have to use 2D measurements with lower positional accuracies.

In theory, one should be able to calculate position with little if any error. In practice, this is not the case. First, the mapping community is dependent upon reference datums which become more precise every day but still contain error. Second, there are limitations on receiver equipment (hardware and software) which are variable according to the cost of the unit (more expensive receivers generally provide better accuracies). Third, there is error introduced by the ionosphere and troposphere which is handled by ground control corrections and software but not totally eliminated. Fourth, there is human error introduced by improper operation of the receiver but controlled through training and repeated use of the equipment. Fifth (and foremost) is the ability of the DOD to degrade the satellite signal at any time. A process called *selective availability* (SA) degrades the C/A code through manipulating navigational message orbit data and by manipulating satellite clock frequency so that receivers may miscalculate positions by as much as one hundred meters. DOD does this to ensure that no tracking mechanisms have equal or better positioning capability than their own machinery or weaponry. DOD has also developed the ability to encrypt the P code (*anti-spoofing*) to guard against false transmissions of satellite data.

There is a technique to avoid the majority of positional errors introduced by all five of these errors that has become very common practice for those collecting GPS data. The process is called relative positioning, or more commonly, *differential correction* and involves using two receivers to collect the field data. One receiver is used as a "base station" while the second receiver is used as the "rover" or field data collection unit. The base station is placed over a previously surveyed point where the exact latitude, longitude, and altitude is known. Then operating at the same time, the rover is used to collect the field data. Because the base station is located at a known point, error in the GPS signals can easily be identified. This same amount of error difference can be applied to the rover unit because the satellites are in such a high orbit that errors measured by one receiver will be nearly the same for any other receiver in the same area (300 mile or 500 km radius) (Trimble Navigation 1989 and 1993). That error difference is subtracted from the rover's data, and errors can be reduced from one hundred meters to usually two to five meters. In fact, many manufacturers are currently advertising units with improved software capabilities that will give submeter positional accuracy.

GPS receivers have many different types of capabilities with a range of prices. Receivers can be broken down into three broad categories (Sennott 1993). The first category includes the survey grade receivers, which have P-code capability (centimeter accuracy) and cost between $10,000 and $40,000. The middle category comprises the L1 geodetic and resource grade receivers (meter accuracy), which cost from $5,000 to $10,000. The bottom category consists of the recreational and low-cost resource grade receivers, with a cost ranging from as low as $200 to $5,000 (10–100 meters accuracy). Gilbert (1995) further refines these categories to specifically classify GPS receivers which function as GIS data capture tools and range in price from $3,000 to $20,000. He points out that receivers that fall into the $250–$1,000 price range are generally only useful for navigational and recreational purposes and do not contain the hardware and software that allows a receiver to obtain and record spatial data for a GIS.

As noted above, accuracy is related to the cost of receivers. Most receivers today have no problem obtaining 3D positions, which generally results in higher accuracy of x,y (horizontal) positions. However, only the survey grade receivers produce high accuracy in the z (vertical) dimension. While the resource grade receivers require the z dimension for better accuracy in the x,y dimension, that does not necessarily relate to better accuracy in the z dimension (vertical). Therefore, resource grade receivers generally are not a good tool to use for mapping elevation.

Examples in Natural Resources

Touted originally as a new navigational instrument and then as a revolutionary surveying aid, GPS has become a necessary tool in every form of computer mapping including environmental or natural resources mapping. The following section begins with examples of GPS use in natural resources applications included from the literature related to GPS and GIS. From this the reader can obtain an idea of the applications where GPS is a helpful tool as well as the limitations of using GPS in natural resources management. The section concludes by citing examples of projects with which the author has had personal experience.

The effect of tree canopy on satellite signal reception and signal accuracy is important in all GPS applications but is often critical in natural resource applications when time in the field is limited by both environmental and financial constraints. In forested areas the forest canopy, tree trunk size, and topography changes affect the expected skytrack of the satellites and can contribute to signal loss. Topography will be a major consideration in mountainous areas where a clear view of the sky from horizon to horizon will be obstructed. In a report on using GPS for recreational uses such as hunting, the receiver was very effective in leaf-off deciduous conditions, but heavy evergreen canopy blocked signal reception (Archdeacon 1995).

Using differential correction to get accurate positions is extremely important, especially when working in forested areas where some data loss due to signal block is expected. Kruczynski and Jasumback (1993) reported five-meter accuracy 95 percent of the time when using differential corrections from a suitable base station on GPS data for forest management applications.

Use of a helicopter for the collection of data for forest management using GPS often eliminates canopy problems but can be expensive and requires additional training. The GPS unit must be mounted so that the aircraft itself does not block signals, and the pilot must be assisted in navigation in order to obtain the desired mapping detail for a particular project (Drake and Luepke 1991; Bergstrom 1990). A helicopter-based GPS is especially effective for mapping forest boundaries during fires; maps indicating burning areas can be delivered quickly to fire crews (Drake and Luepke 1991). Thee (1992) reported the innovative use of tethered helium balloons to get the GPS antenna above tree canopy in the Pantanal of Brazil. GPS was deemed an essential tool when traversing the rain forest.

As compared with many traditional processes of cartographic data collection and data entry, GPS is often hailed as a mapping tool that saves time and money on many mapping projects. Bergstrom (1990), compared a traverse survey to a GPS survey for approximating the size of timber stands and found the GPS survey to be as accurate as the traverse but requiring significantly less time and labor. Wurz (1991) used GPS to survey a site in southeastern New York State that is a wintering ground for bald eagles. GPS was used in survey mode and mapping mode, and it was determined that by using GPS the project cost was one-sixth of the original estimate for a conventional survey. In another project GPS was used in natural areas management to help delineate boundary lines which, when done traditionally by tracing lines on aerial photos, consumed 75 percent of project time. GPS significantly cut down field mapping time (Lev

1992). Russworm (1994) used GPS to map unique habitats of an endangered squirrel. Researchers were able to make more accurate population estimates with the new maps, which gave them better information to make management decisions.

GPS is also an excellent inventory tool. The U.S. National Park Service used GPS to inventory Native American art (petroglyphs) in the southwestern United States (Fletcher and Sanchez 1994). GPS allowed for more rapid inventory, which saved time, but was of more limited use when artifacts were in close proximity (within meters). A mapping project in Idaho used GPS to locate archaeological sites on forty thousand acres containing more than six hundred sites. The GPS was valuable especially in foggy weather and cut the project time in half (Druss 1992).

As mapping technologies such as GIS and image analysis become easier to use and integrate with one another, GPS helps them become even more powerful. Bobbe (1992) states that GPS is a perfect complement to satellite and airborne remote sensing imagery. The two technologies are being used worldwide to map vast areas, correct satellite image distortion with GPS points, and pinpoint objects of interest (such as rare or endangered plant species) on the images (Hough 1992).

GPS on the Cherokee Trail

GPS was used to map segments of a remnant Native American Indian trail. The Cherokee Trail was a primary transportation and trade route prior to European settlement of the area. Today most of the trail is paved over with modern highway or other developments; however, a few sections remain untouched. Working with a local historical society, a mapping team was taken to various points along the trail which were tagged by GPS and various attribute data. It is hoped that by putting this historical data in digital format an important piece of southeastern U.S. history can be saved.

Using GPS in Marine Environments

In a project designed to study underwater sand migration off the coast of South Carolina, transect data were collected using a sonar imager which was geographically referenced with GPS. Transect data were downloaded at the end of each working day onto a portable PC using PATHFINDER post-processing software and stored as a Standard Storage Format (SSF) file. The data were converted into GIS files with output coordinates in Universal Transverse Mercator (UTM).

Transect files were transferred into a UNIX workstation environment, imported into ARC/INFO, and stored as separate layers or coverages. Digital files compiled by the U.S. Geological Survey (called Topologically Integrated Geographic Encoding and Referencing system, or TIGER) at a scale of 1:100,000 were used as a reference map, specifically the roads and hydrology layers. Transect coverages were overlaid on the TIGER files to check for proper registration.

Sonar images were interpreted for presence or absence of sand and other sediments. Attribute data were entered in the INFO database and then related to the existing transect coverages. Transects were classified according to the sand attributes and plotted in order to determine the spatial pattern of sand movement within the study area.

An analysis of the transect maps revealed that migrating sand (that type which naturally nourishes a coastline) is only found in small amounts immediately offshore of the coastal islands within the study area. Most of the sand was associated with the transects that ran parallel to the shore, and was only on the shore side of the transects. It appears that man-made dams and jetties (breakwaters) as well as the dredged harbor channel all act as barriers to sediment movement and decrease the sediment supply to the coastal islands.

GPS proved successful in tagging coordinates to the transect lines and in providing an accurate spatial reference for the sonar transects. At the map scales used for this project, differential corrections applied to transect lines did not noticeably produce more accurate results. High accuracies of positions may have been the result of working at sea level.

USING GPS FOR WETLANDS DELINEATION

This project involved using new technologies for wetland species detection and mapping. The primary objective of the project was to use a process called subpixel image analysis for species level mapping. GPS was required for georeferencing of sample plot data, canopy maps, and 30-meter Landsat TM data. A Trimble Navigation Limited Pathfinder Professional receiver was used in tandem with data gathered simultaneously with a Trimble Community Base Station. By using two receivers in tandem, data that is normally scrambled by DOD to produce positions with 15–100 m error was differentially corrected to produce positions with only 2–5 m error. The Pathfinder Professional is a six-channel receiver, which gives it the ability to track or lock on to six satellites at one time and therefore provides optimal position solutions with the lowest error. In contrast, a single or dual channel receiver locks on to one satellite at a time until it finds four satellites that give the best 3D position. This is very time-consuming and problematic when signals are being blocked. The multichannel capability is essential when working under dense canopy field sites such as the sample plots in this project.

Use of GPS in Locating File Plots   Two sets of GPS data were collected— ground control points and plot location points. The ground control points were ground features that were readily visible on the aerial photographs of the study area, and where reliable 3D reception was available (i.e., no obstruction of the satellite signals from dense canopy or other barriers). These control points were marked on the aerial photographs as the GPS data were collected.

The plot location points were actually a set of three points for each field plot. The three points corresponded to the center, northeast corner, and southwest corner of each plot. These three points were evaluated for agreement and a 20-meter plot boundary was fitted to the points. The plot boundary, the plot center, and the ground control points were transformed from latitude and longitude to the coordinate plane of each photograph that contained field plots. The plot boundary and center point locations and control points were then mapped at the scale of the photograph on clear acetate. This piece of acetate was overlaid on the photograph to locate the field plot on the photograph. At this point the field-drawn canopy map was compared with the photograph data and the precise position of the plot was determined. The canopy map was then redrawn from the photograph, using a zoom transfer scope, to better reflect the aerial view of the plot. This photo-drawn plot map was digitized, converted from vector to raster format, and transformed to the coordinate system of the TM imagery.

Refinement of Plot Center Data   Much of the data collected for the field plots was 2D data. This data was of varying quality. The use of 2.5-meter airborne multispectral imagery data for the plots made it highly desirable to locate the plot centers as accurately as possible. Because the GPS software can sometimes be limited in its ability to perform project-specific statistical analyses, the following process was used to refine the 2D data. The standard deviation of the point clusters (three minutes' worth of data at one point per second were collected at each point) for each of three points for a plot were compared in an attempt to determine the reliability of the collected data. Also, since the three points were at known distances from each other, their relative positions were evaluated for agreement. The data for each point were analyzed for clustering to test for the existence of modes. Different central tendency measures (mode, median) were assessed to find the one that best reflected the plot center rather than relying on the arithmetic mean provided by the GPS software. This evaluation allowed for the use of the best combination of points from the set of three. The plot boundary inferred from these points was weighted toward the most reliable points.

Waypoints   The waypoint itself is just a single latitude and longitude that has been assigned a name and number for easy reference. Once the waypoint has been assigned, the user can navigate back to it from any point on the earth. The GPS receiver software calculates the shortest distance between the user and the waypoint along a great circle arc. After a waypoint is selected, the GPS receiver will display the range and azimuth to that waypoint until it is located. GPS was used to assist in the field verification of potential detections of the wetland target species. After subpixel image analysis had been used to produce an image with all of the possible or potential locations of a particular target species, the GPS was used in the wayfinder mode to locate the targets in the field. By taking map or image coordinates of the species detections and storing them into the memory of the GPS data logger as a waypoint, it is possible to navigate to these points to confirm information from the images.

Technology Transfer Concerns

TRAINING

Training is a critical component if an organization wishes to utilize GPS as one of its spatial analysis tools. Personnel need to understand the hardware and software of the receiver system as well as data in order to do project work successfully. Currently, in the United States the most notable provider of training related to GPS is the "Navtech Seminars" series. Navtech offers courses at locations all over the world and covers the three main topic areas of (1) *GPS and Differential GPS*, (2) *GPS for Systems Integration*, and (3) *GPS for Surveying, Positioning, and GIS*. Several of the larger GPS manufacturers offer training courses through their own facilities or through their distributors. Some consulting groups offer periodic GPS training courses or workshops. Several universities also provide GPS training, especially those associated with groups that use GPS extensively in their day-to-day activities.

Training courses for technicians and natural resource managers who need GPS capabilities should include the following themes and topics:

1. An introduction to mapping/cartography, geodetic datums, and geographic reference systems
   a. Map projections (Mercator, Lambert, Albers, Conic, Polyconic, Equidis - tant, Azimuthal, etc.)
   b. Coordinate systems (State Plane, UTM, Latitude/Longitude)
   c. Horizontal and vertical datums (NAD 83, WGS-84, international da   - tums)
   d. Explanation of the ellipsoid and the geoid and their relationship to positioning
   e. Introduction to surveying and positioning (history of surveying, instruments of the trade, remote sensing, and satellite surveying systems)
2. Fundamentals of the GPS
   a. Worldwide 24-hour position and time information
   b. System segments (space segment, control segment, user segment)
   c. Receiver architectures (number of channels, multiplexing, etc.)
   d. GPS signals (messages, codes)
   e. GPS error sources
   f. Differential correction (post-processed or real-time)
3. GPS and field work
   a. Data base design (for GPS software and for incorporation into GIS)
   b. Utility software (data formats, RINEX)
   c. Mission planning (GPS almanacs, field data collection problems, topography effects)
   d. Data collection (field crew management)
   e. Data problems (excessive error, data loss, file management)
   f. Equipment problems
   g. Software problems

4. Integrating technologies—GPS, GIS, remote sensing
    a. Integrating GPS data with vector and raster data
    b. Compatibility issues with coordinate systems and map projections
    c. GPS and GIS attribute data
    d. GPS as control data for satellite imagery

There are numerous details that can be interwoven through the above topics. However, the most important detail to be included in training is allowing ample time for use of the receivers in real-world conditions. There is no substitute for experience, and the user will learn far more by planning a field mission and carrying it out than by listening to an instructor explain GPS.

In addition to taking formal classes or workshops, the user can also participate in self-education through reading the vendor manuals, journal and magazine articles, and textbooks. This is not the preferred method of learning GPS, as the user will likely experience the myriad of technical problems that most first-time users encounter. It is much easier and cost-efficient to take a course or attend a workshop and learn from the mistakes of others.

SUPPORT

The GPS industry is growing at a phenomenal pace. Only a few years ago just two or three companies dominated the market. Today there are dozens of companies in the GPS marketplace with hundreds of products to choose from. Receiver sizes continue to get smaller and smaller, disk storage capacity and memory continues to grow, and software continues to improve in utility and ease of use. For example, in the late 1980s the Trimble Pathfinder receiver with a Polycorder data logger contained two channels, weighed over five pounds, would not record attribute data, and cost more than $20,000. As of 1994, the lightweight Trimble Geo Explorer fits in the palm of your hand, has six channels, locks onto satellites faster, updates positions faster, collects attribute data and allows you to change the attribute data library in the field, and costs around $3,000. Likewise, companies such as Magellan, Rockwell, Motorola, Garmin, and Corvallis Microtechnologies are all making smaller, better, and less expensive receivers.

According to *GPS World*'s 1995 "Receiver Survey," there were at least twenty-three different manufacturers that produced GPS receivers capable of obtaining data that would be compatible with GIS mapping activities. Just one year later, *GPS World*'s 1996 survey cited fifty-two manufacturers producing over 340 models of receivers. Of those, there are more than eighty models that can function as a GIS data capture tool and that are priced under $10,000 (see appendix 1).

In the United States, those in the natural resources mapping community who are using GIS appear to favor either units manufactured by Magellan or Trimble. This is primarily because those manufacturers have put forth great effort to make sure their products work easily with GIS and other mapping software. Currently, one advantage of using Trimble equipment in the United States is that a network of base stations exists with excellent coverage in certain parts of the country and growing coverage in other parts. This allows the user to apply differential

TABLE 6.1 *Useful Internet Addresses on the World Wide Web*

1. United States Coast Guard Navigation Center
   http://www.navcen.uscg.mil/
2. The Global Positioning System
   http://wwwhost.cc.utexas.edu/ftp/pub/grg/gcraft/notes/gps/
   gps.html
3. NAVSTAR GPS Internet Locations
   gopher://unbmvs1.csd.unb.ca:1570/
   0EXEC%3aCANGET%20GPS.INTERNET.SERVICES.html
4. NAVSTAR Global Positioning System
   http://tycho.usno.navy.mil/gpsinfo.html
5. GPS
   http://www.zilker.net/~hal/geoscience/gps.html
6. GIS, Remote Sensing, GPS and   Geoscience
   http://www.zilker/net/~hal/geoscience/
7. A Practical Guide to GPS
   http://www.fys.uio.no/~kjetikj/fjellet/GPS1.html
8. Leick GPS, GLONASS, Geodesy
   http://www.spatial.maine.edu/leick.html
9. GPS—General Information Sites
   http://www.inmet.com/~pwt/gps_gen.htm
10. University NAVSTAR Consortium (UNAVCO)
    http://www.unavco.ucar.edu/
11. *GPS World* magazine's Home Page
    http://www.advanstar.com/GEO/GPS/

corrections to their data without having to own two receivers. Usually, base station data can be obtained at a nominal cost, sometimes free from the base station operators. The U.S. Forest Service, U.S. Coast Guard, U.S. Army Corps of Engineers, and the Federal Aviation Administration have taken the lead in setting up these base stations in the United States for their own use, but the data is, for the most part, available to the public.

In order to receive technical support from a receiver manufacturer, the user generally must pay a software and hardware maintenance fee which, in some cases, can cost more than the receiver itself. While this is recommended if an institution can set aside funds for this kind of support, realistically many organizations cannot afford to pay maintenance fees. It may be necessary for an organization to become involved with or form a GPS users group with other agencies, institutions, businesses, and organizations. Benefits from interacting in this manner include learning how other groups are incorporating GPS into their project work, sharing data, sharing software and hardware, and forming partnerships to do future projects. In addition, others in the users group may have access to equipment, information, or people that would help you. For example, new information on GPS is appearing on the Internet every day (table 6.1). Direct access to the Internet may be variable within a group, but one member could distribute new GPS information within days of its publication.

GPS Training in Costa Rica

One of the essential components of the USAID project (see part four, this volume) was the collection of ground truth data for the satellite imagery analysis. The ground truthing involved the use of GPS receivers to identify the precise location of sites, which were then verified in the classification accuracy assessment procedures. By using a base station receiver located on a surveyed point in conjunction with a field receiver, differential correction was used to obtain locational accuracies ranging from two to five meters.

A two-step training process was initiated when the project team member from Costa Rica (Jorge Fallas) visited Clemson University. The training program involved a general introduction to GPS and showed how it is integrated into the GIS and remote sensing hardware and software. This was followed by one-on-one instruction with Trimble's two GPS software packages, Pfinder and Proplan. This instruction, given over the course of an afternoon, was meant to provide a familiarity with the software in order to utilize the GPS receiver in the field. The visiting scientist was taken on a GPS field course and shown the differences in collecting point and line data and how the field (rover) receiver relates to a base station receiver. He was also given written material to review between the time of the first session and the next scheduled training session in Costa Rica.

Out of the training experience with GPS, a list of potential GPS hardware and software options was developed for consideration by the Regional Wildlife Management Program for Mesoamerica and the Caribbean (PRMVS) at the Universidad Nacional (UNA). Using this list in conjunction with brochures describing the various products, in addition to consultations with vendors and with all the project staff, PRMVS decided to purchase GPS equipment from Trimble Navigation, Ltd. The system which met both the financial and scientific needs of the project included a Pathfinder Basic Plus, a six-channel receiver, and a Pathfinder Community Base Station.

The second GPS training session occurred on site in Costa Rica. A North American team member traveled to Costa Rica to deliver the GPS equipment and to assist with system setup and continue with on-site GPS training. The week's proposed agenda included Pathfinder Basic Plus software and hardware installation and review in Heredia, site visits to northern and central Costa Rica, Pathfinder Community Base Station software and hardware installation in Heredia, and site visits to eastern Costa Rica.

System setup proceeded on schedule with no problems encountered with the Pathfinder receiver or the Pathfinder software. Site visits in northern Costa Rica included Santa Rosa National Park and Palo Verde National Park. Both of these sites were within the dry tropical forest zone. The low and sparse canopy conditions afforded excellent satellite signal reception (continuous 3D, the most accurate signal). Results of this included mapping of certain roads and trails that had never been accurately mapped before. A site visit to Carara Biological Reserve (transitional tropical forest) proved more challenging in collecting the GPS data. Dense canopy interrupted satellite signal reception, forcing researchers to accept less accurate 2D readings.

Two days were spent at the UNA, where trainees were instructed on techniques of data transfer from the GPS receiver to the PC and on data manipulation within the Pathfinder software. These days were also used to set up and test the Pathfinder Community Base Station hardware and software. Scheduling problems prevented placement of the base station at its permanent surveyed site; however, the system was deemed to be operational and would be moved as soon as was practical.

The last full day in Costa Rica was utilized for two additional site visits to test the GPS receiver in more diverse conditions. The first site was Poas Volcano National Park. GPS points were collected successfully at the crater where forest canopy was not a problem. However, when attempting to map the trail from the crater to the lagoon, the researchers traveled through a low but dense canopy forest and satellite signal reception was again interrupted. In retrospect, the use of an antenna extension would have been very helpful in that situation to get above the canopy. The last site to be visited was La Selva Biological Station of the Organization for Tropical Studies (OTS; see chapter 7). GPS points were taken at various locations along one of the forest trails. The high dense canopy of this wet/humid tropical forest provided better GPS signal reception than anticipated. When signals were blocked, just moving a few meters down the trail allowed a 3D signal.

By the end of the week, the Costa Rican team members were familiar and comfortable with the GPS equipment and procedures. The initial testing of the GPS indicated it can be a valuable mapping tool for the diverse landscapes of Costa Rica. Additional testing of the effectiveness of base station data used with rover data outside the Central Valley remains to be investigated.

THE HUMAN DIMENSION

The human dimension of GPS is the critical piece of the information puzzle. There are numerous instances where organizations have committed huge financial resources to computing hardware and software yet have failed to adequately train the personnel who are responsible for use and maintenance of the system. For GPS to be an effective tool, the technology must be adapted to the people using it. The utility of the system has to sell itself. There is little doubt that the utility of GPS is great, but to ensure positive results, users of GPS must have a solid training foundation.

Effect of Canopy, Topography, and Other Factors on Accuracy

One of the most common concerns related to collecting GPS data in the field is obtaining consistent GPS signals under canopy. This is of particular concern in the tropics or any regions where dense canopy can be found. A list of twenty-nine tips for obtaining good GPS signals follows. The intent of the list is to help GPS users avoid common planning and technical pitfalls. For easier reference, this list is organized into four topic areas: planning, equipment, environmental factors, and human factors. Using these tips along with a commonsense approach to field data collection should produce a successful field experience. These tips are based upon a presentation given by Thomas Lyman (personal communication, Second International GPS/GIS Conference, Newport Beach, California, 1992) and on Slonecker et al. (1992).

Planning

1. Every organization should have its own checklist for GPS missions. The checklist should contain pre-mission activities, GPS receiver standard settings and operations, other equipment needs and post-mission activities. The list should be tailored to fit the organization's needs and will help give every technician a logical visual aid to carry out each GPS project.

2. Sometimes GPS just does not work. Do not waste your time if it is not the right tool. You may be in a situation where a mountain or even a single tree consistently blocks satellite reception. It may be necessary to use your best estimate or no data at all for that particular spot or area.

3. Sometimes you must be satisfied with collecting only a certain percentage of your data with GPS. Whether there are physical barriers such as mountains blocking signals or time constraints where you or your staff can only go out in the afternoon or budget constraints that limit your team to going out just one time for one particular project, you must take all of these into consideration when constructing a mapping database.

4. Unless the scale of your maps is such that a few meters in error will not cause any problems, always remember to subtract the height of your antenna from your elevation readings. This may seem insignificant to many and also an undesirable extra step in data processing. However, when you consider all of the potential situations that can add error to GPS signal reception, any opportunity to decrease error should be used.

5. GPS receiver manufacturers always give recommended angle masks and DOP (precision) level masks for optimum signal reception and accuracy. However, under dense canopy it may be desirable to use a satellite with a high DOP as opposed to obtaining no signals. Do not be afraid to change your angle masks and DOP levels to pull in more satellites, even if it means a slightly less accurate position.

6. If your GPS software has a mission-planning component, make sure to use

it. The more time you spend in pre-mission planning, the less problems you will encounter in the field.

7. If you cannot get a signal, come back at a later time if possible (even on the same day) since at a different time satellites will be in a different arrangement in the sky. You will be surprised at how unpredictable the GPS can be, and returning to a site under almost the exact same environmental conditions you will get better satellite signal reception. Sometimes the DOD will take satellites out of service without notifying the Coast Guard or a satellite will be out of service (even though it says "healthy" on your satellite almanac) for several hours before it passes a monitoring site which can then turn it off and label it "unhealthy." Sometimes, no matter how much pre-mission planning you do, the health of the satellite constellation is unpredictable.

8. Whenever you are going into the field for a prolonged period of time, do not forget spare parts. The more you can carry without it being a burden, the better off you are. Weight is always a factor when doing fieldwork, but if you only get one chance at a particular site you are much better off having the parts for a repair and carrying that extra weight.

9. When spending extended time in the field, it is helpful to use short (small) files. Again, it will help to write down all of your files with a short description of what each file contains so you can stay organized when you return to your office. The loss of one of many small files is not as great as the loss of a single large file.

10. Immediately before collecting field data, the GPS user should go to a known surveyed point and collect data for three minutes. By calculating the error after differentially correcting this point, you will know the relative error of the differentially corrected field data gathered that day.

Equipment

1. Radio transmitters in close proximity can wipe out data on a data logger or on diskettes. Always know the specifications of any equipment you are using in conjunction with your GPS receiver. Call a manufacturer to find out if using the units together will in any way interrupt data collection or destroy previously collected data.

2. Keep static bags available to store disks. They eliminate static electricity. If you know the environment you will be working in, then you will have an idea whether or not static electricity is going to be a problem. If you are not familiar with the area, then bring along a bag just in case a problem should arise.

3. The GPS antenna cable is the most likely element to fail in the field. The cable is prone to getting stepped on, dragged through water and dirt, run over by vehicles, and jammed into bags and gear trunks. In addition, under heavy canopy many technicians like to use an extended antenna pole, which means extra cable and extra possibilities of the cable getting twisted, crimped, cut, etc. Always carry a spare.

4. Always carry a wrench, especially for the nuts on a serial port connection.

Most if not all of the time you will want your port connections tight so that cables do not become disconnected in the middle of collecting data on a critical point.

5. Check for dirt or other foreign particles or bent pins in the serial port and at other connection points. These elements can cause interruptions in signal reception and can ultimately damage the GPS equipment. Be especially careful in marine environments where saltwater spray can cause corrosive damage.

6. Take a clipboard or notebook with you and keep good field notes: time, date, byte count, and attributes are just a few of the things you might want to manually tally with each data file. This will all be worth it the first time you return from the field to download data files and some of them are corrupted or missing entirely. Your field notes can be a great backup device in case you have to manually retrieve data.

7. Always take the receiver manual(s) out into the field. Unless you use GPS every day, you will never remember all of the settings and parameters that might help you get your data and increase the accuracy of your positions. Again, this adds extra weight to the total package you take into the field, but in the long run it could save you valuable time.

8. Sometimes when collecting data for natural resource applications, you will need to map infrastructure such as roads and therefore will need to use the GPS receiver from your vehicle. Often access roads or logging roads have never been mapped, or even roads that have existed for ten years are not on the base map you are using. When it is necessary to do this type of mapping and you are collecting large volumes of data while in a vehicle, use a dedicated power source other than the cigarette lighter. The lighters are just not reliable over a long period of time.

9. Use some type of strain relief on all your cable connections. It is easy while walking through thick underbrush, crossing a stream, or crawling over a downed tree to snag a cord and pop it off or just loosen it enough to lose a signal. When moving from one data collection point to another, always recheck your cables and connections.

ENVIRONMENTAL FACTORS

1. Use GPS as a registration point in clear areas so you have a reference when you move into obstructed areas. Measure off from known areas into areas where no signals are possible. You may have to use traditional bearing and distance measurements to get a positional measurement for a point of interest under canopy or blocked by some other physical obstacle. This can be fairly accurate when you measure in from a known GPS point nearby and under relatively open skies.

2. It is harder to obtain signals under deciduous canopy. In temperate zones the evergreens tend to have leaves or needles with much less surface area than deciduous species. In the tropics even the evergreens may have broad leaves which can directly block or weaken signals.

3. Moisture, often in the form of dew or raindrops, causes multipath error. The water causes the signals to travel different lengths and contributes to the

total error in the signal measurement. Collect data when the forest canopy is relatively dry—this generally means in the afternoon when most of the dew has evaporated off the leaves.

4. Often under heavy canopy and no matter how much you adjust your antenna, you will only get 2D coverage. Although most GPS receiver manufacturers recommend against it, you can input your elevation data manually. What this means is that because the accuracy of your horizontal position depends upon the accuracy of your vertical position, whatever error you introduce by estimating an elevation will also be reflected in your horizontal position. In other words, if you cannot estimate your elevation accurately, your 2D positions may have huge errors. A pocket altimeter can help and is essential in some cases.

5. At night the ionosphere has less interference and therefore gives a more accurate signal. But collecting data at this time is often not possible because of unfamiliar or potentially dangerous field conditions or because work schedules simply do not permit it. However, if at all practical, collect data at night.

6. Before venturing into an area of heavy canopy for data collection, turn on your receiver and let it begin collecting point positions out in the open. Once it is "warmed up," then move into the area of interest under the canopy. You will stand a better chance of collecting continuous data under canopy by proceeding in this manner.

7. When collecting data under heavy canopy, move your antenna around at different angles, elevate or lower it, or even move it a meter or so from the spot you need to record. Even though you may increase your positional error by a few meters, it may be better than obtaining no signal at all.

8. In areas with low but dense canopy, it may be advantageous to use an extension pole or retractable pole to elevate the antenna above the canopy. It is cumbersome to carry and manipulate equipment in this type of environment, but it will avoid the necessity of a return visit.

9. In areas with high dense canopy, it is often the tree trunks that obscure satellite signal reception and not the canopy itself. It may be necessary to collect data away from your desired target in order to obtain signal reception and then proceed with a measuring tape and compass back to your target location.

HUMAN FACTORS

1. Make sure there is clear communication with project team members regarding designation of responsibilities for a particular GPS mission. A checklist outlining responsibilities for each member can be helpful.

2. Be patient!

Utility of GPS in USAID Project

Within the project, GPS was used as a complementary data source in conjunction with aerial photographs and existing maps. GPS was used to help automate a significant amount of the geographic data collection. Location of boundaries as well as establishing new or revised boundaries and location of species sitings were all assisted with GPS. GPS was also useful for helping establish ground control for the imagery that was used for land use classification and for integration of spatial data into the image processing and GIS software.

Using waypoints to aid in navigation to remote sites was useful but not entirely practical for pinpointing locations because with just one GPS receiver only 10 to 100-meter accuracy can be guaranteed. There is great potential for real-time differential correction for wayfinding and other GPS data collection, but the establishment of GPS base stations to form a usable network in Central America may take years.

Some problems were encountered when using GPS to collect field data. The GPS was successful only in open areas. It was not used in dense canopy areas—but primarily because of physical movement limitations, not because of GPS capability. Those areas could not be visited with or without GPS even though GPS wayfinding could get them there. It was a problem of physical access.

Training for the Costa Rican team, especially learning GPS, was essential even given the time constraints of the project. GPS proved to be a useful tool for team members and is a technology they will be able to utilize in mapping projects in the future.

References

Archdeacon, T. 1995. Campfire tales: Taking GPS on a hunting expedition. *GPS World* 6(9): 36–42.
Bergstrom, G. C. 1990. GPS in forest management. *GPS World* 1(5): 46–49.
Bobbe, T. 1992. Real-time differential GPS for aerial surveying and remote sensing. *GPS World* 3(7): 18–22.
Drake, P. and D. Luepke. 1991. GPS for forest fire management and cleanup. *GPS World* 2(8): 42–46.
Druss, M. 1992. Recovering history with GPS. *GPS World* 3(4): 32–37.
Fletcher, M. and D. Sanchez. 1994. Etched in stone: Recovering Native American rock art. *GPS World* 5(10): 20–29.
Gilbert, C. 1995. You get what you pay for: The differences between GIS data capture tools and consumer-oriented GPS receivers. *Earth Observation Magazine* 4(12): 40–41.
GPS World (editors). 1996. *GPS World* receiver survey. *GPS World* 7(1): 32–50.
GPS World (editors). 1995. *GPS World* receiver survey. *GPS World* 6(1): 46–67.
Hough, H. 1992. Satellite synergy: GPS and remote sensing. *GPS World* 3(2): 18–24.
Kruczynski, L. R. and A. Jasumback. 1993. Forestry management applications: Forest Service experiences with GPS. *Journal of Forestry* 91(8): 20–24.
Leick, A. 1987. GIS point referencing by satellite and gravity. In R. T. Aangeenbrug and Y. M. Schiffman, eds., *International geographic information system (IGIS) symposium: The research agenda*, 305–17. Washington, D.C.: Association of American Geographers and the National Aeronautics and Space Administration.

———. 1995. *GPS satellite surveying.* 2d ed. New York: Wiley.

Lev, D. 1992. Park management and GPS. *GPS World* 3(5): 35.

Russworm, C. 1994. Ancient forests and modern technology. *GPS World Showcase* 5(8): 36.

Sennott, J. 1993. GPS receiver sales: The sky's the limit. *GPS World Showcase* (August): 10.

Slonecker, E. T., J. W. Owecke, L. Mata, and L. T. Fisher. 1992. GPS: Great gains in the great outdoors. *GPS World* 3(8): 24–34.

Thee, J. R. 1992. GPS tames the jungle. *GPS World* 3(5): 34.

Trimble Navigation. 1989. *GPS: A guide to the next utility.* Sunnyvale, Calif.: Trimble Navigation.

Trimble Navigation. 1992. *General reference for the GPS Pathfinder Professional system.* Sunnyvale, Calif.: Trimble Navigation.

Trimble Navigation. 1993. *Differential GPS explained—an expose of the surprisingly simple principles behind today's most advanced positioning technology.* Sunnyvale, Calif.: Trimble Navigation.

Wells, David: Prepared under the leadership of David Wells by Norman Beck, Demitris Delikaraoglou, Alfred Kleusberg, Edward J. Krakiwsky, Gérard Lachapelle, Richard B. Langley, Mete Nakiboglu, Klaus-Peter Schwarz, James M. Tranquilla, Petr Vanícek, and David Wells. 1987. *Guide to GPS positioning.* 2d ptg. with corrections. Fredericton, N.B., Can.: Canadian GPS Associates.

Wurz, B. E. 1991. National treasures: GPS helps preserve a bald eagle habitat. *GPS World* 2(3): 28–33.

PART THREE

Uses of GIS—Examples in Costa Rica

7

GIS Design and Implementation at La Selva Biological Station

Elizabeth A. Wentz and Joseph A. Bishop

BIOLOGICAL research stations are growing in number and becoming more sophisticated in the services they provide. It is not uncommon for researchers to have access to full meal services, air-conditioned laboratories, libraries, and computers (NSF 1992). More comfortable living combined with access to research equipment allows researchers the opportunity to stay longer at the site, thereby becoming part of an atmosphere that promotes the integration of data, information, and knowledge. One of the mechanisms available for this integration is access to computer-based tools such as GIS and Database Management Systems (DBMS).

Techniques associated with GIS and DBMS are not new to research and government agencies. Their popularity also extends into various disciplines including geography, ecology, and biology (Cromley and Cromley 1987; Michelmore et al. 1991; Roughgarden, Running, and Matson 1991; Wright 1991; Moreno and Heyerdahl 1992). In these fields GIS allows for the combination of diverse, geographically referenced data in a computer environment for storage, query, and analysis. Additionally, GIS provides users with a structured environment in which data from various sources can be integrated and analyzed. For example, it becomes possible to examine impacts of socioeconomic development on biological conservation (Scott et. al. 1993; Sader, Stone, and Joyce 1990). Before the availability of such tools, combining data from multiple sources was difficult and often not attempted. Tools such as a GIS/DBMS in the data collection environment makes this possible.

This case study shows how the installation of a GIS/DBMS at one field station—La Selva Biological Station in Costa Rica—is bringing tools for multidisciplinary research directly into the research environment. The important aspects addressed are the differing needs of the station administrators and the researchers, the integration of station-managed databases with researcher data sets, and the techniques used to provide data, computer access, and training. These concepts will be described by discussing the design study, the actual implementation, and the impact the system has had on administration and research at the station.

La Selva Biological Station

The Organization for Tropical Studies (OTS), founded in 1963, is an international consortium of about fifty universities, colleges, museums, and research institutions with the common goals of education, research, and conservation in the tropics. OTS promotes and supports a wide variety of basic and applied research at three field stations in Costa Rica. The largest of these is La Selva Biological Station, located in northeastern Costa Rica.

As a result of improvements in roads, public transportation, and dedicated OTS staff, La Selva has grown from a small isolated field station to an easily accessible research facility. This growth can be seen by the increase in the number of researchers that have visited the station: from fifty-seven researchers in 1982 to 240 in 1992. In 1992 alone La Selva hosted more than one hundred undergraduate and graduate courses as well as a variety of conferences and workshops in such diverse fields as agroforestry, biology, botany, ecology, herpetology, mammalogy, and ornithology (Clark 1993). In addition to growth in research and education, the physical plant has been expanded to include a library, air-conditioned laboratories, conference rooms, and housing for up to seventy people per night. Even the actual size of the station has grown to include approximately 1,500 hectares of lowland tropical rain forest. The property consists of primary and secondary forest, abandoned pastures and plantations, managed habitats, and a 45-kilometer trail system (figure 7.1).

The administrative activities at La Selva are also expanding at an increasing rate. In 1985, as part of La Selva Master Plan, OTS implemented a database policy (OTS 1992). This policy requires researchers to submit key data for archive when requested by the station administrators. Before this policy researchers would collect data and return to their home institutions, thus restricting the data access of other researchers.

The station's growth, coupled with the need to examine data historically and across disciplines, demanded a new environment to manage station and researcher data; simply archiving was not enough. This need forced station administrators to investigate new computer tools, including GIS and DBMS, as a means to support the increased growth.

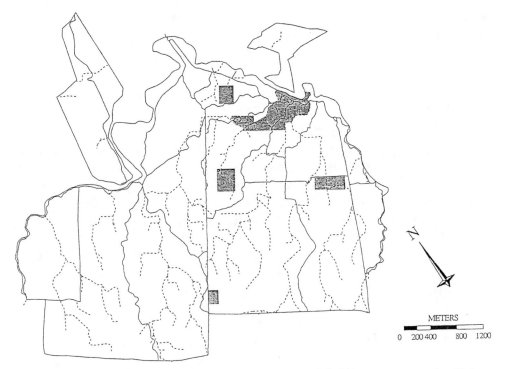

FIG. 7.1 Map of La Selva Biological Station property. Solid lines represent the divisions among the various sectors of the property or the existing trail system. The dotted lines represent the stream system. The dark boxes are restricted areas.

The Design Study

Before an integrated GIS/DBMS system can be successfully implemented, a design study should take place to identify the needs of all potential users. Systems implemented without designs often fail, not from technological limitations but because the system has not met the needs of the users (Marble 1989). Design studies are either undertaken from within the organization or outside consultants are hired. In the case of La Selva, the study was conducted through a graduate-level geography course offered at Ohio State University.

THE OHIO STATE DESIGN STUDY

Following the design approach recommended by Dr. Duane Marble, twenty Ohio State University graduate students divided into groups and formed questions for La Selva administrators and researchers (Marble and Wilcox 1991; Marble 1983). The researchers were selected based on their potential interest in GIS applications as indicated by the station's codirectors, Drs. Deborah A. Clark and David B. Clark. Questions focused on the database design and expected outcome:

1. What data do you expect to be included (e.g., soils, topography)? what scale?
2. What data would you provide? what is the original format of the data?
3. Do you have any previous GIS experience?
4. What products/analyses do you expect?

In brief, the goal of La Selva GIS is to be a tool shared by students, administrators, and researchers so that the combined use of the system generates cross-disciplinary research and data integration. To meet this goal, the geographic database was fashioned in a hierarchical form, beginning with a detailed station survey and then expanding the database to the surrounding region. The hierarchical database allows for expansion so that researchers can contribute to the system at all geographic scales. Another result of the study was identifying the need for a full-time person to work at La Selva for user support. This would allow the system to support the on-site needs of the station administrators and the researchers. A final result focused on the physical components of La Selva's infrastructure that are necessary to support a sophisticated computer system. To clarify these design results, a more thorough discussion of each follows.

Design Results   As a result of the design study, the following system goals were identified:

1. Build a geographically referenced database to facilitate new approaches to research at La Selva.
2. Assist the station administrators in making the decisions that directly affect the quality and type of research that takes place at the research station. For example, it is possible to use the GIS to analyze existing plot locations, trail locations, and forest cover to identify the locations of new research plots (Wentz and Castro 1993).
3. Design methods to help researchers use the database for project planning and spatial analysis.
4. Provide the flexibility to include regionally based projects so researchers can take advantage of the system's ability to manage large data sets.
5. Develop on-line demonstrations and training documents to help provide the means for everyone to use the facility.

It became apparent that La Selva system needed to include a nongeographic DBMS in addition to GIS. Tabular lists of flora and fauna, published and unpublished documents, and other information were in various forms at La Selva. To develop an integrated system effectively, these data needed to be included but were clearly not part of the geographic database. The DBMS portion of the database thus contains two types of data—those collected by researchers to be made publicly available, and the data maintained by La Selva staff. Researchers provide digital data in a predetermined format with limited constraints to their accessibility as described in the database policy document. The core database maintained by OTS contains data representing general interests of the researchers and administrators such as researcher biographies, lists of flora and fauna, weather data, and herbarium records. The DBMS operates with the GIS so that relationships between the spatial distribution of certain features are associated with their nongeographic counterparts. For example, one of the geographic data layers is the distribution of researcher study plots. The user is able to link this geographic data layer with the lists of researchers involved in a particular study, resulting publications, key words, and collected data. The researcher data and the station-supported data all contribute to data archived at the station in both geographic and tabular forms.

Geographic database development started for La Selva region independent of OTS but, coincidentally, was concurrent with the design study. This database included topography, roads, hydrography, park boundaries, and political boundaries obtained from maps published by the Instituto Geográfico Nacional (IGN) (Wilcox 1989). During the user interviews and with the aid of these data, it became apparent that a detailed survey of the research station was necessary. The interviews revealed that research scales vary from the entire station (approximately 1,500 hectares) to smaller than single hectare plots where individual plants are mapped. Even in the research projects involving the entire station, the maps published by IGN at 1:50,000 scale would not contain the detail necessary to identify spatial patterns for analysis. OTS decided to fund the development of a database with sufficient detail at the station level. Maintaining the plan for a hierarchical database, researchers have seen the database grow to be larger and more regionally defined, one that includes data from the adjacent national park as well as the initial data from the IGN maps.

In addition to the GIS-based data, remote sensing data are also incorporated into La Selva GIS and are being used by the researchers. These include images from airborne scanners, aerial photographs, and readings from radio telemetry (Luvall et al. 1990). Uses of remote sensing in the tropics can include examination of forest/land-cover types to estimate deforestation rates and land use patterns, animal tracking through radio telemetry, and monitoring biodiversity (Sader and Joyce 1988; Stoms and Estes 1993; Campbell, unpublished).

During the design study, the computer resources in Costa Rica were found to be extremely limited, including technical support and personnel to run the machines. As a result, a system was designed to best support the users in a way that limited downtime would occur should problems arise with either the hardware, software, or databases. A second system running at the research station provides the first backup. A third system was donated by OTS to the Universidad Nacional (UNA) in the School of Geographic Sciences to help maintain and establish further links with the Costa Rican universities and to provide La Selva researchers with a system near San José. A fourth system plus technical support is provided through the Department of Geography at Ohio State University. This system is accessible to authorized La Selva users through Internet.

Providing multiple systems in several locations supports researchers while they are at the research station and when they are at their home institutions.

The users of the GIS/DBMS are mostly biologists who are usually not trained in the use of GIS and may not wish to take the time to be trained in the technical aspects of GIS. In fact, many are not even aware of the hours required to design applications, enter data, perform analyses, and output the products typical to basic GIS projects. The users want quick results to sometimes fairly complex questions. To resolve some of these issues, the GIS at La Selva is designed to have these components:

1. a database manager to assist researchers with the design of projects that involve a GIS component;
2. menu-driven programs to aid in the development of geographically refer-enced databases;
3. programs to assist with the output of these data either in the form of maps or digitally transferable files; and
4. general recommendations on where to look for additional information about GIS and methods for analysis upon their return to home institutions.

These components, designed with the system objectives in mind, consist of databases and programs that are transportable to other systems, thus providing options and flexibility to the administrators and researchers. Details regarding these databases and programs will be discussed in the implementation section of this case study.

During the design study, a few potential problems were identified that would determine whether the computers required for the system would function at the research station. La Selva is a tropical research station where high temperatures and humidity are normal. Also, rural areas in Costa Rica do not always have consistent electric power. Power fluctuations and shortages that could damage the computers occur frequently. OTS addressed most of these problems long before the design study. The two laboratories, as well as the library, are air-conditioned, and an electric generator capable of supplying power to the entire research station was in place for several years prior to the GIS/DBMS installa-tion. In addition, surge protectors and uninterruptable power supplies were purchased for the GIS/DBMS. These are designed to help guard against electric surges and to maintain consistent power during the ten seconds it takes the generator to provide electricity.

Implementation

Critical to the development of an integrated database was the construction of a precise geographic database. As indicated by the design study, the publicly available maps would not contain the necessary detail for mapping and analysis.

OTS needed to construct a grid detailed enough to provide practical and accurate locations by researchers in the field. To meet these objectives, it was decided to construct a 50 × 100 meter topographic survey of the station. The accuracy of the grid is ± 20 cm in the x,y direction and ± 10 cm in the z direction. Also included in the survey were the trails, streams, station boundaries, building locations, and primary research plot boundaries. These data form the foundation from which the remainder of the geographic data are constructed.

To assist researchers in the field with the collection of geographically based data, a steel tube was placed at the intersection of each 50 × 100 meter grid line and labeled with a unique identification number. By using the fixed tubes, researchers can now map the location of trees, plants, animal sightings, study plots, and so forth based on the survey with a compass and a tape measure. Although no protocols regarding quality control on data collection are established, the grid provides a better system for recording study locations. Previously, researchers would estimate their location based on approximate distances from unsurveyed positions on the trail. With the survey, data collected from the grid can be entered directly into the GIS and combined with the existing information in the hierarchical database.

To complement the hierarchical database design, remote sensing data were collected for the region. Sets of black-and-white aerial photographs from 1960, 1971, 1976, 1981, and 1983 were purchased from IGN. Each of these sets, at minimum, covers the research station property and most include significant portions of the surrounding area. The Canada Centre for Remote Sensing tested radar sensors in Costa Rica on two occasions and both included La Selva. Data from the first project, conducted in 1977, are not available. Data from the second radar project were collected in 1992 and are in place at La Selva. These include the radar data and a set of low-level color aerial photographs.

The National Aeronautics and Space Administration (NASA) also collected data from the area around La Selva. In 1988 NASA conducted a project to test two airborne multispectral scanners, as reported in Luvall et al. (1990). The two sensors, a Thermal Infrared Multispectral Scanner (TIMS) and a Calibrated Airborne Multispectral Scanner (CAMS), were tested over La Selva and most of the adjacent national park. Copies of aerial photographs taken as part of the project were donated by NASA. They include a natural color set and a false color infrared set for their entire study area. The TIMS and CAMS digital data are on-line at La Selva.

The nongeographic data were more difficult to compile because existing tabular databases were in several unorganized formats. Some data existed only on paper; others were in various software packages; some were in many stages of completeness; and most were maintained by different people, on different computers, and in different countries. To compile these data it was decided to start simple and begin with databases that were already in digital form in Costa Rica. Concurrent with the construction of the tabular database in Costa Rica, a comprehensive structure was designed with the idea that new databases could be added without disrupting the initial design (figure 7.2). An interface was structured to provide a direct connection between the GIS software and the DBMS software as the data were being compiled. Part of this link included the capability to transport the geographic and tabular data in ASCII format or in one of the export formats of the GIS or DBMS software in order to provide researchers a mechanism to take data home.

The GIS software being utilized is ARC/INFO because it provides a high level of programmer and user flexibility. Additionally, many of the OTS member institutions use it, thereby helping researchers apply what they have learned from La Selva to the systems at their home institutions. Sybase was purchased as the DBMS software because it is one of a small group of DBMS software packages

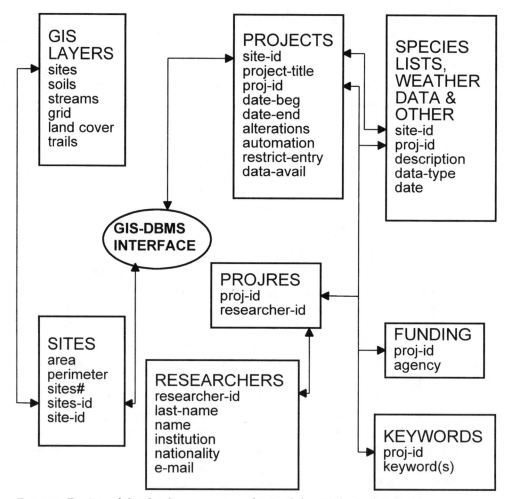

FIG. 7.2 Design of the database structure for La Selva Biological Station

with direct integration capabilities to ARC/INFO. The decision was made to use a DBMS software because they provide a Structured Query Language (SQL) interface not available through INFO alone. The hardware at the research facility includes two UNIX-based Sun workstations, two large digitizers, and two eight-color pen plotters. A local area network was installed, which includes three IBM compatible PCs and several Macintosh computers. These were established to facilitate data transfer and to allow for access to the databases from the administrative and public computers. The selections of hardware were made because the functionality of ARC/INFO increases at the workstation level and workstations have the ability to support multiple users.

Examples of Use

There are several potential applications that demonstrate how GIS is well suited to assist station administrators. The administrators need to maintain physical structures and monitor the research areas. The research use throughout La Selva can be monitored in GIS to avoid conflicts and maintain the quality of the forest (Wentz and Castro 1993). This type of site management is challenging because of the many variables to be considered: surface topography, trails, and existing research plots. GIS combines these variables, and the output is a composite of the variables that OTS can use to assist researchers locate new study plots based on their specific criteria and existing environmental conditions. For example, researchers may wish to locate a study area in a region that can be cleared; thus criteria might include presence of alluvial soils, little change in slope, and a specified distance from existing sites. GIS can combine these variables and display areas fitting these criteria. If researchers choose to locate their plot in this location, the new site boundaries and information about the researchers can then be added to the system.

Station administration was not the first project to utilize the GIS. A pilot project was established to polish the design and identify holes in the implementation. This project was a sixteen-month comparative ecological study of two of the primate species that coexist at La Selva: *Ateles geoffroyi* (red spider monkey) and *Cebus capucinus* (white-faced capuchin). A major component of the study included a comparison of the feeding patterns of these primates. Research included studies of feeding behavior as well as the spatial and temporal distribution of food resources used by the monkeys. While observing the monkeys, all trees that were used for feeding were marked with flagging. These trees were later mapped to the 50 × 100 meter grid. Before installation of the GIS at La Selva, each tree was plotted by hand on a paper map of the study site. After the installation, all mapped feeding trees used by both primate species were entered as point data into the project database. Associated attribute data (observation date, tree species, monkey species, etc.) were also entered to produce the feeding tree database.

Possibilities for GIS use in primate field research are vast and virtually untapped. Some of the topics being explored in this and future research serve to illustrate how GIS has expanded the possibilities for approaching challenging research questions such as understanding how the animals use forest space. The GIS calculated overall use area by comparing a variety of techniques. For example, area of use can be calculated by counting the number of 100×100 meter grid squares that contain feeding trees, identifying a minimum convex polygon, or buffering the feeding trees. Examining how the use areas vary over time is critical in understanding how seasonal variation of food resources affects use of the forest. Area size is only one component to analyzing the spatial distribution of the species. Other factors to be considered are tree species density and diversity of habitat.

The specific results of these applications are unpublished and hence are not included in this document. The application of GIS to this study, however, has given the researchers insights into the spatial patterns of the food resources that could not have been obtained using previous methods (e.g., paper maps). As a result, future primate field studies by this investigator will likely expand on results obtained in the current study and include GIS in the initial project design.

Not all research projects at La Selva, however, are based on the movement of animals. Many studies are based on sedentary organisms (e.g., trees). Geographic analysis for these studies may examine tree growth spatially and temporally compared to slope, elevation, and soil type. Using the GIS and the 50×100 meter grid, one project examined seven palm species found at La Selva (Clark et al. 1993). When comparing the mapped locations to soil type, topographic position, and accessibility for harvesting, four of the species displayed highly significant nonrandom distributions. It would have been difficult to obtain these results without the GIS.

The data collected and entered into the GIS from the primate project were among those used in the development of a poster and an on-line demonstration. The goals of the poster and demonstration were to introduce the concepts associated with GIS and DBMS and to begin to give potential users hands-on experience. Both were designed to illustrate the goals of the GIS at La Selva to appeal to students, administrators, and researchers and to aid in the evolution of their ideas for the GIS. Utilizing data collected from the primate project promotes data integration objectives to other researchers. In addition to the poster and demonstration, extensive training manuals were written to document the entry of data and the procedures for making maps and to provide samples of spatial analysis. For more information regarding GIS, users are encouraged to follow the training documents supplied with the ARC/INFO software. Although all projects at La Selva do not require explicit geographic analysis, these researchers benefit through the management of data sets, standard trail maps of the station, and the archive of databases.

Lessons Learned

When establishing a system like La Selva's GIS/DBMS, the primary goal is to create a solid foundation from which the system can continue to grow. This can only happen through adjusting the initial design and educating the researchers and administrators in the use of the tool. The design continues to be improved through interviews with users as they visit the station and interact with the training and demonstration materials. The user interviews identified and continue to emphasize the need for a common database for administrators and researchers. It is especially valuable to researchers because it is unlikely that individual researchers would construct a detailed system for personal use or integrate their data with other researchers. An advisory committee is being formed to formulate the future goals of the system. This group will be involved in setting priorities for the purchase of hardware and software, staff training, and database development and integration.

In general, the idea of data integration is supported by researchers but it is rarely practiced. It is also true that administrators have little control over data collection techniques and thus data quality. Various protocols can be written by station administrators, but they must be implemented and maintained. Despite these difficulties, the growth in research facilities demands better management of station resources, and a GIS/DBMS is one possible solution to these problems. This kind of facility should be maintained because it can be viewed as a centralized data archive for cross-disciplinary data and historical records of the research site.

The main objective for most researchers going to a research station is to collect data. Working at a computer in a laboratory can be viewed as inefficient use of resources during difficult financial times. A major problem with most GIS/DBMS is that the software programs are complex and training is expensive. As a result, many researchers are self-taught, and this requires a time commitment that may be impossible in some cases. As the technology becomes integrated into the research environment, researcher resistance to a new mode of working will diminish. Unfortunately, the technical staff available on the premises to train researchers and construct new databases is a further constraint. OTS operates on a limited budget primarily funded through grants and station fees. The problem is being addressed by providing users with portable databases, user-oriented programs, documentation, and systems based at home institutions.

Conclusions

There are many similarities between La Selva and other field-based research facilities. On-site facilities provide many benefits by addressing both researcher and administration needs—creating a framework for multidisciplinary research and providing for easy and uniform archiving of data. These needs can be met through implementing a software and administrative system that institutionalizes data sharing and standardization by providing a framework for storage and analysis. Researchers can perform preliminary analysis on-site so that more or different data can be collected quickly. Data can also be verified and re-collected if errors are found. These benefits will be more apparent as the technology is incorporated into the normal operating procedures of the researchers at the station.

Addendum

This paper represents the initial development phase of the GIS at La Selva. During this time database development, user training, initial applications, and training of a database manager occurred as described. Further work has taken place following this initial phase as new data have been developed and new applications have utilized these data. Although this paper does not address these new developments, it does provide the framework on which they were implemented. Information regarding the current status of the GIS can be obtained by contacting Bruce Young at the Organization for Tropical Studies (OTS).

Acknowledgments

The authors of this paper would like to express their appreciation to Dr. Duane F. Marble, Dr. Donald E. Stone, Dr. Deborah A. Clark, Dr. David B. Clark, Aimee F. Campbell, Marco V. Castro Campos, Dr. Donna J. Peuquet, Dr. Wayne L. Myers, and the Organization for Tropical Studies for their participation and assistance with the project. Thanks also go to the National Science Foundation, Andrew W. Mellon Foundation, Sun Microsystems, Inc., and Environmental Systems Research Institute, Inc.

References

Campbell, A. F. Unpublished. Use of radio-tracking on Neotropical rain forest monkeys.

Clark, D. A. 1993 (May). Personal communication with E. A. Wentz.

Clark, D. A., D. B. Clark, R. Sandoval, and M. V. Castro Campos. 1993. Edaphic and human effects on palm species distributions within a Neotropical rain forest. *Proceedings, 78th Annual Meeting of the Ecological Society of America.* University of Wisconsin, Madison, July 31–August 4, 1993.

Cromley, E. K. and R. G. Cromley. 1987. A GIS for local health services planning. *Proceedings, International GIS Symposium* 3:551.

Luvall, J. C., D. Lieberman, M. Lieberman, G. S. Hartshorn, and R. Peralta. 1990. Estimation of tropical forest canopy temperatures, thermal response numbers, and evapotranspiration using an aircraft-based thermal sensor. *Photogrammetric Engineering and Remote Sensing* 56: 1393–1401.

Marble, D. F. 1983. On the application of software engineering methodology to the development of geographic information systems. In D. J. Peuquet and J. O'Callaghan, eds., *Proceedings, United States/Australia Workshop on Design and Implementation of Computer-Based Geographic Information Systems*, 102–11. Washington, D.C.: U.S. National Science Foundation.

———. 1989 (May). Personal communication with E. A. Wentz.

Marble, D. F. and D. L. Wilcox. 1991. Measure twice - cut once: a structured approach to successful GIS design and implementation, *Proceedings, Eleventh Annual ESRI User Conference* 2: 585. Redlands, Calif.: Environmental Systems Research Institute.

Michelmore, F., K. Beardsley, R. Barnes, and I. Douglas-Hamilton. 1991. Elephant population estimates for the Central African forests. *Proceedings, Eleventh Annual ESRI User Conference* 1: 49. Redlands, Calif.: Environmental Systems Research Institute.

Moreno, D. D. and L. A. Heyerdahl. 1992. GIS help revegetation efforts at hazardous waste site. *Geo Info Systems* 2: 46.

National Science Foundation (NSF; U.S.). 1990. *Development of a research infrastructure in a tropical rainforest research station.* U.S. National Science Foundation grant DIR 90–13191.

———. 1992. *Data management at biological field stations.* Battle Creek: W. K. Kellogg Biological Station, Michigan State University.

Organization for Tropical Studies (OTS). 1992. *Master Plan for the management and development of the La Selva Biological Station of the Organization for Tropical Studies.* Durham, N.C.: OTS.

Roughgarden, J., S. W. Running, and P.A. Matson. 1991. What does remote sensing do for ecology? *Ecology* 72: 1918–22.

Sader, S. A. and A. T. Joyce. 1988. Deforestation rates and trends in Costa Rica, 1940 to 1983. *Biotropica* 20: 11–19.

Sader, S. A., T. A. Stone, and A. T. Joyce. 1990. Remote sensing of tropical forests: An overview of research and applications using non-photographic sensors. *Photogrammetric Engineering and Remote Sensing* 56: 1343–51.

Scott, J. M., F. Davis, B. Csuti, R. Noss, B. Butterfield, C. Groves, H. Anderson, S. Caicco, F. D'Erchia, T. C. Edwards Jr., J. Ulliman, and R. G. Wright. 1993. *Gap analysis: A geographical approach to protection of biological diversity.* Wildlife Monograph no. 123 (41 pp.). Bethesda, Md.: The Wildlife Society.

Stoms, D. M. and J. E. Estes. 1993. A remote sensing research agenda for mapping and monitoring biodiversity. *International Journal of Remote Sensing* 14: 1839–60.

Wentz, E. A. and M. V. Castro Campos. 1993 (May). Management of research areas at a biological field station. *Proceedings, Thirteenth Annual ESRI User Conference* 1:303–14. Redlands, Calif.: Environmental Systems Research Institute.

Wilcox, D. 1989 (June). *Components of the OSU ARC/INFO 1:50,000 database for Greater La Selva, Costa Rica.* Columbus, Ohio: Geographic Information Systems Laboratory, Department of Geography, Ohio State University.

Wright, J. P. 1991. GIS foundations for electric utility applications. *Proceedings, Eleventh Annual ESRI User Conference* 1: 609. Redlands, Calif.: Environmental Systems Research Institute.

8

Use of Digital Elevation Models in Tropical Rain Forest Basins to Extract Basic Hydrologic and Land Use Information

G. Arturo Sánchez-Azofeifa

ASSESSMENT of environmental damage due to deforestation and its impacts on evapotranspiration, infiltration, and runoff requires better climatic, geomorphological, and geographical databases. These databases will require new technological tools based on remote sensing, spatial statistics, and nonparametric statistics for quantitative impact analysis. These observational and analytical methods are not only important for assessing current environmental deterioration trends but may also have the potential to clarify future impacts of land use changes on the environment.

Two of these tools—the generation of land use information from satellite images and the extraction of topographic characteristics from digital elevation models (DEMs)—have proved to be important in a wide variety of fields (Sader and Joyce 1988; Sader, Powell, and Rappole 1991; Vesrtappen 1977). These can be especially helpful in studying impacts of land use changes on water resources management.

Topographic properties extracted from DEMs, such as drainage networks and catchment boundaries, can be related to different hydrologic and geomorphologic characteristics such as sediment erosion, production and transport, stream-discharge characteristics, and climatic patterns (Jenson 1991; Jenson and Domingue 1988; Joyce, Luvall, and Sever 1990; Klingebiel et al. 1987; Levine et al. 1993; Martz and Garbrecht 1992; Sader and Joyce 1988; Sader, Powell, and Rappole 1991; Vesrtappen 1977). Additionally, DEMs can be used in conjunction with GIS as decision-making tools for developing sustainable land use policies in tropical environments where other geographic data is poor or nonexistent. The main objective of this paper is to further explore the use of DEMs in the tropics in order to generate drainage boundaries, drainage networks, and to assess their potential on sediment and land use studies. To accomplish this objective, a regulated rain forest basin located in Costa Rica was selected as a case study.

Use of DEMs in Water Resources and Hydrologic Studies

Atmosphere-terrain interactions can often be correlated with topography. Topographic attributes are important in hydrologic analysis both at mesoscales and microscales (Moore, Grayson, and Ladson 1991). There are many correlations between topographic attributes and hydrologic response. Moore, Grayson, and Ladson (1991), quoting Speight (1974; 1980), presented over twenty different topographic-hydrologic attributes that can be directly evaluated within a catchment and that are topographically driven.

DEMs have proven to be very successful for studying aspects of catchment hydrology. During the last decade several authors have studied the hydrologic applications of DEMs (Band 1986; Jenson 1985; Klingebiel et al. 1988; Martz and Garbrecht 1992; Quinn et al. 1991). A series of experiments regarding the use of DEMs in hydrologic studies were conducted by Jenson and Domingue (1988) for four case studies in the United States. Drainage basins were defined for gaging stations on the Susquehanna and Genegantslet river basins (New York), for the south fork of the Lower Willow Creek River Basin (Montana) using a 1:250,000 DEM, and for the dam site of the Tujunga Reservoir (California) using a 1:24,000 DEM.

On the Susquehanna and Genegantslet Creek river basins, the authors reported 97 percent agreement of drainage basin form between the numerically generated basin and the basin that was manually delineated from topographic maps. A 98 percent agreement was reported from similar comparisons for Big Tujunga Reservoir and Willow Creek watersheds. A visual comparison of digitized and manually delineated drainage networks on a raster display device was also reported. Results showed that main channels are described almost identically.

These four case studies indicated the potential that DEMs can have for water resource and hydrologic studies. Use of DEMs can be extrapolated from catchment-subcatchment hydrologic simulations to analyses at larger scales using geostatistical approaches in combination with remote sensing and GIS. It might also be possible to link this level of watershed analysis with regional assessments of land cover change or greenhouse gas emissions.

The Reventazon River Basin

The Reventazon catchment (642 km^2) is located in eastern Costa Rica between 9°30′ and 10°00′ of north latitude and 83°40′ and 84°04′ west longitude (figure 8.1). The basin drains the area from the upper headwaters of the Talamanca mountain system, in the center of the country, eastward to the Caribbean Sea. The area of interest for this project was defined as the Upper Reventazon River Basin controlled by the Cachí Reservoir. The basin is rich in hydropower potential and is a major source of drinking water for the capital city. Its rich soils are used for the production of potatoes, vegetables, and coffee (Dirección General de Estatística y Censos 1987).

The topography of the area is characterized by steep slopes near volcanic areas (northern and southern parts) and more undulating slopes in the central part of the basin. Mojica (1972) states that three quarters of the area has slopes 20 percent or higher, with some slopes greater than 40 percent. There are areas with

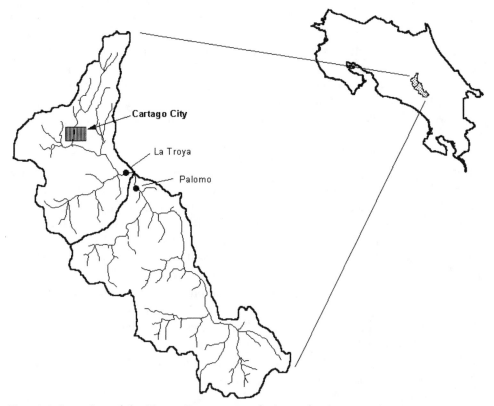

FIG. 8.1 Location of the Upper Reventazon drainage basin

slopes over 100 percent (mountain regions of the Talamanca system). The Cartago urban area has an undulating landscape with gentle slopes (5 to 15 percent). North of Cartago, slopes range from 20 to 40 percent due to the Irazu Volcano. The southern part of the basin has slopes ranging from 20 percent to 40 percent or more in ridges of the Talamanca mountain system. These topographic characteristics, in conjunction with the mean annual precipitation (of 3,490 mm) create conditions conducive to erosion.

The Upper Reventazon Basin can be divided into two subcatchments with significantly different land use patterns. The subcatchment La Troya (271 km^2), drained by the Navarro River network, has been developed for pastures and agricultural land use which consists mostly of coffee, vegetables, and potatoes. The area also includes a growing urban area (the city of Cartago). The subcatchment Palomo (371 km^2) is drained by the Grande de Orosi river network. Primary forest (protected), some limited pasture areas near the river valley, and the Pan-American highway are the main land uses. The union of the Navarro and Grande de Orosi river systems forms the Reventazon River.

Since colonial times (the 1700s), the upper part of the Reventazon catchment has undergone land use change. Initially, development was based on small-scale farms (Saénz 1980). After the 1950s, Costa Rica experienced increased economic growth, resulting in environmental deterioration that was detected in water quality, sediment, and streamflow statistics (Jansson and Rodríguez 1992; Rodríguez 1989; Sanchez-Azofeifa 1993; Sanchez-Azofeifa and Harriss 1994). The main element driving this deterioration was deforestation and agricultural land use. During the 1956–1986 time period, the Upper Reventazon showed a reduction of 0.15 km^2/km^2 in forest density (forest area/basin area).

Methods

BASIC INFORMATION

To accomplish the objectives of this study, three tools were used: (1) maps (scale 1:50,000) from Costa Rica's Instituto Geográfico Nacional; (2) a three arc-second DEM (90 m $\times$ 90 m); and (3) software generated by Susan Jenson and coworkers at the Earth Resources Observation System (EROS) Data Center, Sioux Falls, South Dakota.

DEM CHARACTERISTICS

The primary source for this research was a DEM generated from 1:250,000 topographic maps. This DEM consists of a matrix of geo-referenced digital elevation values on geographic coordinates (Petrie and Kennie 1990). There are three possible sources with which to generate a DEM: (1) aerial photography, (2) topographic maps, and (3) stereoscopic satellite images. The DEM used in this research was derived from 1:250,000 topographic maps by digitizing contour values. The DEM was geographically registered from the geographic coordinate systems to Lambert Conformal Conic using an algorithm developed at the U.S. Geological Survey–EROS Data Center (USGS 1991).

DEM Algorithms

The main goal of the algorithms used in this research is to "provide the analyst with the ability to extract from DEMs information on morphologic features and properties" (Jenson and Domingue 1988). The software consists of twelve programs that when combined produce (1) drainage basin boundaries, (2) drainage networks, (3) overland-flow directions, and (4) hypsometric curves (figure 8.2). The overall process is accomplished through a three-conditional-phase process, described below.

Conditional Phase One: Filling Depressions in the DEM   During the generation of a DEM, errors can be introduced. They usually take the form of "pits," or small depressions, that do not represent real topographic features. These and other errors produced during the surface generation process are corrected in this first conditional phase. These corrections are made using an algorithm that "smoothes" depressions by raising the values of cells in depressions to the lowest values of the surrounding neighbors (Jenson and Domingue 1988).

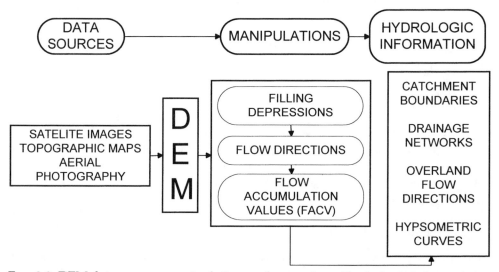

FIG. 8.2 DEM data sources, manipulation, and extraction of hydrologic information (From Sanchez and Harriss 1994)

Conditional Phase Two: Definition of Flow Directions   Flow directions are computed for each cell in phase two. In this conditional phase, flow directions for each cell are quantified into the eight possible directions of its neighboring cells. Possible directions are encoded as a function of the surrounding cells.

Conditional Phase Three: Generation of a Flow Accumulation Data Set   Flow accumulation value is defined as "the total count for each cell of how many upstream cells would contribute to it based on their flow directions" (Jenson and Domingue 1988). In this last step the flow accumulation value (FACV) for each cell of the DEM is computed.

After these three phases are accomplished, data sets can be further processed to define catchment boundaries and drainage networks. Frequently, an automatic procedure is used to "seed" drainage basins at all confluences with the same FACV, generating drainage networks and catchment boundaries. However, such "seed" points can also be automatically generated or specified by the user (e.g., for a dam site). Drainage networks in different stages of topologic development can be extracted as a function of threshold value. Therefore, the smaller the threshold value, the more dense the drainage network will be; subsequently, more subcatchments can be generated.

Extraction of Basic Hydrologic Information from DEMs

GENERATION OF CATCHMENT BOUNDARIES

The primary objective of this section is to compare drainage boundaries extracted from DEMs generated from 1:250,000 topographic maps with those manually delineated from 1:50,000 topographic maps. Total drainage area and geometric form are the variables selected for comparison.

Results show that catchment boundaries and drainage basin areas extracted from DEMs are in good agreement. The drainage areas generated from the DEM and the topographic maps are 657 km^2 and 642 km^2, respectively. This is a difference of only 2.4 percent. Agreement is also observed in terms of the geometric form of the automatically generated drainage basin. Figure 8.3 shows the southern sector of the study area. The topographically and numerically generated drainage boundaries are essentially identical. Due to the characteristics of mathematical solution and scale resolution, small positive and negative differences can be observed. However, these differences would not significantly influence any analysis of basin hydrologic properties.

Drainage boundaries extracted from the three arc-second DEM were used to clip the study area from a Landsat TM image. Information extracted from this

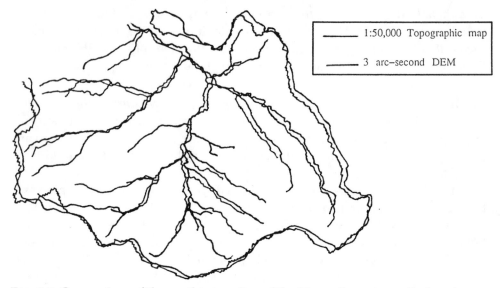

FIG. 8.3 Comparison of the southern section of the Upper Reventazon basin using drainage basin boundaries and drainage networks extracted from 1:50,000 topographic maps and a three arc-second DEM

image was used to create a land use classification map and construct a deforestation time series for the study area.

Drainage Network Development

In order to compare the drainage network generation algorithm with the one extracted from 1:50,000 topographic maps, the modification made by Strahler (1957; 1964) of the original Horton's Law (Horton 1945) for stream order definition was used. Under Strahler's approach, all headwater streams on a drainage basin have order one. When two streams with the same order join downstream, their order increases by one. However, when two streams with different order are joined downstream, the new branch takes the order of the higher rank.

Using the Strahler approach, stream order and the number of streams in each class were defined from drainage networks extracted from topographic maps and the DEM. Four artificial stream networks, with FACV of 10, 60, 100, and a drainage network visually extracted (table 8.1) were compared in a semilogarithmic graph (figure 8.4).

From this analysis, it can be concluded that low FACV (less than 60) correlates well with 1:50,000 topographic maps. The correlation between the drainage network extracted from the topographic maps and the one with a FACV of 10 is considered the best. In addition, it is important to observe that the correlation decreases as the FACV increases.

TABLE 8.1 *Number of Streams per Strahler Class Extracted from a Three Arc-Second DEM[a] and 1:50,000 Topographic Maps*

Stream Order	1:50,000 Map	DEM Visual[b]	DEM FACV10	DEM FACV60	DEM FACV = 100
1	194	122	220	63	42
2	50	35	42	16	12
3	15	11	15	5	2
4	2	3	3	2	1
5	1	1	1	1	0

[a]Three arc-second DEM (90 m × 90 m resolution).
[b]DEM visual: Drainage network visually extracted.

Extraction of Land Use Information Using DEMs

In order to identify potential sources of sediment in the Upper Reventazon Basin, land use classification was extracted through supervised land classification of a clipped TM satellite image (30m × 30 m) using a three arc-second DEM. Both images were geographically registered to Lambert Conformal Conic. Three ag-

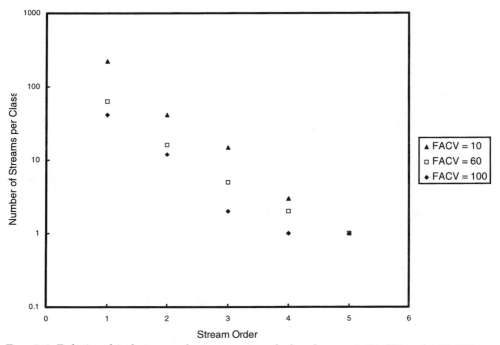

FIG. 8.4 Relationship between drainage network development, FACV, and 1:50,000 topographic maps. FACV less than 60 correlates well with 1:50,000 topographic maps. The correlation between the drainage network extracted from the topographic maps and the one with a FACV of 10 is considered the best.

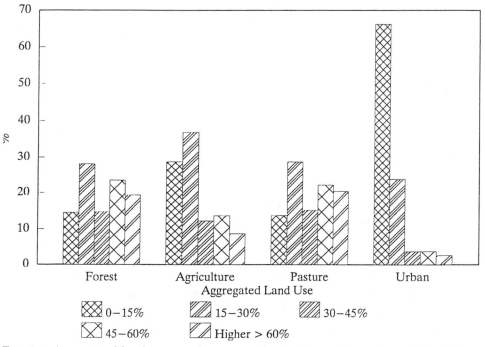

FIG. 8.5 Aggregated land use per slope range for the Upper Reventazon Basin (information extracted from TM information and a three arc-second DEM)

gregated land classes were considered: forest, pasture, and agricultural lands. In addition, slope was extracted in ranges of 15 percent using a median slope calculation method (USGS 1991) from the three arc-second DEM grid. A raster-based GIS (ERDAS 1991) was used to extract land use as a function of slope. As a result of this analysis, figure 8.5 presents the aggregated land classification by slope and land use.

Results indicate that agricultural areas are developed on 28.7 percent of the 0–15 percent slope range, 36.8 percent in the 15–30 percent range, and 34.4 percent above the 30 percent range. Agricultural land use is more intense in basin La Troya than Palomo. At the same time, pastures are concentrated on the 15–30 percent range (28.7 percent), the 30–45 percent range (22.2 percent), and the range higher than 60 percent (20.4 percent). Most of the urban area (90 percent) is concentrated on the 0–30 percent slope range. The distribution of forest remains stable in ranges over 30 percent in the southern section of the basin (Sanchez-Azofeifa and Harriss 1994).

The spatial distribution of land use by slope suggests a major development of the upper area (La Troya) due to its close proximity to the urban area. The southern part of the basin (Palomo) has less agricultural development in the whole slope range due to conservation policies.

Conclusion

A better understanding of tropical systems and their response to land use change is necessary in order to achieve sustainable use of the natural resources present in these areas. This goal can only be achieved with better technological tools such as the ones presented in this paper.

The use of DEMs as a source of basic information on topographic properties of tropical environments has been shown to be an important new tool for hydrologic studies. The different processes outlined in this paper and their results indicate that DEMs can be used when cartographic information is poor or limited. It is also useful when the analyst or planner is interested in obtaining an accurate definition of areas for deforestation studies or in the effects of land use change on tropical rain forests.

Results of this research indicate that information extracted from DEMs generated from 1:250,000 topographic maps can be used to determine drainage boundaries, drainage basins, and hypsometric curves at a level of accuracy similar to data extracted from 1:50,000 topographic maps. The result of a less than 3 percent difference for drainage basin area, plus good agreement of the basic form as well as 98 percent agreement on the drainage network with a FACV of 10, all indicate that the DEM has potential benefit in water resources planning in tropical environments.

Finally, the potential application of three arc-second DEMs in tropical environments with poor topographic information can be extended to hydrologic simulations where a catchment/subcatchment concept is used and no hydrographic information is available. This study suggests that the DEM can be an important tool of hydrologic studies in changing environments.

References

Band, L. 1986. Topographic partition of watersheds with digital elevation models. *Water Resources Research* 22(1): 15–24.

Dirección General de Estatística y Censos. 1987. *Censo Agropecuario.* San José, C.R.: Ministerio de Economia, Industria y Comercio.

ERDAS. 1991. *ERDAS: Field Guide (Version 7.5).* 2d ed. Atlanta, Ga.: ERDAS.

Horton, R. E. 1945. Erosional development of streams and their drainage basins: A hydrophysical approach to quantitative morphology. *Geological Society of America Bulletin* 56: 275–370.

Jansson, M. and A. Rodríguez. 1992. *Sedimentological studies in the Cachí Reservoir, Costa Rica: Sediment inflow, reservoir sedimentation, and effects of flushing* (UNGI rapport 81). Uppsala, C.R.: Department of Physical Geography, Uppsala University.

Jenson, S. 1985. Automated derivation of hydrologic basin characteristics from Digital

Elevation Model data. International Symposium on Computer-Assisted Cartography, Washington, D.C.

———. 1991. Applications of hydrologic information automatically extracted from digital elevation models. *Hydrologic Processes* 5(1): 31–44.

Jenson, S. and O. Domingue. 1988. Extracting topographic structure from digital elevation data for geographic information system analysis. *Photogrammetric Engineering and Remote Sensing* 54(11): 1593–1600.

Joyce, A., J. Luvall, and T. Sever. 1990. Application of remote sensing in tropical forests. Conferencia Espacial de las Americas, San José, Costa Rica.

Klingebiel, A. A., E. H. Horvath, D. G. Moore, and W. U. Reybold. 1987. Use of slope, aspect, and elevation maps derived from digital elevation model data in making soil surveys. *Journal of the SSSA*, Special Publication (no. 20): 77–90.

Klingebiel, A. A., E. H. Horvath, W. U. Reybold, D. G. Moore, E. A. Fosnight, and T. R. Loveland. 1988. A guide for the use of digital elevation model data for making soil surveys. Open-File Report 88–102. Reston, Va.: U. S. Geological Survey.

Levine, D., C. Hunsaker, S. Timmins, and J. Beauchamp,. 1993. *A geographic information system approach to modeling nutrient and sediment transport.* Oak Ridge, Tenn.: Oak Ridge National Laboratory (Environmental Sciences Division 3993).

Martz, L. W., and J. Garbrecht. 1992. Numerical definition of drainage network and subcatchment areas from digital elevation models. *Computers and Geoscience* 18(6): 747–61.

Mojica, I. H. (1972). Effects of changes in land use on the streamflow of the Reventazon River, Costa Rica. Ph.D. diss., University of Washington, Seattle.

Moore, I. D., R. B. Grayson, and A. R. Ladson. 1991. Digital terrain modelling: A review of hydrological, geomorphological, and biological applications. *Hydrologic Processes* 5(1): 3–30.

Petrie, G. and T. J. M. Kennie, eds. 1990. *Terrain modelling in surveying and civil engineering.* Glasgow: McGraw-Hill.

Quinn, P., K. Beven, P. Chevallier, and O. Planchon. 1991. The prediction of hillslope flow paths for distributed hydrological modelling using digital terrain models. *Hydrologic Processes* 5: 59–80.

Rodríguez, R. 1989. Impactos del Uso de la Tierra en la Alteracion del Regimen de Caudales, la Erosion y Sedimentacion de la Cuenca Superior del Rio Reventazon y los Efectos Economicos en el Projecto Hidroelectrico de Cachí, Costa Rica. Unpublished diss. (Master of Science), Centro Agronómico de Investigación y Ensenanza, Turrialba, C.R.

Sader, S. A. and A. T. Joyce. 1988. Deforestation rates and trends in Costa Rica, 1940 to 1983. *Biotropica* 20: 11–19.

Sader, S. A., G. Powell, and J. Rappole. 1991. Migratory bird habitat monitoring through remote sensing. *International Journal of Remote Sensing* 12: 363–72.

Saénz, A. 1980. *Algunos aspectos basicos agrologicos de Costa Rica* (Some basic agrologic aspects of Costa Rica). San José, C.R.: Editorial Costa Rica.

Sánchez-Azofeifa, A. 1993. Environmental change in a tropical rain forest basin. Paper presented at the annual meeting of the American Association for the Advancement of Science '93: Science and Education for the Future, Boston, Mass.

Sánchez-Azofeifa, G. A. and R. Harriss. 1994. Remote sensing of watershed characteristics in Costa Rica. *International Journal of Water Resources Development* 10: 117, 130.

Speight, J. G. 1974. *A parametric approach to landform regions.* Special Publication Institute of British Geographers (Vol. 7, pp. 213–30): Institute of British Geographers, London.

———. 1980. The role of topography in controlling throughflow generation: A discussion. (Vol. 5).

Strahler, A. N. 1957. Quantitative analysis of watershed geomorphology. *Transactions American Geophysical Union* 38: 913–20.

———. 1964. *Quantitative analysis of watershed geomorphology: Handbook of applied hydrology.* New York: McGraw-Hill.

U.S. Geological Survey (USGS). 1991. *LAS: Land Analysis System (Version August 1991)* [Satellite images interpretation and processing]. Greenbelt, Md.: LAS Support Office.

Vesrtappen, H. 1977. *Remote sensing in geomorphology.* Amsterdam: Elsevier Scientific Publishing.

9

Using a GIS to Determine Critical Areas in the Central Volcanic Cordillera Conservation Area

Grégoire Leclerc and Johnny Rodriguez Chacón

THE Foundation for the Development of the Central Cordillera (FUNDECOR) is a nongovernmental organization whose mission is to preserve and promote sustainable development of the natural and cultural patrimony of the Central Volcanic Cordillera Conservation Area (ACCVC; Area de Conservación Cordillera Volcanica Central). It promotes the self-financing of the national parks as well as activities of the private sector within ACCVC which are deemed sustainable, such as ecotourism or "green" forest management. FUNDECOR's actions are based on the principle that conservation and development are complementary and can coexist in harmony.

ACCVC, which is part of the National Parks Service of Costa Rica (NPS), is located in the central sector of the country (figure 9.1). It covers approximately 300,000 hectares. About 71,500 hectares correspond to protected areas by law as national parks while another 100,000 hectares are covered by dense rain forest in the buffer areas. The remainder is used for pasture and agriculture.

FUNDECOR and ACCVC/NPS support the protected areas to preserve and guarantee biodiversity, water quality, and scenic beauty through self-financing, territorial consolidation, and improved administration and planning. In the buffer zones FUNDECOR preserves all the area covered by rain forest through sustainable management of the forest resource. Both groups promote reforestation in the deforested areas.

Part of the strategy for conservation and development in the ACCVC, developed by FUNDECOR, USAID, NPS, and the Direction General Forestal (DGF—the Costa Rican equivalent to the U.S. Forest Service) with the technical assistance

FIG. 9.1 Location of the Central Volcanic Cordillera Conservation Area (ACCVC) in Costa Rica

of the Centro Agronomico Tropical de Investigacion y Ensenanza (CATIE), consisted of building a model to predict areas where the forest and water (the principal natural resources of the zone) are more prone to be affected by human activities. FUNDECOR would focus its resources in these areas and perform emergency corrective actions.

This paper presents a methodology using a raster-based GIS to determine critical areas based on the advice of a panel of experts. The method is standard multicriteria analysis, where weights have been assigned by pair-wise analysis of the threats to natural resources. The technique to normalize (standardize) the parameters will be described in detail.

Determination of Critical Areas in ACCVC

Definition of critical areas has been fundamental to the development of FUNDE-COR's strategy. Proper management activities in the area require the input of limited resources. To help in the selection of sites where FUNDECOR should intervene to preserve natural value, a scale of priority has been assigned to each hectare (the pixel size) in the ACCVC. These areas are referred to as *critical areas* throughout this paper. In this respect, a critical area is defined as an area with physical and socioeconomic characteristics such that it has a high probability of damage or deterioration from human pressure. In these areas FUNDECOR will promote actions that minimize the negative impact of human activities on natural resources.

With a raster GIS the factors that are associated with pressure on (threats to) the natural resources are combined to create the critical areas map that shows these dangers to the resource. This map corresponds qualitatively to a deforestation probability (if the resource is the forest) or to a water contamination risk (if the resource is water). To construct this map, the resources themselves are prioritized, and each threat is given a relative weight. The spatial variation of a given threat is then determined, and the threat is normalized in order to combine threats quantitatively.

PRIORITIZING THE NATURAL RESOURCES

Forest and water have been identified as the most important resources to protect since they represent the principal source of natural richness of the ACCVC. We considered them to be equally important but treated them individually because they require different types of protective actions.

Aquifers were classified in two categories—superficial and deep (with the first being given a priority twice as large as the second). With the normalizing procedure below, a weight of 1.04 was assigned to superficial aquifers, and a weight of 0.52 was applied to the deep aquifers. This particular weighting ensures that, on average (taking into account their areas), aquifers have a weight of 1. Primary and secondary rain forest were also given a weight of 1.

PRIORITIZING THE THREATS

Several criteria defined the degree of threat or pressure on the resources. These were (1) population density, (2) roads and trails, (3) terrain slopes, (4) logging activities (i.e., forest management plans), and (5) the land distribution plan initiated by the Instituto de Desarrollo Agrario (IDA, or Institute of Agrarian Reform), the government agricultural development and land reform agency. To assign a weight to these factors is not an easy task since they are interrelated. We chose a pair-wise analysis using Saati's method (1977), which has been implemented in the module WEIGHT of the GIS IDRISI (IDRISI 1993). This method ensures that the resulting weights are those that minimize the distortion of our conceptions of these factors, based on the analysis of the principal eigenvectors of the pair-wise comparison matrix. A group of ten experts analyzed the threats by pairs, using the following scale to define by consensus the level of threat a given resource was experiencing. The level of threat and the weights assigned were:

TABLE 9.1 *Relative Perceived Threats to Forest and Water*

Threats to Forest

	a	b	c	d	e
a	1	3	5	⅓	1
b	⅓	1	3	1	⅓
c	⅕	⅓	1	⅓	⅓
d	3	1	3	1	3
e	1	3	3	⅓	1

Threats to Water

	a	b	c	d	e
a	1	½	3	⅓	1
b	2	1	3	½	3
c	⅓	⅓	1	⅓	½
d	3	2	3	1	3
e	1	⅓	2	⅓	1

NOTE: The relative perceived threats for the top row of threats versus each of the lower ones. Threats were (a) population density, (b) roads and trails, (c) terrain slopes, (d) logging activities (i.e., forest management plans), and (e) Institute of Agrarian Reform (IDA) land distribution.

Equally threatening—1
Slightly more threatening—2
More threatening—3
Much more threatening—4
Absolutely more threatening—5

The weights were then used to construct tables of relative perceived threats (table 9.1). Next, using the module WEIGHT of IDRISI, we obtained weights that will be later referred to as *absolute weights,* for the resources forest and water. The absolute weights for forest were (a) population density, 0.15; (b) roads and trails, 0.26; (c) terrain slopes, 0.08; (d) logging activities (forest management plans), 0.38; and (e) IDA land distribution, 0.13. The absolute weights for aquifers were (a) population density, 0.23; (b) roads and trails, 0.15; (c) terrain slopes, 0.06; (d) logging activities (forest management plans), 0.35; (e) IDA land distribution, 0.21. The weights for a particular resource category (forest or aquifer) sum to one.

MODEL

To construct the map of critical areas, we have to combine quantitatively the different factors with their absolute weights. Each threat k is given an absolute weight P_A^k determined by the pair-wise analysis (as described in the preceding section). Within a specific threat, spatial variations are represented by $P_R^k(i,j)$ where (i,j) denotes the position of cell (pixel) (i,j).

Multicriteria modeling can be defined as follows: Given N types of independent threats k, the resulting threat A(i,j) for each cell (i,j) is given by:

$$A(i, j) = \sum_{k=1}^{N} A^k(i,j) \qquad \text{Equation (1)}$$

where

$$A^k(i,j) = P_R^k(i,j) P_A^k \qquad \text{Equation (2)}$$

An example on how we combine two threats having a weight of 0.7 and 0.3 is shown in figure 9.2.

The absolute weights P_A^k are scaled from 0 to 1, the sum being equal to 1 as

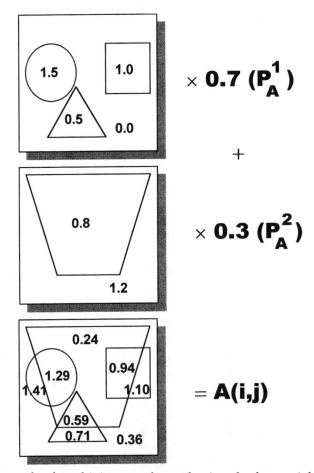

FIG. 9.2 An example of combining two threats having absolute weights of 0.7 and 0.3 in order to obtain a total threat A for each pixel (i,j)

mentioned earlier. The relative weights $P_R^k(i,j)$ are also normalized to 1, with the result that, on average (weighted by the areas covered by each threat), $P_R^k(i,j)$ is 1. Hence, multiplying $P_R^k(i,j)$ by P_A^k will produce the threat $A^k(i,j)$ for each cell, that will average over the entire area to a value equal to P_A^k. The methodology for the normalization is described below.

NORMALIZING THE PARAMETERS

Given initial values for weights $P(i,j)$ for a given threat k, the normalized values $P_R(i,j)$, or relative weight, is given by:

$$P_R(i,j) = \frac{P(i,j)}{<P>} \qquad \text{Equation (3)}$$

where $<P>$ is the weighted average of the $P(i,j)$ within the map. We will now explain how to compute $<P>$ for different spatial distributions.

Factors Covering a Well-Defined Area   This is the simplest case that applies to slope classes and aquifers. Once a weight P^l is assigned to each class l within a threat k, a scale factor $<P>$ is calculated from the area occupied by each class l relative to the total area of interest. Given the set of class weight P^l, each having an area S_l, we obtain:

$$S_T = \sum_l S_l \qquad \text{Equation (4)}$$

and

$$<P> = \sum_l P^l(i,j) \frac{S_l}{S_T} \qquad \text{Equation (5)}$$

where $P^l(i,j)$ is the weight of each class l at cell (i,j). Within IDRISI, the areas S_l are computed with AREA.

Factors That Vary Continuously in Space   This is the case for population density and threat from distance to roads. The problem can be illustrated by a simple example. Let us consider an infestation by insects at a given point of the ACCVC. At a given time, the density of insects will decrease with the distance from the infestation nucleus. Insects could be found at any place in the area but are scarce far from the nucleus. If we want to use equation 5, we have to determine the area of influence, S_T, of the insect infestation. If we consider all the ACCVC (the area of interest) as the area affected by insects, the scaling factor $<P>$ as in equation 5 will be very small since the insects are concentrated near the infestation nucleus (i.e., S_l is small). On the other hand, if we set a threshold to define S_T, saying that if the density of insects is lower than x percent it is considered negligible, then the value that S_T will take will depend on the choice of x.

Therefore, there is no well-defined area to weight a distribution that varies slowly in space, and the task of normalizing this distribution is by no means simple. There is, however, a way to use equation 3 with such distribution. For a continuous distribution, equation 5 is represented by a volume integral:

$$<P> = \int_{AOI} P(x,y)\frac{dS}{S_T} \qquad \text{Equation (6)}$$

where AOI denotes the area of interest of surface S_T. Such an integral can be evaluated numerically if the distribution is discretized. In GIS, discretization is done by reclassifying the continuous map in a large number of discrete classes. This is already done if the map is represented by integer numbers. For these new classes, one can calculate the average value of the threat (obtaining the P_1), and their areas (S_1), and compute <P> with equation 5. With IDRISI this is done with the modules RECLASS (to obtain the discrete map from the continuous map), EXTRACT (to extract the average value of the continuous map within each discrete class), and AREA (to obtain the area of each discrete class). Then one can compute <P> with equation 5.

Details of the Threats

Roads and Trails   In Latin America, building a new public road results in the colonization of the area within a short time along the road. The natural tendency is to develop agricultural and cattle production and wood extraction simply because it is easier to bring the products to market. It also results in an increase in the standard of living in the region and increased demand for products.

We digitized roads from 1:50,000 scale maps and made the assumption that the pressure of the human activity along them is decreasing exponentially with the distance to the road. All types of roads (from highway to gravel) have been given the same weight. The choice of the exponential comes from the hypothesis that the probability of penetrating a given distance in the forest (and therefore to deforest at that point) is a constant. Consequently, the probability $P(d + \Delta d)$ of going from a point at d to a point at $(d + \Delta d)$ within the forest is proportional to the probability $P(d)$ of being at d (i.e., having logged up to that point).

$$P(d + \Delta d) = P(d)\left(1 - \frac{\Delta d}{d_0}\right) \qquad \text{Equation (7)}$$

where d_0 is a constant called the *characteristic distance*. Therefore:

$$P(d) = \exp^{-\frac{d}{d_0}} \qquad \text{Equation (8)}$$

Hence the probability of entering the forest up to a distance d_0 is $P(d_0) = 1 / e$ = 0.37. This function (figure 9.3) applied to roads is shown in the map in figure 9.4. We estimated that a characterestic distance of 1 km was a reasonable figure for the area.

Forest Management Plans   The forest management plans in the ACCVC approved by the DGF after 1989 have been mapped at a 1:50,000 scale, which provides an overview of where the logging activity was concentrated between 1986 and 1992. Some of the plans have already been executed within the Braulio Carrillo protected area, as a consequence of the private ownership of these lands. In these areas the loggers (principally locals) have contracts with the owners of the land covering a period of from one to five years. The management plans have to be approved by DGF. This is a long and tedious process which involves several revisions, but approval is eventually conceded.

To simulate the pressure that the logging activity can bring to an area, we selected a buffer zone of 1 km around the actual management plans and gave it a weight of 1. The management plans supervised or approved by FUNDECOR have been given a weight of 0, which implies that these plans do not present any

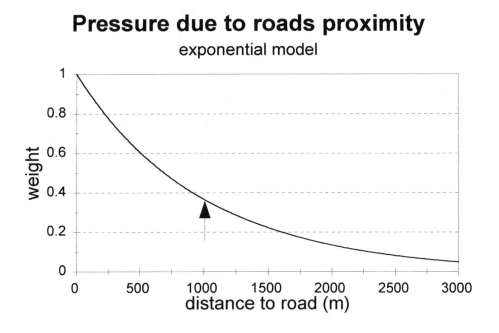

Pressure due to roads proximity
exponential model

FIG. 9.3 Graph of the threat due to the proximity to a road in function of the distance of the latter, following equation 8. The arrow shows the value of the function for the characteristic distance d_0 (1000 m).

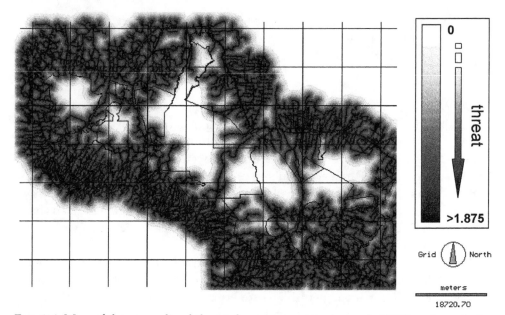

FIG. 9.4 Map of the normalized threat due to proximity to roads (1000 m characteristic distance, exponential model).

risk to the environment (figure 9.5). Adjacent to these areas, however, FUNDE-COR has a responsibility because the logging activities, although well managed, imply road construction which opens the way to uncontrolled logging in the buffer zone.

Population Density The forest and other natural resources that are close to population centers are under constant pressure. More families will need more land for construction and agriculture, and will represent a larger threat to the forest. In addition, water pollution is likely to increase closer to the villages. Locating population centers and estimating the population density will help focus efforts where human activity is greatest.

Since 1945 Costa Rica has put tremendous effort and money toward improving education, and as a consequence it has a lower rate of illiteracy than the United States. As soon as there are more than six children in an area, a school is built and a teacher assigned. Numbers of schools allowed us to generate a better estimate of population density than from the villages that appear on the outdated maps. The schools, digitized as points from the 1:50,000 scale maps of the Ministry of Education, were assigned a weight equal to the number of registered students. Then, by applying successive passes of a 3 × 3 average filter, we generated a Gaussian distribution centered on the school (which represents student density) and converted this to population density by knowing the number of family members and students per family. Here, however, we are only interested in the normalized distribution.

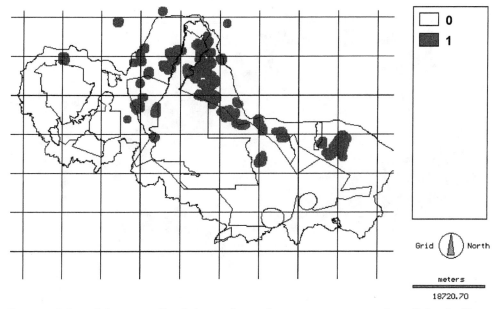

FIG. **9.5** Map of the normalized threat due to forest management plans (1 km buffer zone)

In the remote areas of the ACCVC the children will walk a maximum of 2.5 km to go to school (those that have to walk a longer distance will eventually have a school built closer to their homes). Knowing this fact, we can estimate the extent of the population distribution. The average filter that IDRISI provides (FILTER) computes, for each cell (i,j), the average of the values of its nearest neighbors. Given E(i,j), the registration for a school located at cell (i,j), the value after 1 pass of the filter will be

$$E(i,j) = \frac{1}{9} \sum_{k=i-1}^{k=i+1} \sum_{l=j-1}^{l=j+1} E(k,l) \qquad \text{Equation (9)}$$

Each time the filtering operation is done on the map resulting from the preceding filter, the population distribution becomes more Gaussian, is flattened, and extends radially. On a raster map with a square pixel of 100 m, one hundred successive passes of the average filter produces a distribution with a width at half height $R_{E/E0=50\%}$ of about 1,000 m and a maximum radius of approximately 2.5 km. This distribution represents the density of students per hectare (since the pixel is one hectare). The normalized map resulting from this operation is shown in figure 9.6. Table 9.2 shows how the distribution changes with the number of consecutive passes of the average filter. In this table, E/E_0 represents the height of the center of the distribution (for example, the height of the distribution after one hundred passes is 0.0024 of the original height E_0, which is the number of

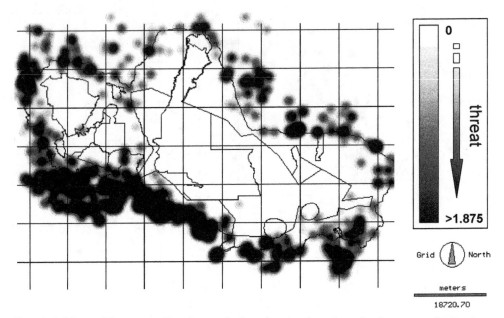

FIG. 9.6 Map of the normalized population density (one hundred passes of a 3 x 3 average filter). The map was produced starting from a point coverage of the schools, where the value of the school is equal to the number of registered students.

registered students). R_{max} is the value where the distribution is close to zero, although the absolute zero is reached at a distance equal to the number of passes times the size of the pixel (i.e., for one hundred passes, 100×100 m = 10 km; see figure 9.7).

IDA Land Distribution   As an important criterion to determine a potential threat to natural resources, FUNDECOR considered the proximity occasioned by the IDA's land repatriation plan. In fact, IDA has given extensive areas of forest free to families in order to promote agriculture and development. A way to add

TABLE 9.2 *Distribution Changes Produced by Passes of a 3×3 Average Filter*

Number of Passes (f)	$R_{E/E0=50\%}$	R_{max}	E/E_0
10 times	400 m	1,000 m	0.0218
50 times	750 m	2,000 m	0.0047
100 times	1,000 m	2,500 m	0.0024
150 times	1,300 m	3,500 m	0.0018

NOTE: Effect of consecutive passes of the filter in the IDRISI program (FILTER) on the width of the distribution at 50 percent of maximum height, its maximum width (1 percent of maximum height), and the height of the distribution.

Population distribution
number of passes of 3x3 mean filter

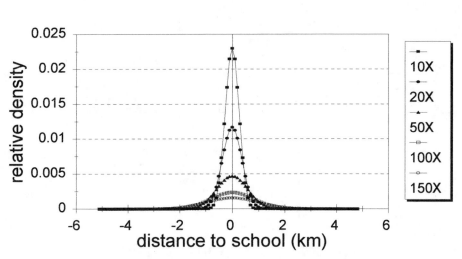

FIG. 9.7 Graph depicting the effect of the number of passes of an average filter on a point distribution having an initial value of 1. The resulting distribution is very close to Gaussian and hence becomes smaller and broader with increased filtering.

value to the land, however, is to cut down the forest. To simulate the fact that new IDA colonies can be located in the neighborhood of existing colonies, we considered a simple 1 km buffer. The IDA colonies and the buffer zone have been given a weight of 1 (figure 9.8).

Slopes   The criterion of reduced slopes as a threat to the natural resources is based on the fact that steep slopes are a natural barrier for logging and for expansion of the population. Flat areas, to the contrary, are prone to be invaded rapidly. The threat for slope classes has been computed using the inverse of the average slope in a given slope class, and has been normalized using the area of each class (equation 5). The calculated weights for slopes are 5–15 percent slope = 3.838; 15–30 percent slope = 1.706; 30–45 percent slope = 1.023; 45–60 percent slope = 0.731; 60–75 percent slope = 0.569; 75 percent slope = 0.465. Note that there is no area of less than 5 percent slope in the ACCVC. The resulting map is shown in figure 9.9.

Conflicts Between Threats   The parameters used by the model are globally as independent as possible, but there may be areas where two parameters are redundant. For example, where population is concentrated there is sometimes a

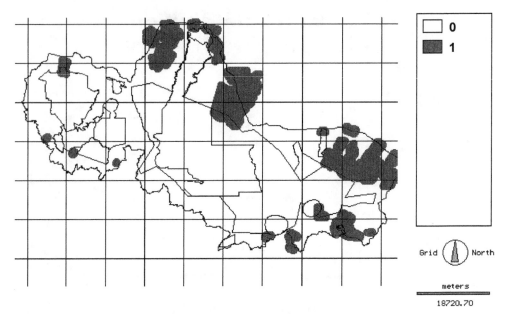

FIG. 9.8 Map of the normalized threat due to IDA colonies

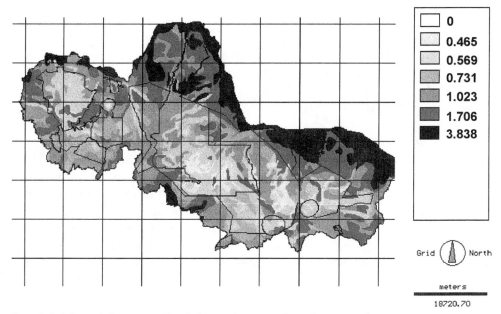

FIG. 9.9 Map of the normalized threat due to reduced terrain slopes

greater density of roads and the region is usually flatter, and the simple sum of the weights resulting from these parameters will overestimate the threat. To overcome this situation, we combine population and roads into a single threat:

$$P(\text{population} + \text{roads}) = MAX[P(\text{population},P(\text{roads})]$$

Equation (10)

This operation is done after the normalization of the respective parameters. It is this combined threat that is used as a specific threat P_R^k in equation 2.

Results and Discussion

MAP OF CRITICAL AREAS

The critical areas map is the result of combining the distinct layers representing different threats, as in equation 1 (for the total threat maps, see figures 9.10 and 9.11), and of overlaying the total threat map with the map showing the natural resources of interest (normalized after prioritization). Figure 9.12 shows the

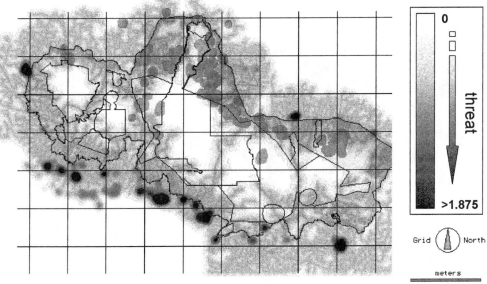

FIG. **9.10** Map of the total threat to forest which results in combining the preceding normalized threat maps with the weights appearing in the text (under the section "Prioritizing the Threats"), according to equation 1. Darker areas have already been deforested or are more prone to deforestation.

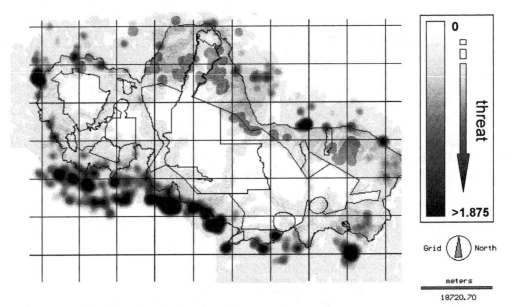

FIG. 9.11 Map of the total threat to aquifers which results from combining the preceding normalized threat maps with weights appearing in the text (under the section "Prioritizing the Threats"), according to equation 1. Darker areas are more prone to contribute to water contamination.

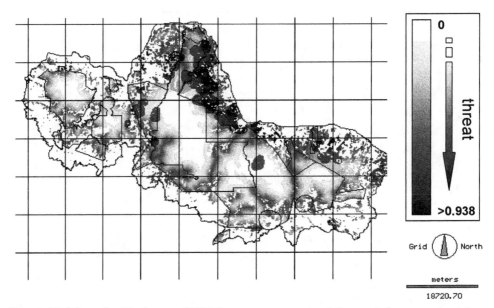

FIG. 9.12 Map of critical areas (1986 forest cover mask of the total threat map of figure 9.10)

critical areas map for forest, in this case a simple mask of the total threat map with the 1986 forest cover map (see folowing section).

These maps contain quantitative real values that we can now reclassify to obtain a qualitative map that is easier to interpret visually. For example, we earlier defined five levels of criticality:

1—No threat (0–0.2)
2—Light threat (0.2–0.4)
3—Moderate threat (0.4–0.6)
4—Great threat (0.6–0.8)
5—Extreme threat (>0.8)

LAND USE CHANGE AND MODEL VALIDATION

We used Landsat TM satellite imagery and aerial photographs for cloudy areas to estimate land use changes in the ACCVC for the period 1986–1992 (figure 9.13). To validate the model, the critical areas map (real values) from figure 9.12 was reclassified in twenty levels in intervals of 0.05. For different regions of the ACCVC out of the national parks (buffer zone), the area deforested was determined for every level of threat (figure 9.14).

For low levels of threats, deforestation was erratic, probably due to errors in

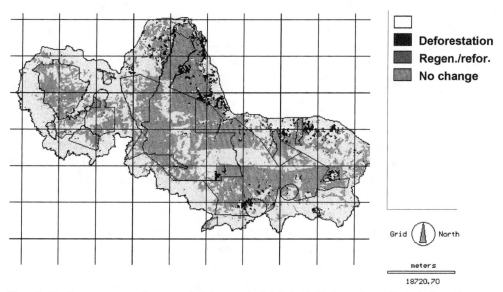

FIG. **9.13** Forest cover changes for the period 1986–1992, based on digital classification of Landsat TM images and on the interpretation of aerial photos. Due to persistent cloud coverage in 1992, three 1992 scenes of different dates were combined with information from several aerial photos in order to obtain a better coverage. Still, there were considerable areas with cloud cover, located mainly over protected areas on very steep terrain and likely undisturbed.

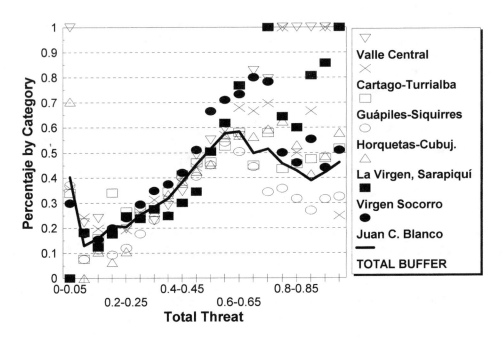

FIG. 9.14 Graph of the deforestation percentage by 0.05 threat range, as a function of the threat, in the buffer zone and excluding the protected areas. The linear behavior for threats between 0.1 and 0.7 confirms the validity of our model. For lower threats, erratic behavior is probably due to errors in the registration/classification of the forest cover maps. For very high threats, the model again loses precision, probably due to social factors not considered in the analysis.

the land use change map (slight misregistration of the 1986–1992 maps) and to differences in the pixel size of the source imagery. For the intermediate levels of threat the precision of the prediction improves considerably, and a linear relationship is found (which is to be expected if the model is correct). In the zones with the greatest threat, the prediction of the model loses precision as evidenced by the divergence of the curves for each region. This is an indication of other factors that differ among regions. The present analysis can help to identify the factors that do not contribute to deforestation. For example, for high threat levels, the average deforestation rate seems to become constant or decrease. This phenomenon could be explained in some areas by the proximity of the forested land to national parks, where the owners prefer to maintain the forest cover in the hope that the government will purchase the land to enlarge the core areas of the parks.

In general, the model correctly predicts land use change or deforestation in

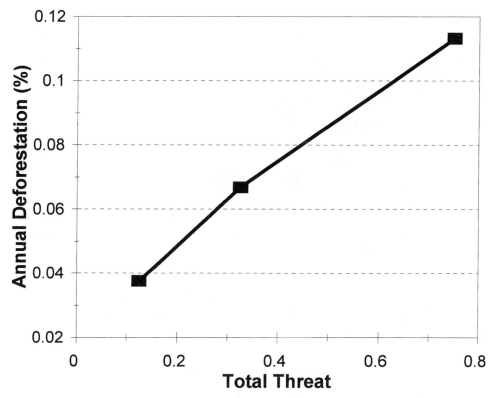

FIG. 9.15 Graph of the average annual deforestation rate as a function of the total threat (reclassified threats) in the buffer zone (excluding the protected areas)

the buffer zone. GIS technology has enabled the model to be used as a flexible tool that can be easily improved, modified, and updated.

This model is now part of FUNDECOR's activities. For operational purposes the critical areas map has been reclassified in three levels in order to obtain a linear relationship for deforestation (figures 9.15 and 9.16), showing low-, average-, and high-priority areas. When a farmer requests help and financing from FUNDECOR, the farm is mapped on the critical areas map and the average level of priority for that farm is obtained. Farms are then ranked with respect to their average priority levels, and preference for support is given to high-priority areas even if their commercial value is not as high.

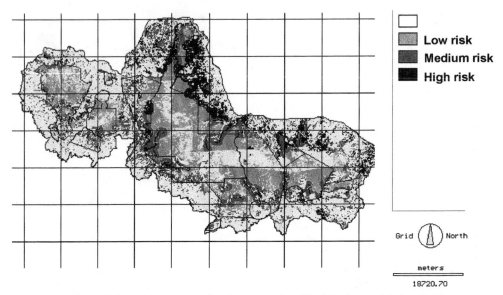

FIG. 9.16 Map of the critical areas for forest, reclassified in three risk levels. Low, medium, and high risks correspond to approximately 0.04 percent, 0.07 percent, and 0.11 percent deforestation rates.

Acknowledgments

Thanks are due to the technical team that contributed to the development of this methodology. In particular, we would like to mention the tremendous efforts put forth by Franz Tattenbach, Jan Engert, Grettel Vargas, and Froylan Castañeda of FUNDECOR, and Carlos Herrera of the National Parks Service of Costa Rica. This work has been financed by the United States Agency for International Development (USAID).

References

IDRISI. 1993. *IDRISI 4.1 (Technical Reference and Update Manual)*. Worcester, Mass.: Clark University.

Saati, T. L. 1977. A scaling method for priorities in hierarchical structures. *Journal of Mathematics and Psychology* 15: 234–81.

10

Application of the HEP Methodology and Use of GIS to Identify Priority Sites for the Management of White-Tailed Deer

Wilfredo Segura López

THE white-tailed deer (*Odocoileus virginianus*) in the Guanacaste area is an important species in tropical dry forest. As part of the social and cultural environment, human populations from this area have benefited from the availability of this resource for many years, using its meat, leather, and antlers (Solís 1986). The Guanacaste area contains the main population of this animal in the country (Solís and Rodríguez 1986). The evaluation of the white-tailed deer's potential habitat in this area is very important since, in order to manage and conserve this valuable game-ranching species, it is necessary to know the quantity and quality of available habitat.

Different methods and techniques have been developed to analyze and evaluate the physiobiological variables of wildlife habitat in order to develop indices and models that will allow for the deduction of the appropriateness of a habitat for a specific species (Gysel and Lyon 1985; Thomas 1982). For this purpose the following methods have been commonly used: biophysical habitat mapping (Demarchi 1986); the regional evaluation of landscape for wildlife (Anderson, Wentz, and Treadwell 1985); multiple linear regression models (Gaudette and Stauffer 1988); exponential regression models (Patton 1984); habitat gradient models (Short 1982); wildlife and fisheries habitat relationships (Thomas 1982); and habitat evaluation procedures (U.S. Fish and Wildlife Service 1991). The last method is the most widely used in evaluating wildlife habitat.

The habitat evaluation procedure, widely known as HEP, is a method developed by the U.S. Fish and Wildlife Service to measure the impact of changes carried out by land and water development projects (U.S. Fish and Wildlife

Service 1991). This method adapts to different management situations, including project planning, evaluations of environmental impacts, mitigation, compensation, and habitat management for fauna (Cole and Smith 1983; Matulich et al. 1982; Rhodes, Cloud, and Haag 1983; Schamberger and Farmer 1978).

On the other hand, GIS actually represents a basic tool in gathering and analyzing data from the evaluation of land and aquatic habitats (Anderson et al. 1985; Ward and Weigle 1993; Welch et al. 1988). Therefore, the use of this technology is fundamental to obtain a better combination and interpretation of the factors involved in habitat evaluation.

The aim of this work is to construct a model to evaluate potential habitats for *Odocoileus virginianus* in the central district of Bagaces, Guanacaste, and to encourage future management strategies such as reintroduction, improvement of habitat quality, and the establishment of game ranching.

Study Area

The area of study is located in the medium and low basins of the Tempisque and Bebedero rivers. It comprises an area of 600.8 km² and belongs to the central district of Bagaces, Guanacaste (figure 10.1). According to Bolaños and Watson's *Mapa de Zonas de Vida de Costa Rica* (Ecological map of life zones in Costa Rica) (1993), the following wildlife zones are identified for this area of study: tropical dry forest, wet premontane forest, and tropical wet forest. The average annual rainfall is 1,624 mm.

Materials and Methods

Fieldwork

Location and Installment of Plots   For the vegetation sampling, secondary and tertiary paths commonly used for horses were followed. These paths are well distributed throughout the area of study. Each path was mapped and subdivided into segments of 100 m length (for example one path with a length of 1,500 m, was divided into fifteen segments of 100 m each). To set the sample points, the sites were chosen at random from the N segments available in each path.

Once the sample point was located on the map, it was decided at random whether it would be on the right or left side of the path. In this manner a base map was created of the different sites where the sample points would be placed. In each of the sites identified as a sample point, five circular plots of 100 m² each

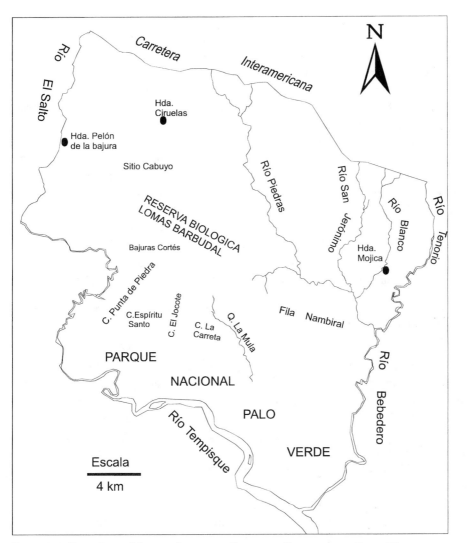

Fig. 10.1 Location of the study area at Bagaces, Guanacaste, Costa Rica

were installed, twenty meters apart from each other. Five plots were installed in each sample point in order to obtain a better representation of the area and to maximize time and resources.

Some 0.01 percent of the total area was sampled. This percentage represents approximately 60.000 m^2, or six hundred circular plots of 100 m^2 each. To obtain the same sample intensity for the vegetation in all categories, the plots were distributed according to the percentage that represents the area of each category from the total area of study.

Recording of Field Information In each plot the following information was collected:

1. *Abundance of species.* All species of plants, bushes, and trees larger than 2 cm in diameter at breast height were recorded.

2. *Horizontal visual obstruction (vegetation cover).* The horizontal visual obstruction was measured with a piece of material 1.2 × 1.2 m divided into twenty-five black and white squares. Each square represented an area equivalent to 4 percent of the surface area of the material. The material was placed in the center of the plot at ground level, and the observer stood twenty meters from the material and recorded the number of visible squares. The number of visible squares was subtracted from the twenty-five total panels, and the percentage of covered area was calculated. Four measurements were obtained in each plot, with one reading from each cardinal point. Next, an average was obtained for each plot and for each category of current use and ground vegetation cover.

3. *Number of feces.* Only one count was made of fresh feces that were left by the deer on each of the established plots in order to obtain a preliminary validation of the model.

LABORATORY WORK: CREATING A DATABASE FOR THE AREA OF STUDY

For a better analysis of the potential habitat of this species, a digital database of the zone of study was created using GIS, GPS, and remote sensors. The information sources that were used included the following maps:

1. *Map of current use and ground vegetation cover.* This map was based on the photo interpretation of aerial pictures with a scale of 1:35,000 (furnished by IGN), and it was complemented with a digital analysis of a Landsat satellite image (furnished by the TELESIG-UNA Laboratory). Next, the map was verified in the field.

2. *Map of springs.* In order to construct this map, each spring was visited and its position registered (latitude and longitude), with a 100 m margin of error using a GPS (Trimble Navigation 1992).

From the maps previously mentioned, the database included the following geospatial information provided by different institutions: map of land possession, map of communication lines, map of life zones, map of slopes, map of climate, map of permanent rivers, map of human settlements, map with the location of Stage II of the Arenal-Tempisque Irrigation Project, and map of capacity use for forest lands.

Later each map was digitized using the Roots program (Corson-Rikert 1990). The vector data were then exported to the IDRISI program (Eastman 1992). In IDRISI the files were stored in a 25 × 25 m format raster file. The commands used for the different analyses were AREA (area calculations), OVERLAY (superimposition of maps), DISTANCE (measurement of distances), and CROSSTAB (distribution of a variable in relation to a second variable).

DESIGN OF THE MODEL FOR THE WHITE-TAILED DEER'S POTENTIAL HABITAT

The scheme for the creation of the model was based on HEP methodology. This methodology assumes that the value of a wildlife area can be estimated using a habitat quality index with a scale of 0 to 1. The model structure consists of the following phases.

Assigning and Obtaining HSI (Habitat Suitability Index) Values   The first step in the creation of the model was to assign HSI values (from 0 to 1) to each of the chosen variables and for each habitat present in the zone. Each habitat was assigned a value for the following variables: food, horizontal coverage, and slope of the terrain. This value (which varied between 0 and 1) represents the importance of the variable for the species. Next, by using GIS (IDRISI, command DISTANCE), HSI values were assigned to the other three variables (human activity, bodies of water, and distances between habitats) in the model since they are based on a distance analysis.

Once the HSI values were defined and assigned for each of the variables, six maps were designed that included the spatial distribution for each of the variables (with their corresponding HSI values). Then, using the SUM function from the IDRISI-OVERLAY command, the six maps were superimposed in the following manner. A map was obtained that included, for each site, six different HSI values (which represented six variables). Next, an HSI point average was calculated for the six variables to represent the final HSI for a specific site or point in the area of study. Mathematically, the formula to calculate the final HSI values is represented as:

$$\text{HSI} = (2v1 + 2v2 + 2v3 + v4 + v5 + v6) / 9 \quad \text{Equation (1)}$$

where the variables are: v1 = distance to bodies of water; v2 = food; v3 = vegetation cover for protection; v4 = slope; v5 = interdistances between habitats; v6 = human factors. Ecologically, this formula means that the variables for water, cover, and food will determine the habitat use of deer to a greater degree.

Finally, based on the distribution map for the different HSI values and on the limitation of the principal variables (water, food, and vegetation cover), the final map of quality of habitat potential was obtained for the species.

Relationships and Assumptions for Variables Used in the Model   The present model was developed to evaluate the quality of habitat potential for the white-tailed deer (*Odocoileus virginianus*) during the dry season. At the study area, the species is very vulnerable during this period owing to the decrease in vegetation cover caused by the loss of foliage and the frequent burning of pastures and woods. Furthermore, water is more scarce during the dry season, which favors the concentration of animals around water sources; this encourages illegal hunting (Rodríguez et al. 1985).

Role of the Variables in the Model

Food. According to Gallina (1995), the sites deer prefer are those that present higher plant diversity and biomass. For the present model, it is assumed that the more richness, abundance, and frequency of plants consumed by the deer in a determined area, the higher the value of that area for food resource.

Slopes. How slopes affect this species has not been evaluated in the zone nor in the rest of the country. However, X. Izurieta (personal communication, biologist, Universidad de Quito, Ecuador, 1994) carried out a study in the zone of the Cotopaxi National Park in Ecuador and found that 96.8 percent of the deer (*Odocoileus virginianus*) sampled were found in areas with slopes less than 30 percent. Through a regression analysis he confirmed that deer prefer those sites that present a more regular topography. Based on this, the model assumes that the habitats with a slope of less than 30 percent will have double the value of those located in terrain with slopes greater than 30 percent.

Interdistance between habitats. The importance of plant diversity and the juxtaposition of patches of habitats for white-tailed deer have been reported by many investigations (Suring and Vohs 1979; Williamson and Hirth 1985). According to Suring and Vohs, white-tailed deer use pastures that are immediately adjacent to forest to a great extent. Williamson and Hirth indicate that the cost to obtain food for the deer will increase when the animal searches for food resources around the center of open areas; therefore, the distance from cover will be greater and will present more exposure to predators.

The model assumes that as distance increases from the edge of the forest toward the center of a pasture, then the probability of use decreases. The size of the home range used for this model (178 ha, average radius of 750 m) was obtained from an average of home ranges for the dry season in different zones of the dry forest on Costa Rica's Pacific side (Calvopiña 1990; Rodríguez et al. 1985, Saénz 1990).

Water. The distribution of bodies of water influences the use of habitat by white-tailed deer in the dry season. The evaluation of this variable was based on the average radius of the home range of the species for the dry season (750 m). In this way, four categories were created, where the maximum value was assigned to those areas located at less than 750 m from water (i.e., the resource is available within the average home range).

Vegetation cover for protection. Six categories of cover in each different habitat were calculated using a quantitative field method. With the use of six categories a gradient for coverage was created that assumed that the more horizontal vegetation cover present, the safer the deer from its predators.

Human factors. The combination of the above variables can indicate if a determined habitat is appropriate for the species; however, the presence of small settlements and human activity could negatively affect the deer's use of habitat. The categories used to evaluate this variable are subjective because the true effects of human activity on the deer's behavior have not been evaluated. The model assumes that the species will make the most use of those zones located further away from human presence.

Preliminary Verification of the Model

Through the use of GIS, the map of plot locations was superimposed on the distribution map for HSI values. Next, for each of the sectors where the plots were installed, the average number of feces groups was calculated for that sector (polygon), which corresponds to a determined HSI value. A correlation coefficient was calculated for the HSI values and the average number of feces groups (in 100 m^2) (Cole and Smith 1983; Cook and Irwin 1985; Gaudette and Stauffer 1988; Irwin and Cook 1985), using the statistical tests of Spearman's Coefficient (Siegel 1986; Sokal and Rohlf 1981; STSC 1989).

In order to relate qualitatively the presence of the species to the quality of the habitat, a map of points was designed for those sites with the presence of deer (sightings and signs such as feces and tracks), which was then superimposed on the map of the quality of habitat potential.

Results

According to the developed model, a total of fourteen different HSI values exist for the study area (figure 10.2). Based on these values and the presence or absence (limiting factor) of the variables with major importance in the model (water, food, and vegetation cover), seven categories of quality of habitat potential were obtained (table 10.1):

1. High: all factors of well-being for the species are present
2. Medium (food): presents food as the limiting factor
3. Medium (cover): presents vegetation cover as the limiting factor
4. Medium (water): presents water as the limiting factor
5. Low (cover, food): presents food and vegetation cover as the limiting factors
6. Low (cover, water): presents vegetation cover and water as the limiting factors
7. Inappropriate: all factors for well-being are limited.

The results indicate that the majority of the area of study is potentially optimal habitat for white-tailed deer. Approximately 22,500 ha are found in this category, and approximately 50 percent are located in the protected wildlife areas in the zone (Palo Verde National Park and Lomas Barbudal Biological Reserve),

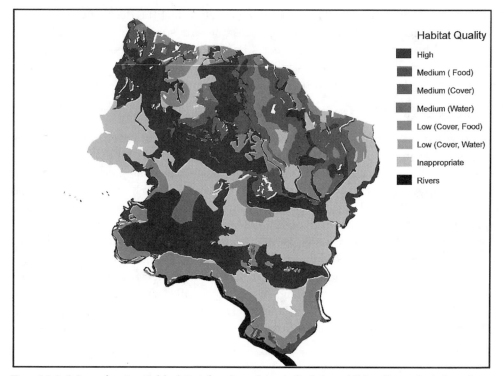

Fig. 10.2 Map of potential habitat for the white-tailed deer (*Odocoileus virginianus*) in the study area (1994)

Table 10.1 *Area for Each Category of Habitat Quality Potential for* Odocoileus virginianus *Present on the Study Area (Bagaces 1994)*

Habitat Quality	Area (ha)	Percent
High	21,512.25	35.8
Medium (food)	854.50	1.4
Medium (cover)	9,363.00	15.6
Medium (water)	868.00	1.4
Low (cover, food)	11,633.62	19.4
Low (cover, water)	38.25	0.1
Inappropriate	15,810.44	26.3
Total	60,080.06	100.0

with the other half in private farms and government farms of Costa Rica's Instituto de Desarrollo Agrario (IDA, or Institute of Agrarian Reform). Approximately 25 percent (15,810.4 ha) of the total area does not provide minimal conditions for deer (inappropriate habitat). The rest of the 21,891.7 ha have limits in some of the habitat requirements for the species.

A preliminary verification of the model indicated a significant correlation between the HSI index and the average number of feces/plot/site (r_s = 0.64, d.f. = 44, p<0.01).

Discussion

The present model is designed to provide comparisons between different areas at a fixed time or among time periods for a given area. It is not a load capacity model because not all factors that influence animal abundance are included in the model. However, an HSI of 0.9 can indicate better habitat quality than an HSI of 0.48, and it is possible that the former could represent a potentially higher load capacity.

Even though this model did not include other variables of interest (e.g., competition and diseases), it is a tool for decision making in species habitat management. Sites with excellent characteristics for deer are identified (high quality) as are sites with limiting factors for the species (medium, low, and inappropriate quality). One of the potential applications of this model is selection of sites for reintroduction of the species.

Because the medium-quality sites have some limiting habitat requirements, they could be improved with management techniques or simply fulfill other functions equally important for the management and conservation of the species. For example, these habitats can provide buffer for the high-quality habitats and serve as biological corridors that connect high-quality habitats (provided that the vegetation cover is not a limiting factor).

Currently, most efforts in classifying and mapping terrain in order to under-stand the distribution of habitat requirements of a species are directed toward threatened or endangered species. Halls (1984) indicated the necessity of carrying out investigations on common or widespread species, such as this one, since the habitat mapping for species like the white-tailed deer had not been given suffi-cient importance due to their extensive distributions. With better habitat manage-ment techniques, we will be able to prevent common species from becoming rare in the future.

References

Anderson, W., W. Wentz, and B. Treadwell. 1985. Una guía sobre información de sensores remotos para biólogos especializados en vida silvestre. In R. Rubén, ed., *Manual de Técnicas de Gestión de Vida Silvestre*, 305–20. Bethesda, Md.: The Wildlife Society.

Bolaños, R. A. and V. C. Watson. 1993. *Mapa de Zonas de Vida de Costa Rica: Hojas Liberia y Nicoya. Escala 1:200.000* (Ecological map of life zones in Costa Rica: [According to the system of classification of life zones of the world by L. R. Holdridge; nine map sheets at] 1:200,000 scale). San José, C.R.: Centro Científico Tropical (Tropical Science Center).

Calvopiña, J. 1990. Reintroducción del venado cola blanca (*Odocoileus virginianus*) a Cobano, Puntareanas, Costa Rica. Tesis de Maestría, Sistema de Estudios de Postgrado, Programa Regional en Manejo de Vida Silvestre. Heredia, C.R.: Universidad Nacional.

Cole, C. and R. Smith. 1983. Habitat suitability indices for monitoring wildlife populations—an evaluation. *Transactions of the North American Wildlife and Natural Resources Conference* 48: 367–75.

Cook, J. and L. Irwin. 1985. Validation and modification of a habitat suitability model for pronghorns. *Wildlife Society Bulletin* 13: 446–48.

Corson-Rikert, J. 1990. *Roots User's Manual*. Harvard University, Graduate School of Design Laboratory for Computer Graphics in Spatial Analysis. Washington, D.C.: Conservation International.

Demarchi, D. 1986. *Biophysical habitat mapping: Draft methodology*. Victoria, B.C.: Mapping Standards Committee, Ministry of Environment.

Eastman, J. R. 1992. *IDRISI (Version 4.0)*. Worcester, Mass.: Clark University.

Gallina, S. 1995. Uso del hábitat por el venado cola blanca en la Reserva de la Biosfera La Michilia, México. In C. Vaughan and M. Rodríguez, eds., *Ecologia y Manejo del Venado Cola Blanca en Mexico y Costa Rica*, 299–314. Heredia, C.R.: Editorial UNA.

Gaudette, M. and D. Stauffer. 1988. Assessing habitat of white-tailed deer in Southwestern Virginia. *Wildlife Society Bulletin* 16: 284–90.

Gysel, L. and L. Lyon. 1985. Análisis y evaluación del hábitat. In R. Rubén, ed., *Manual de Técnicas de Gestión de Vida Silvestre*, 321–44. Bethesda, Md.: The Wildlife Society.

Halls, L. 1984. Research problems and needs. In L. Halls, ed., *White-tailed Deer: Ecology and Management*, 783–90. Harrisburg, Penn.: Stackpole.

Irwin, L. and J. Cook. 1985. Determining appropriate variables for a habitat suitability model for pronghorns. *Wildlife Society Bulletin* 13: 434–40.

Matulich, S., J. Hanson, I. Lines, and A. Farmer. 1982. HEP as a planning tool: An application to waterfowl enhancement. *Transactions of the North American Wildlife and Natural Resources Conference* 47: 111–27.

Patton, D. 1984. A model to evaluate Abert squirrel habitat in uneven-aged ponderosa pine. *Wildlife Society Bulletin* 12: 408–14.

Rhodes, M., T. Cloud, and D. Haag. 1983. Habitat evaluation procedures for planning surface mine reclamation in Texas. *Wildlife Society Bulletin* 11: 222–32.

Rodríguez, M., C. Vaughan, V. Villalobos, and M. McCoy. 1985. Notas sobre los movimientos del venado cola blanca. In G. Estrella, ed., *Investigaciones sobre Fauna Silvestre de Costa Rica*, 37–46. San José, C.R.: Editorial Universidad Estatal a Distancia.

Saénz, J. 1990. Ecología de dos grupos de venados cola blanca (*Odocoileus virginianus*) liberados en un nuevo hábitat. Tesis de grado: Ingeniería en Ciencias Forestales, Grado Académico Licenciado, EDECA. Heredia, C.R.: Universidad Nacional.

Schamberger, M. and A. Farmer. 1978. The habitat evaluation procedures: Their application in project planning and impact evaluation. *Transactions of the North American Wildlife and Natural Resources Conference* 43: 275–83.

Short, H. 1982. Development and use of habitat gradient model to evaluate wildlife habitat. *Transactions of the North American Wildlife and Natural Resources Conference* 47: 57–72.

Siegel, S. 1986. *Estadística no Paramétrica*. Mexico City: Editorial TRILLAS, S.A.

Sokal, R. and F. J. Rohlf. 1981. *Biometry*. 2d ed. New York: W. H. Freeman.

Solís, V. 1986. La alternativa de la educación ambiental. In V. Solís, M. Rodríguez, and C. Vaughan, eds., *Actas del primer taller nacional sobre el venado cola blanca* (Odocoileus virginianus) *del Pacífico Seco, Costa Rica,* 63–71. Heredia, C.R.: EUNA.

Solís, V. and M. Rodríguez. 1986. El venado cola blanca en Guanacaste, retrospección histórica. In V. Solís, M. Rodríguez, and C. Vaughan, eds., *Actas del primer taller nacional sobre el venado cola blanca* (Odocoileus virginianus) *del Pacífico Seco, Costa Rica,* 15–18. Heredia, C.R.: EUNA.

STSC. 1989. *Statgraphics (Version 4.0).* Rockville, Md.: Manugistics.

Suring, L. and P. Vohs. 1979. Habitat use by Columbian white-tailed deer. *Journal of Wildlife Management* 43: 610–19.

Thomas, J. 1982. Needs for and approaches to wildlife habitat assessment. *Transactions of the North American Wildlife and Natural Resources Conference* 47: 35–46.

Trimble Navigation. 1992. *Operating the GPS Pathfinder basic receivers.* Sunnyvale, Calif.: Trimble Navigation.

U.S. Fish and Wildlife Service. 1991. *Habitat evaluation procedures (HEP).* Washington, D.C.: Division of Ecological Services, Department of the Interior.

Ward, L. and B. Weigle. 1993. To save a species: GIS for manatee research and management. *GIS World* 6: 34–37.

Welch, R., M. Remillard, and R. Slack. 1988. Remote sensing and geographic information system techniques for aquatic resource evaluation. *Photogrammetric Engineering and Remote Sensing* 54: 177–85.

Williamson, S. and D. Hirth. 1985. An evaluation of edge use by white-tailed deer. *Wildllife Society Bulletin* 13: 252–57.

11

The Paseo Pantera Project: A Case Study Using GIS to Improve Continental-Scale Conservation Planning*

J. David Lambert and Margaret H. Carr

Background

Because of the accelerating loss and fragmentation of Central America's wildlands, the rich biodiversity that once characterized the isthmus may disappear unless there is a coordinated regional effort to protect the remaining pristine wildlands and restore degraded lands that could provide landscape linkages between the remaining wildlands of the isthmus. Biological corridors have been recommended by many researchers as a way to overcome the negative effects associated with fragmentation (Forman and Godron 1986; Harris and Atkins 1991; Soulé 1991). An ambitious regional wildlands conservation project called Paseo Pantera was initiated in 1990 to address this threatening scenario. The five-year project was implemented by a consortium composed of the Wildlife Conservation Society and the Caribbean Conservation Corporation in collaboration with several educational institutions and research organizations in the United States and Central American governmental and nongovernmental organizations. It was funded in part by the Regional Environmental and Natural Resources Management Project (RENARM), initiated by the USAID Regional Office for Central American Programs.

Paseo Pantera provided a comprehensive multinational viewpoint on biodiversity conservation and aggressive advocacy for the design and implementation

*This case study is an updated and revised work which draws substantially from other previously published work by the authors (Lambert and Carr 1993; Carr, Lambert, and Zwick 1994).

of a biological corridor system linking protected areas throughout Central America. The project addressed the need for improved wildlands management in Central America through both regional and site-specific activities. Some of the consortium's activities included field research on techniques of buffer zone management, research and promotion of ecotourism as a strategy for sustaining conservation programs, development of environmental education programs, and coordination of international seminars.

The project's Spanish name (Paseo Pantera, or path of the panther) was derived from the fact that for millions of years the Central American land bridge provided a pathway for the interchange of wildlife species, and genetic information, between the Northern and Southern hemispheres and resulted in increased diversity in both. The panther, also known as the puma or mountain lion, is found from the Andes to the Rocky Mountains and is an appropriate symbol for an effort to maintain this historic linkage.

The regional approach that characterizes the Paseo Pantera project is summarized by the Wildlife Conservation Society's Dr. Archie F. Carr III:

> By thinking in terms that reach beyond the cramped political boundaries of modern-day Central America, we may intelligently address the challenge of biodiversity conservation in the entire region. Paseo Pantera originates from a phenomenon of nature, but its successful completion will breach a human phenomenon in the region, the partitioning of the isthmus into seven small nations, whose isolation and independence from one another is considered by economists and historians to be a major factor contributing to the chronic underdevelopment of the region. Whatever else divides the human inhabitants of the Western Hemisphere, the Paseo Pantera silently unites us.
>
> (Carr 1992)

At the request of the Paseo Pantera Consortium, a multidisciplinary research and planning team was formed at the University of Florida in 1992 to explore the potential for using GIS technologies to aid in the design of a Mesoamerican biological corridor network. Partial funding was provided by the USAID Guatemala-Central American Program (G-CAP). The team's initial goal was the mapping of a continuous biological corridor, stretching from Colombia to Mexico, in order to (1) demonstrate that a continuous corridor is still feasible, considering that many areas have already been developed; (2) generate support for a Central American corridor network; and (3) determine the accuracy and availability of information needed to define a detailed and feasible corridor network. Following the preliminary study, more detailed studies would be conducted for specific linkages, with the major objective being the generation of the technical information required to support the development and implementation of management, restoration, and land acquisition plans and funding strategies.

A secondary goal of this study was to facilitate the effective use and distribution of conservation funds earmarked for land acquisition. The planning team hoped that analysis and mapping of a corridor network would assist Central American governments and nongovernmental organizations in the identification and prioritization of key areas for preservation and protection. A spin-off benefit of this project is a preliminary GIS database of the entire Central American isthmus which has been shared with many government agencies in Central America, other scientists, land use planners, and conservation organizations that are also working to preserve and manage the natural treasures of Central America.

Database Development and Evaluation

The GIS database development component of the corridor study was designed as a two-phase process to complement the preliminary and more detailed analysis efforts. Initially, due to limited funding, only the data layers that were required to support the preliminary corridor potential study would be developed. Subsequently, with additional funding, the team would develop more comprehensive databases to support more detailed study of specific potential linkages.

The logical first step for the team was the identification and collection of existing digital data sources that could be obtained inexpensively. Unfortunately, the team found that, although there were several GIS projects being conducted in Central America, the GIS databases these projects were creating varied widely in scale, projection, content, theme, date, and digital format. There were apparently no regional efforts being made to develop a standardized database for the entire isthmus.

Fortunately, an affordable source for base map features called the *Digital Chart of the World* (*DCW*) had just become available (ESRI 1993). The *DCW* provides base map features such as roads, hydrography, political boundaries, population centers, and topography (at 1,000-foot intervals) for the entire world. This database was created by digitizing the U.S. Defense Mapping Agency's 1:1,000,000 scale Operational Navigation Chart map series. A license for the ARC/INFO version of the *DCW* database was purchased from Environmental Systems Research Institute, Inc. (ESRI) in the fall of 1992. At first, the team was skeptical about the suitability of this database because the scale of the source data limits typical spatial accuracy to approximately plus/minus one kilometer. However, the alternative of digitizing base map features for all of Central America motivated the team to test the database. After working with the database, the team found the *DCW*'s spatial and attribute accuracy to be quite adequate and appropriate for the objectives of this preliminary, multinational study.

An important point to make about the *DCW* is that its availability allowed the planning team to concentrate its own limited funding on the generation of the new databases required for analysis and on the preliminary design of the corridor rather than on the digitizing of base map feature layers. However, a second important advantage to using the *DCW* was that it allowed the team to get off to a quick start. All too often in the past, ambitious GIS managers have promoted this technology successfully to their cautious colleagues, only to find themselves explaining later, to now impatient colleagues, why it takes so long to demonstrate any substantial results from a technology that was supposed to save time and increase productivity. Being aware of this potential scenario, and the fact that GIS technology and methods are still new to many of the participants in the Paseo Pantera project (especially some of the cooperating institutions in Central America), the corridor planning team recognized the need to demonstrate the utility of GIS as quickly as possible to its sponsors. The *DCW* made this possible. Although the *DCW* will not be appropriate for all projects, this project demonstrates the potential value of the *DCW* to those faced with continental-scale environmental problems and dwindling budgets.

The second step in the initial phase of GIS database development involved the team in a process of weighing the costs of producing each new data layer against the relative potential contribution of that data to the preliminary analysis. Several new data layers were subsequently developed, including boundaries of existing and proposed protected areas; forested/deforested areas; potential biological communities based on the Holdridge system of life zone classifications (Holdridge 1967); population density and major population centers; and areas occupied by indigenous populations. The GIS data layers listed above represent the conversion of more than seventy-five source maps to digital format. It is important to point out that these data sets represent only a preliminary effort, limited by modest funding, and that the study team recognizes the need for much more detailed information as it enters the second phase of this study.

Once the databases described above were developed, the team explored ways to use them to analyze the potential for a continuous biological corridor. The following four criteria were selected for use in the model based on the evaluation of the available data: (1) size of protected areas, (2) uniform national designation of protected areas, (3) population densities, and (4) forested/deforested areas.

The protected areas were divided into two size classes—large (50,000 hectares and greater) and small (less than 50,000 hectares). These classes were based on suggestions for minimum core area size in Noss (1991).

Because of the variations in terminology used by each country to classify its protected areas, the team developed a set of "uniform national designations" based on current management practices. These designations were: national park (or equivalent), anthropological reserve, extractive reserve, private reserve, and proposed reserve. "Uniform national designation" was selected as an important criterion because the management practices used in each protected area determine its value to the preservation of biological diversity. An uninhabited national park will contribute differently than an inhabited anthropological reserve.

Owing to variations in the ranges used for population density categories for each country, the team had to determine a generalized population density classification scheme for the entire region. Five density classes were used, with the following ranges: 0 to 10 people per square kilometer, 11 to 25, 26 to 50, 51 to 100, and 101 people or more per square kilometer. Population density was considered a critical criterion because, according to Redford and Robinson (1992), where densities are higher there is less potential to maintain biodiversity.

The fourth criterion utilized in the preliminary analysis was the classification of "forested/deforested" (or natural/altered) areas. This generalized data was digitized from the map supplement ("The Coexistence of Indigenous Peoples and the Natural Environment in Central America") contained in the spring 1992 issue of *Research and Exploration,* a publication of the National Geographic Society. This classification was considered to be a significant discriminator, at this resolution of analysis, because it is generally accepted that natural areas will have higher "natural diversity" than deforested, human-altered areas.

After an evaluation of the remaining available spatial databases, several were not used in the model developed for our initial analyses because of their incomplete classification or content. These data sets included roads, hydrography, and population centers. Holdridge's life zones and areas of indigenous populations were not used because the team could not substantiate the prioritization of one life zone over another, and there was controversy over whether or not historical ranges of indigenous populations were predictive of corridor potential.

Biological Corridor Suitability, Potential, and Feasibility Analyses

All analysis from this point in the method was accomplished by using ESRI's raster GIS software called GRID. The vector data layers used in the analysis were converted into layers of four-square-kilometer grid cells. This was the highest reasonable resolution based on the spatial accuracy of the combined source data layers.

A weighted criteria analysis method was used to generate a biological corridor suitability map that would subsequently be used as an input to the corridor potential and feasibility analyses. There were three steps in the weighted criteria analysis. The first was to determine the relative values for the range of options within each of the four criteria discussed above. The second was to determine the relative importance among the four criteria (i.e., to assign a weight to each criteria). The third was to calculate the normalized, cumulative scores, which results in values ranging from 1 to 100. These values represent the relative overall suitability of any area for inclusion in a biological corridor. Several alternative weighting schemes have been explored for assigning the values within and among the criteria.

In the first step, for the criterion of "size of protected area," lands contained in larger protected areas were considered relatively more valuable than lands found in smaller protected areas, based on theories put forth by MacArthur and Wilson (1967). Lands with no protection received the lowest relative value for this criterion. Similarly, for the criterion of "uniform national designation," lands in "national park (or equivalent)" were determined to be of highest value, lands in "proposed reserves" to be of a lower value, and lands not in a protected area to be of no relative value. For each category of protected area, the stricter the limits on use (as determined by management practices), the more important its potential contribution to protection of biodiversity was considered to be. Within the criterion for population density, areas of high density were considered to be a detriment to the development of a corridor network, whereas low-density areas were assumed to be of higher relative value. Finally, lands with natural forest cover were considered to be of much greater relative value than altered lands.

The corridor suitability database provided the relative cost information needed for the next step in the corridor analysis. The cells with high corridor suitability were redefined as cells with low relative "costs" for inclusion in the corridor. The cells with low corridor suitability were redefined as having high relative "costs" for inclusion. The resulting "cost" surface was the input for the assessment of corridor potential. This analysis used the GRID analysis function CORRIDOR to calculate the relative accumulated "cost" of developing a corridor between two sources. In this case, the two sources were Mexico and Colombia. The CORRIDOR function generated a value for each four-square-kilometer pixel along the least cost path to each of the sources. In figure 11.1, the values have been divided into five classes of equal area. These results represent continuous biological corridor potential based on the criteria used.

The areas of highest corridor potential were not simply along the shortest route between Colombia and Mexico, but represented a combination of distance and other influences assigned through the four criteria used in the weighted criteria analysis. The result was a bias toward large, forested national parks with low population density in close proximity.

In the final step of the analysis, the boundaries of the area represented by the classes of highest corridor potential were used to "clip out" the corresponding suitability classifications developed in the weighted criteria analysis step. The resulting map (figure 11.2) represents biological corridor feasibility. The area within these limits had the highest potential for a continuous corridor, but the feasibility factor was not homogeneous within the limits. Three problem areas became evident: one in northwestern Honduras, another in northeastern Costa Rica, and the third around the Panama Canal.

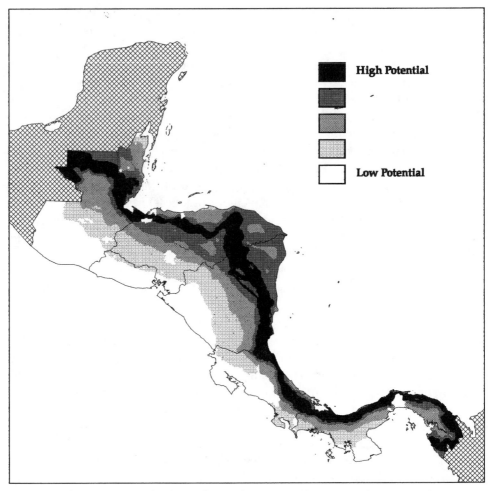

FIG. 11.1 The continuous biological corridor potential in Central America (based upon criteria described in the text)

Conclusions from the Initial Corridor Study and Thoughts on the Next Phase of Study

The authors believe that the methods they used for this preliminary study have great potential to assist in the identification of corridor study areas and in their prioritization. The maps and reports generated from these preliminary (but promising) results have been used widely throughout Central America and the United States to promote the concept of a Mesoamerican biological corridor. There has also been greater appreciation of the contribution that GIS technology can make to conservation planning. The study team is currently focusing on refinements to its methodology to strengthen the relationships between current

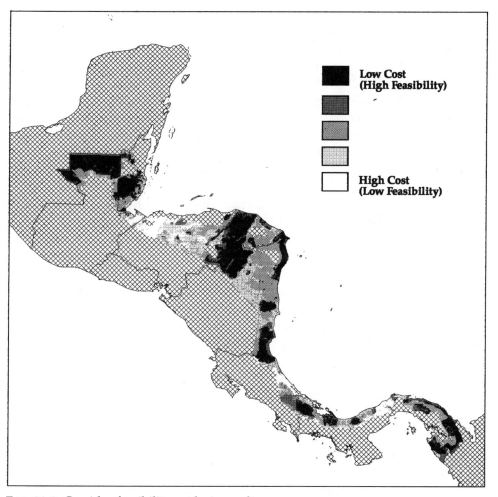

Fig. 11.2 Corridor feasibility analysis results

scientific theories and the relative weights assignments, and on the development of new and improved data sets to support more detailed planning.

As a result of its experience with this study, the team has recommended the use of, and begun development of, 1:250,000 scale data sets to support the next, more detailed phase of regional corridor analysis. A second-phase pilot project, implemented at this scale, was completed by the authors in the fall of 1995 for the trinational region of the Selva Maya (which includes Belize, the Peten district of Guatemala, and southern Mexico). This project was supported by the MAYA-FOR program of USAID / G-CAP. The GIS database was created for the planning of biological corridors but has also been used more generally to support the Regional Conservation Assessment Workshop for the Maya Tropical Forest held in San Cristobal de las Casas, Chiapas, Mexico, in August 1995. This workshop brought together more than sixty representatives from the region to establish conservation needs and priorities for the Selva Maya. The new standardized multinational GIS database provided the participants with a common base map and data which enabled multinational conservation planning that would not have been possible before. Instead of dealing with a different map for each country, the regional database allowed the participants to more effectively plan strategies based on ecological boundaries rather than political boundaries. Additionally, the new standardized database was distributed to over thirty governmental, academic, and conservation institutions in the region in the hopes that their future conservation planning efforts would not be limited by national boundaries.

Based on the experience gained through implementing the MAYAFOR GIS database, the authors recommend that a coordinated and cooperative effort be initiated whereby a standardized GIS database would be developed for the entire isthmus. It is further recommended that this database be freely shared with any parties involved in conservation of the region's natural resources in order to prevent duplication of effort and to make efficient use of limited funding. The team believes that a 1:250,000 scale database has been shown to provide sufficient detail and accuracy for many regional conservation planning needs and is reasonable to develop within the limited funding constraints of the conservation community.

References

Carr III, A. F. 1992. Paseo Pantera Project brochure. New York: Wildlife Conservation Society.

Carr, M. H., J. D. Lambert, and P. D. Zwick. 1994. Mapping of biological corridor potential in Central America. In A. Vega, ed., *Conservation corridors in the Central American region*, 383–93. Gainesville, Fla.: Tropical Research and Development.

Environmental Systems Research Institute (ESRI). 1993. *Digital chart of the world* (CD-ROM Cartographic Database). Redlands, Calif.: ESRI.

Forman, R. T. T. and M. Godron. 1986. *Landscape ecology.* New York: Wiley.

Harris, L. D. and K. Atkins. 1991. Faunal movement corridors in Florida. In W. E. Hudson, ed., *Landscape linkages and biodiversity*, 117–38. Washington, D.C.: Island Press.

Holdridge, L. R. 1967. *Life zone ecology.* San José, C.R.: Tropical Science Center.

Lambert, J. D. and M. Carr. 1993 (May). Utilizing GIS to plan for a Central American biological corridor. *Proceedings, Thirteenth Annual ESRI User Conference* 1: 257–64. Redlands, Calif.: Environmental Systems Research Institute.

MacArthur, R. H. and E. O. Wilson. 1967. *The theory of island biogeography.* Princeton: Princeton University Press.

Noss, R. F. 1991. Landscape connectivity: Different functions at different scales. In W. E. Hudson, ed., *Landscape linkages and biodiversity*, 27–39. Washington, D. C.: Island Press.

Redford, K. H. and J. G. Robinson. 1992. The sustainability of wildlife and natural areas. *Proceedings of the International Conference on the Definition and Measurement of Sustainability,* Washington, D.C.

Soulé, M. E. 1991. Theory and strategy. In W. E. Hudson, ed., *Landscape linkages and biodiversity,* 91–104. Washington, D.C.: Island Press.

PART FOUR

The USAID Case Study in Gap Analysis

12

Overview of Gap Analysis

Basil G. Savitsky

GAP analysis is a "search for biotic communities and species in need of preservation management" (Davis et al. 1990:56). Gap analysis provides a method for assessing present measures to protect biological diversity and for identifying focus areas for optimal conservation efforts (Scott et al. 1987). Gap analysis is a GIS technique which superimposes species distributions with boundaries of ecosystems and protected areas to identify gaps in the protection of species. GIS is used to overlay maps or layers that are geographically referenced to each other and to create new information through the combination of those map files. Image analysis is used to create the vegetation database that provides the framework for the various GIS data layers. GPS has been used in conjunction with field components of image analysis and is beginning to be utilized as a wildlife data collection technology.

One tool that was developed during this project was the Habitat Conservation Decision Cube. The decision cube is covered in detail in chapter 15, but is introduced at this time as it defined the database design for the USAID project. The decision cube can be represented as a three-dimensional box with eight internal cubes (see figure 15.2). The eight cubes represent possible outcomes when three separate axes are viewed for the presence or absence of the three variables used in gap analysis. The three variables are the presence or absence of a species or group of species of wildlife; the presence or absence of suitable habitat for that species; and the presence or absence of protected areas. Each of the eight types of locations require different policy approaches. For example, gap analysis was designed to identify the locations where species and habitat are present that are outside of protected areas. Such locations adjacent to or between protected areas are prioritized in land acquisitions for conservation purposes.

History and Status

There is growing recognition in the United States of the high cost and low efficiency of the species level approach to conservation of biological diversity associated with the 1973 Endangered Species Act (Edwards et al. 1995). Gap analysis is one approach in extending conservation of biological diversity from reactive legislative battles over individual species to strategic planning for habitat conservation.

The methodology for gap analysis is based upon the logic used in evaluating the representation of vegetation communities within protected areas, such as studies performed in the United States (Crumpacker et al. 1988) and Africa (Huntley 1988). Evaluation of wildlife in a gap analysis framework was first performed in the United States in a study in Hawaii. The measurement of the geographic intersection of the home range of endangered forest bird species with protected areas indicated that less than 10 percent of the bird habitat was protected (Scott et al. 1987). In 1989 Idaho initiated a statewide gap analysis project which addressed a wide variety of wildlife species and habitat. Since that time, gap analysis projects have been completed for most of the western states in the United States.

Gap analysis is a technique that is receiving a high level of attention from conservation agencies and organizations (Machlis, Forester, and McKendry 1994). It is an effective tool for decision-makers and policy analysts because it clearly maps out potential conservation priorities and the path used to reach those priorities. Gap analysis results can be combined with economic development needs as constraints or opportunities in geographic selection of sustainable development projects. Thus, gap analysis is likely to be a focal technique in biodiversity and sustainable development research in the future.

The Application of Gap Analysis in the United States

Gap analysis is a biodiversity planning approach which has been embraced by the U. S. Geological Survey, Biological Resources Division (Machlis, Forester, and McKendry 1994). The state of Utah published a report that contained four maps, two CD-ROMs, and documentation of the methodology used and results obtained (Edwards et al. 1995). The four maps include a mosaic of Landsat TM images, habitat classes generated from the image analysis, distribution of public lands, and a combination of habitat data and public lands suitable for consideration in wildlife management plans. The two CD-ROMs contain data on the distribution of 525 wildlife species.

A gap analysis also has been completed for the southwestern portion of the state of California (Davis 1994). The project identified eighteen vegetation communities and forty-two vertebrate species at risk in the region. The minimum mapping unit for the project was one square kilometer (100 hectares), and final results were presented at a scale which utilized 7.5 minute U.S. Geological Survey topographic quadrangle maps as the smallest geographic unit of analysis.

The state of Florida performed a gap analysis for 120 vertebrate species (Cox et al. 1994). This gap analysis was only a subset of the extensive wildlife and habitat analyses performed by the state. Biological data holdings in Florida are rich, with over 25,000 geographically referenced locations of rare plants, animals, and natural communities. These data were combined with statewide land cover maps generated from Landsat imagery to identify strategic habitat conservation areas and a separate set of maps indicating regional diversity hot spots.

International Application of Gap Analysis

Gap analysis projects are beginning to be performed in tropical developing countries. Two Latin American projects have used GIS to present existing biodiversity data and to integrate these data for preliminary strategic assessments. One example of this level of mapping is "Biological Priorities for Conservation in Amazonia" (Conservation International 1991). The content of this map was based upon a workshop of zoologists, systemic botanists, and vegetation ecologists. The geographic methodology utilized in the integration of biological and protected area data was innovative, and the project is sure to be followed with more detailed assessments. However, it should be noted that a map at a scale of 1:5,000,000 is useful only in very broad identification of conservation priorities. The general scale of this level of analysis is evidenced by the fact that the entire country of Costa Rica is smaller than several of the high-priority conservation regions identified in Amazonia.

A more detailed project was performed in Costa Rica (Fundación Neotrópica and Conservation International 1988). Priority conservation regions were identified by superimposing data on the percentage of natural vegetation cover with boundaries of watersheds and protected areas. Although the scale of the vegetation maps used in the study was 1:200,000, the only wildlife data utilized were locations of endangered, threatened, and rare species. The objective of the study was to compare thirty-three watershed units in order to identify national priorities in watershed management.

Both the Amazonia and Costa Rica projects were able to provide only general information on biological diversity because they were limited in available details on either habitat or wildlife data. This author has observed that biodiversity projects in the tropics either have not utilized all of the data layers used in gap analysis projects in the United States (wildlife, habitat, and protected areas) or they have not yet been able to utilize a scale of analysis as detailed as projects in the United States. This project in Costa Rica utilized the habitat and protected area data at a similar scale of analysis as other gap analysis projects in the United States. Since a national survey of wildlife was performed, the wildlife data in the Costa Rica project had a greater level of depth than U.S. gap analysis projects. However, because only twenty-one species of wildlife were evaluated, the level of breadth was lower than most gap analysis projects in the United States. The extent to which the international application of detailed gap analysis becomes more frequent may depend in large part on the ability of the international community to produce viable habitat maps for use in national conservation efforts.

There are positive indications that the international community is moving toward funding projects that will generate regional databases useful for detailed biodiversity assessments such as national gap analyses. Several regional habitat mapping projects (detailed in chapter 5) are being proposed or are in early phases. The 1992 United Nations Conference on Environment and Development (UNCED) drafted *Agenda 21,* a list of action areas for creating a sustainable future. *Agenda 21* addresses biodiversity and information for decision making as two of its twenty-eight platform areas (Parson, Haas, and Levy 1992). The fact that biodiversity is one of four categories funded through the Global Environment Facility (Reed 1991) is indicative of the strategic direction and intention of the United Nations Environment Program, the United Nations Development Program, and the World Bank. All of these mechanisms indicate that natural resource managers in developing tropical countries may have more and better habitat data in the near future upon which to build national analyses. It remains the responsibility of the national agencies, private conservation groups, and academic institutions to collect or integrate the wildlife data.

Critique of Gap Analysis

Gap analysis has been shown to be an effective tool for conservation assessment in statewide applications within the United States. GIS has served as a useful mechanism both for integrating data on wildlife, habitat, and protected areas and for providing mapped information for strategic conservation planning. There is interest in combining the gap analysis model with socioeconomic models to better understand our choices in human-environmental interactions (McKendry and Machlis 1991; Machlis, Forester, and McKendry 1994). This level of interdisciplinary research is indicative of the utility of the gap analysis model in providing biodiversity information that is useful in a broad decision-making context.

Nevertheless, there are numerous limitations to the use of the gap analysis

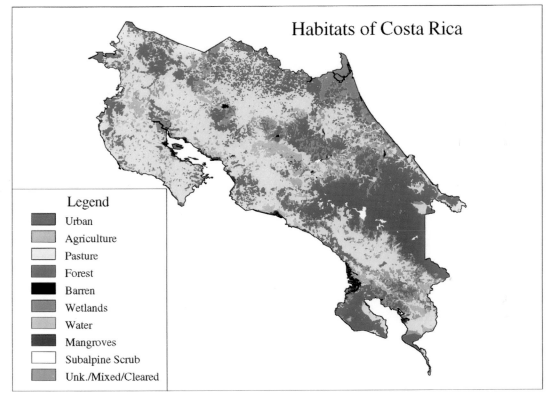

PLATE 1 Habitat map of Costa Rica

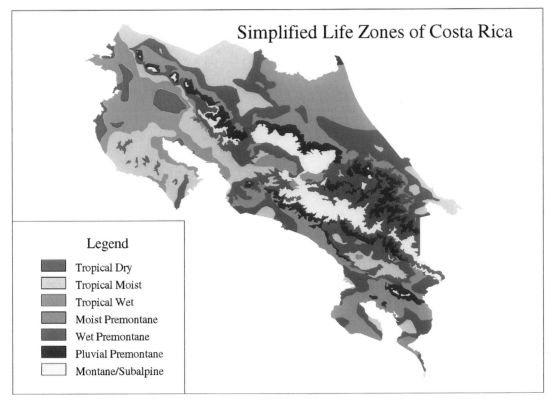

PLATE 2 Simplified life zones of Costa Rica based upon methodology of Holdridge (1971) and maps by Bolaños and Watson (1993). Potential forest types are based upon altitude, precipitation, and evapotranspiration potential.

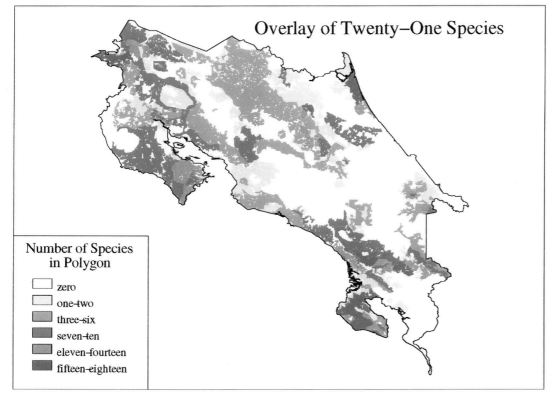

PLATE 3 Overlay map of all twenty-one species

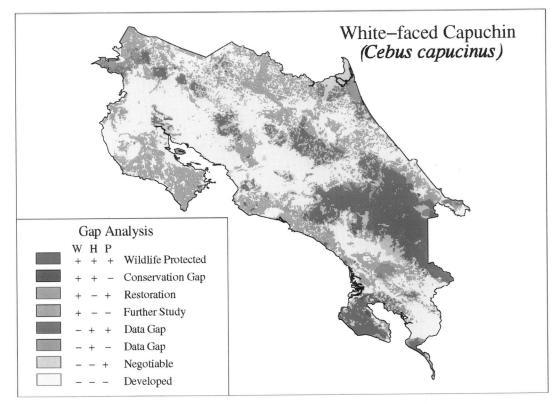

PLATE 4 Gap analysis for the white-faced capuchin (*Cebus capucinus*)

model (Scott et al. 1993), and these are discussed in detail in chapter 14. However, three constraints to the application of the model are noted here. First, since gap analysis is a coarse planning tool designed to indicate regional patterns, results need to be interpreted accordingly and verified in the field at a finer scale of analysis. Second, gap analysis is intended to augment rather than replace efforts to identify and protect individual species of concern and centers of endemism. Third, gap analysis provides information on geographic areas possibly worth adding to the system of protected areas from the biological perspective. Successful implementation of a land acquisition strategy requires data on land ownership which may or may not be readily available for use in a digital format.

Definition of Terms and Concepts

Several terms used throughout the balance of the USAID case study are defined below:

BIOLOGICAL DIVERSITY

Biological diversity has been defined along three hierarchical categories as "the totality of genes, species, and ecosystems in a region" (WRI/IUCN/UNEP 1992:2) The unit of measurement for genetic diversity is either a population or a species. Species diversity is measured within the region of the ecosystem. The region for measuring ecosystem diversity is not as well defined as the regions for the other two units, but it is generally understood to be applied at the national or subnational level. Gap analysis utilizes species diversity data to depict geographic pattern at the ecosystem-diversity scale of analysis.

MAPPING OF HABITAT, LAND COVER, LAND USE, AND VEGETATION

Although there are differences between these four terms, they are used synonymously in this text. The same feature, such as a patch of forest, can be found in the classification schemes of each of the four types of maps. For example, the land cover of forest vegetation, when it occurs within an urban land use (such as a residential neighborhood or a city park), is classified as urban habitat. The focus of the project was on mapping the distribution of vertebrate species that are closely linked to forested habitat. This study does not address variation within forests, such as undisturbed or secondary growth forests.

PROTECTED AREAS

There are five protected area management categories which the World Conservation Union (IUCN) employs. These categories are: strict nature reserves, national parks, natural monuments, habitat and wildlife management areas, and protected landscapes (WRI/IUCN/UNEP 1992). Although the wildlife conservation objectives of these five categories vary, all protected areas are treated equally in the context of this gap analysis project.

REGIONAL LANDSCAPE

The question of scale is at the heart of the discipline of geography. One review of the use of spatial scale in conservation biology concludes that "landscape is the preferable term for describing large natural areas with conservation value" (Csuti 1991:81). Further,

> The regional landscape (generally in the range of 1,000 to 100,000 square kilometers) is a convenient scale at which to integrate planning and management for multiple levels of organization. It is the scale of a constellation of national forests, parks, and surrounding private lands, or of a large watershed or mountain range. The regional landscape is big enough to comprise numerous, interacting ecosystems; to incorporate large natural disturbances; and to maintain viable populations of large, wide-ranging animals. Yet, it is small enough to be biogeographically distinct, and to be mapped in detail and managed by people who know the land well. (Noss 1992:241)

Policy relevant to biodiversity should be formulated at the landscape scale in order to focus on the processes of ecosystem health across human generations rather than on the protection of individual species (Norton and Ulanowicz 1991).

References

Conservation International. 1991. Biological priorities for conservation in Amazonia. Map printed at a scale of 1:5,000,000. Washington, D.C.: Conservation International.

Cox, J., R. Kautz, M. MacLaughlin, and T. Gilbert. 1994. *Closing the gaps in Florida's wildlife habitat conservation systems.* Tallahassee, Fla.: Office of Environmental Services.

Crumpacker, D. W., S. W. Hodge, D. Friedley, and W. P. Gregg, Jr. 1988. A preliminary assessment of the status of major terrestrial and wetland ecosystems on federal and Indian lands in the United States. *Conservation Biology* 2: 103–15.

Csuti, B. 1991. Conservation corridors: Countering habitat fragmentation. In W. E. Hudson, ed., *Landscape linkages and biodiversity*, 81–90. Washington, D.C.: Island Press.

Davis, F. W. 1994. *Gap analysis of the southwestern California region.* Technical Report 94–4. Santa Barbara, Calif.: National Center for Geographic Information and Analysis.

Davis, F. W., D. M. Stoms, J. E. Estes, J. Scepan, and J. M. Scott. 1990. An information systems approach to the preservation of biological diversity. *International Journal of Geographical Information Systems* 4: 55–78.

Edwards, T. C. Jr., C. G. Homer, S. C. Bassett, A. Falconer, R. D. Ramsey, and D. W. Wight. 1995. *Utah gap analysis: An environmental information system.* Final Project Report 95–1. Logan: Utah Cooperative Fish and Wildlife Research Unit.

Fundación Neotrópica and Conservation International. 1988. *Costa Rica: Assessment of the conservation of biological resources* (thirteen pages and four maps at 1:909,091 scale). San José, C.R.: Fundación Neotrópica.

Huntley, B. J. 1988. Conserving and monitoring biotic diversity: Some African examples. In E. O. Wilson, ed., *Biodiversity*, 248–60. Washington, D.C.: National Academy Press.

Machlis, G. E., D. J. Forester, and J. E. McKendry. 1994. *Biodiversity gap analysis: Critical challenges and solutions*. Moscow: University of Idaho.

McKendry, J. E. and G. E. Machlis. 1991. The role of geography in extending biodiversity gap analysis. *Applied Geography* 11: 135–52.

Norton, B. G. and R. E. Ulanowicz. 1991. Scale and biodiversity policy: A hierarchical approach. *Ambio* 21: 244–49.

Noss, R. F. 1992. Issues of scale in conservation biology. In P. L. Fiedler and S. K. Jain, eds., *Conservation biology*, 239–50. New York: Chapman and Hall.

Parson, E. A., P. M. Haas, and M. A. Levy. 1992. A summary of the major documents signed at the earth summit and the global forum. *Environment* 34 (August): 12–36.

Reed, D. 1991. *The Global Environment Facility: Sharing responsibility for the biosphere*. Washington, D. C.: World Wildlife Fund—International.

Scott, J. M., B. Csuti, J. D. Jacobi, and J. E. Estes. 1987. Species richness: A geographic approach to protecting future biological diversity. *BioScience* 37: 782–88.

Scott, J. M., F. Davis, B. Csuti, R. Noss, B. Butterfield, C. Groves, H. Anderson, S. Caicco, F. D'Erchia, T. C. Edwards Jr., J. Ulliman, and R. G. Wright. 1993. *Gap analysis: A geographical approach to protection of biological diversity*. Wildlife Monograph no. 123 (41 pp.). Bethesda, Md.: The Wildlife Society.

World Resources Institute (WRI), World Conservation Union (IUCN), United Nations Environment Programme (UNEP). 1992. *Global biodiversity strategy: Guidelines for action to save, study, and use Earth's biotic wealth sustainably and equitably*. Washington, D.C.: WRI.

13

Wildlife and Habitat Data Collection and Analysis

Basil G. Savitsky, Jorge Fallas, Christopher Vaughan, and Thomas E. Lacher Jr.

Development of Habitat and Wildlife Databases

Costa Rica, with an area of only 51,100 km^2, has one of the highest levels of biodiversity per unit area in the world. According to the Holdridge system of life zones (Holdridge 1967), Costa Rica can be divided into twenty-four life zones, each of which possesses unique characteristics of elevation, temperature, precipitation, and evapotranspiration potential. This high diversity of environmental conditions has generated an equally diverse landscape with an extremely high diversity of plants and animals. Not all species could be included in a wildlife database, and a decision needed to be made concerning the level of detail of the habitat map that would be used as well. This chapter discusses the relevant issues for the creation of wildlife and habitat databases.

Habitat Map

One of the research objectives was to create a habitat map of Costa Rica and superimpose it with map layers on wildlife and protected areas to perform a national gap analysis of Costa Rica. The purpose of the habitat map is to provide a polygon-structured base map to which point-structured wildlife data are related. The polygons need to contain data that are specific enough to be meaningful in diagnosing spatial trends in the wildlife data, but general enough to be manageable in addressing a national database. A target scale of 1:200,000 was selected for the habitat map because the wildlife data and a variety of other data sources were available at this scale. A flow chart of the procedures used to create the habitat map is provided (figure 13.1).

The initial compilation of the habitat map was based upon an unpublished land use and land cover map of Costa Rica produced by the Instituto Geográfico Nacional de Costa Rica (IGN 1984). The IGN map series contained data on the distribution of forty land use and land cover categories at a scale of 1:200,000. In order to approximate the desired classes in the habitat map, the forty classes were generalized using color pens to a set of maps containing eleven classes defined as 1984 Land Use (table 13.1). Boundaries of the simplified polygons were transferred to mylar transparencies. The line work was digitized, and the polygons were labeled using ARC/INFO software. The data were then placed in a grid of 28.5 meter cells and exported to the format of ERDAS software in order to be used in the image analysis of more recent TM data.

The 1984 land use data were confirmed and updated using Landsat TM data. A computer search of all available TM imagery was performed to identify the most cloud-free scenes. Five TM scenes were acquired from 1991–92, providing coverage of the entire country of Costa Rica. The TM images were geographically referenced to 1:50,000 scale topographic maps. Thus, habitat classification maps resulting from TM image interpretation could be generalized to a scale of 1:200,000. Image analysis performed at Clemson University was directed toward a general classification of the imagery for the entire country. Image analysis performed at the Universidad Nacional Autonoma de Costa Rica (UNA) was directed toward providing a more detailed classification of two of the five TM scenes.

The national classification was performed using an unsupervised classification technique. In order to label the unsupervised classes, the land use data were overlaid with the TM classified data. Output from the unsupervised classification resulted in a map indicating forest, nonforest, water, and clouds.

The four-class 1992 TM-derived map was combined with the eleven-class 1984 land cover map in order to (1) confirm the geographic distribution of vegetation classes such as forest, wetlands, and mangroves that remained un-changed since 1984; (2) identify areas of change since 1984 (such as where forest had been cleared and where pasture had been converted to secondary growth); and (3) determine whether polygons indicated as secondary growth in the 1984 land use data had remained as forest or had been cleared. It was assumed that urban and agricultural areas in 1984 had remained in similar land use in 1992 because very few developed areas revert to other land uses in such a short time. Areas covered by clouds in TM imagery were designated with the 1984 land use categories.

The output from this analysis resulted in a ten-category classification scheme called the 1992 TM Update Classes, which differs from the 1984 scheme in several ways (see table 13.1). Wetlands and natural palms were combined into a single

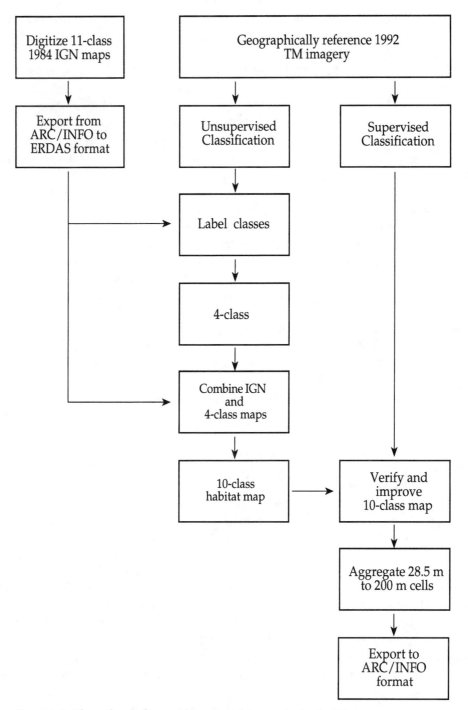

FIG. 13.1 Flow chart of procedures used to create the habitat map

TABLE 13.1 *Land Use in 1984 and 1992 TM Update Classes Used in the Classification Scheme for the Habitat Map*

1984 Land Use	1992 TM Update Classes
Urban	Urban
Agriculture	Agriculture
Pasture	Pasture
Charral / secondary growth	Merged to pasture or forest
Forest	Forest
Subalpine scrub	Subalpine scrub
Wetlands	Wetlands
Natural palms	Merged to wetlands
Mangroves	Mangroves
Barren	Barren
Water	Water
—	Unknown / mixed / cleared

SOURCES: IGN (1984) and author

class. Charral/secondary growth areas were designated either as forest or pasture, depending on the change between 1984 and 1992. A new class was created which indicated unknown habitat, due either to a mixed value (clusters of trees within pastures or along edges of pastures) or to probable but unverified clearing of the area between 1984 and 1992.

A supervised approach was used by staff at UNA for the two TM scenes for which extensive field data and local knowledge were available. The detailed image classification output from this analysis was used in conjunction with aerial photography and other ancillary data sources to improve the results of the national classification described above. Emphasis was placed upon reducing the number of large areas in the unknown/mixed/cleared class by accurately defining the present habitat status of as many polygons as feasible.

The habitat map derived from TM data was complex and voluminous because it was based upon 28.5 meter cells. An aggregation program was performed which used a seven-by-seven moving window to assign cell values to the dominant habitat class. This process removed a significant portion of isolated pixels which are noise at the landscape scale. The resultant habitat database contained 200-meter cells and had a minimum mapping unit of four hectares (see plate 1, table 13.2, and appendix 2). The data were exported to ARC/INFO format in order to combine the habitat data with the wildlife and protected areas data and to perform the gap analysis.

TABLE 13.2 *Area Summaries of Habitat Categories*

Habitat Class	Area (sq. km.)	Percentage
Urban	203	0.4
Agriculture	4,356	8.5
Pasture	23,774	46.6
Forest	16,798	32.9
Barren	154	0.3
Wetlands	1,149	2.3
Water	100	0.2
Mangroves	376	0.7
Subalpine scrub	136	0.3
Unknown / mixed / cleared	4,002	7.8
TOTAL	51,048	100.0

Wildlife Analysis

Wildlife data are the most dynamic of the three major data types utilized in gap analysis (wildlife, habitat, and boundaries of protected areas). Difficulties associated with collecting wildlife data include the problem of sighting some species, the unknown range of the species compared to the point of observation, and temporal variation in species behavior which is seasonally dynamic and which adjusts to long-term habitat alteration. The extent and quality of published species distribution maps are highly variable. Range data are more readily available for mammals, such as primates, or popular species of birds such as parrots. Reptile, fish, insect, and plant range data are not as well documented. Studies performed on the scarlet macaw (Vaughan, McCoy, and Liske 1991) and on the collared peccary (McCoy et al. 1990) indicate the level of effort required to provide comprehensive data on individual species.

The two primary forms of wildlife data collection are to construct the database on personal observation and to rely upon the observations of credible others. The first technique is time-consuming and is typically associated with the field observations of a wildlife biologist who is working on a single species or on a group of species within a small geographic region. Even at this scale, the above problems are still present. For example, for some species difficult to observe visually, it is often necessary to rely upon indirect evidence of their presence, such as tracks, waste, or remains. Maps generated for species distributions from these types of studies are rare but form the best possible source of wildlife data. Indicator species may be selected because the landscape scale of analysis associated with gap analysis precludes this level of data collection. For example, jaguars are known to occur from sea level to nearly 4,000 meters elevation, as long as there is adequate forest cover and prey. Given the high level of fragmentation of forest habitat in countries like Costa Rica, it is virtually impossible for an individual to survey all fragments.

Published maps of species distributions are of variable quality primarily because of the scale utilized and because our understanding of many species distributions is still so rudimentary. Most published species range maps are at a general scale—such as those depicted in field guides which do not show habitat variation within the general range of the species. Even maps of greater detail (perhaps 1:1,000,000 in scale) are constrained by the inability to show habitat where the species is unlikely to occur. On one hand, this is a geographic issue of avoiding map "noise." On the other hand, this is typically an inherent limitation of the wildlife data—one can be certain that a species has been observed in a certain habitat, but one cannot always predict that it will not occur in an adjacent habitat.

In the United States, species distribution data are available through the natural heritage programs (Jenkins 1988). The databases are of a high quality both in terms of number of species and in number of records per species. Since the data are geographically coded, they are conducive for use in a GIS and for gap analysis. Internationally, the implementation of conservation data centers to achieve a similar level of data compilation is increasing, but these have not yet become established enough to meet the data requirements for gap analysis. Tropical nations have very high levels of diversity, and most species are poorly studied. One of the greatest difficulties that a researcher who is trying to construct a distribution map has is the lack of reliable and current geo-referenced data. Costa Rica is one of the most intensively studied tropical countries, with several organizations dedicated to the study of patterns of biodiversity (see chapter 2). Nevertheless, most data are old and the application of traditional techniques of sampling (mark and recapture, banding) is time-consuming and costly.

Thus, for the Costa Rican gap analysis project, the approach implemented was to collect wildlife sighting data through interviews. This approach has the advantage of applying a more uniform sampling scheme to a landscape or region than usually results from other database sightings (which may be spatially biased to points of human observations such as roads, scientific field stations, or park observation centers). The decision to interview has an associated disadvantage, but when compared to national biodiversity programs the limitation is nominal. The drawback in the interview approach is that it usually aims for geographic breadth; thus, the inventory is limited to a select number of species. However, the investment has a high return in that usable data are rapidly available.

SELECTION OF SPECIES

Plant species, vertebrates, and butterfly distributions commonly are utilized as indicator species of biodiversity in gap analysis (Scott et al. 1993). Although plant species do not pose the data collection problems exhibited by the mobility of vertebrates, plant species distributions are often unmapped. Further, vegetation communities are typically defined by the dominant species (which tend to be generalist species). Thus, vertebrate and butterfly data are more useful for gap analysis. There were four major considerations in our choice of species for gap analysis:

1. *Distributions of species in Costa Rica.* Species were selected that had broad, national distributions as were species that were restricted to smaller geographic regions. Having both broad and more restricted distributions was also useful in estimating the frequency of misidentifications or spurious reports.

2. *Taxonomic diversity and habitat requirements.* The species selected should represent several different taxa (reptiles, birds, and mammals) as well as different habitat requirements (forest, estuaries, mangroves, secondary forest, etc.). In this manner, one can evaluate the availability of habitat at the national scale. Some species selected will occupy both undisturbed and disturbed or fragmented areas.

3. *Identification in the field.* The species selected should be easily and unambiguously identified in the field by the individuals who were interviewed.

4. *Value for conservation.* The species selected should serve as indicators of biodiversity.

The utilization of indicator species allows for the use of data on the distribution of select species rather than requiring the mapping of all species. Indicator species must be common enough to be readily mapped but not so common as to occupy the entire landscape, as do generalist species. Threatened and endangered species, although they may be considered in the final conservation recommendations resulting from gap analysis, are not always useful as indicator species, especially when they are exceptionally rare. Likewise, riparian species or other species associated with narrow habitat ranges may not be effective indicator species. Twenty-one species were utilized in this project (table 13.3) and are described in appendix 3. These species met the data collection criteria and were selected on the basis of the expert opinion of Christopher Vaughan and his previous experience with nineteen of the species.

THE SURVEY DESIGN AND RESULTS

The same methodology used to develop the 1983 species data maps prepared by Vaughan (1983) was applied in the development of the 1993 maps. Interviews were held with employees of national resource agencies and registered hunters. Interviews were performed with 406 people at different localities throughout the country (see appendix 4). Fifty percent of those interviewed were involved in agriculture, and another 27 percent were park guards, wildlife inspectors, rural police, or researchers. The truthfulness and quality of the information obtained during the interview process was considered high; 75 percent of those interviewed had resided at the locality of the interview for more than ten years.

TABLE 13.3 *Common and Scientific Names of Twenty-one Species Mapped in Costa Rica Gap Analysis*

Common Name	Scientific Name
MAMMALS	
Howler monkey	*Alouatta palliata*
Spider monkey	*Ateles geoffroyi*
Squirrel monkey	*Saimiri oerstedii*
White-faced capuchin	*Cebus capucinus*
Jaguar	*Panthera onca*
Jaguarundi	*Herpailurus yagouaroundi*
Mountain lion	*Puma concolor*
Margay	*Leopardus wiedii*
Ocelot	*Leopardus pardalis*
Paca	*Agouti paca*
Giant anteater	*Myrmecophaga tridactyla*
Tapir	*Tapirus bairdii*
White-lipped peccary	*Tayassu pecari*
Collared peccary	*Pecari tajacu*
BIRDS	
Great curassow	*Crax rubra*
Harpy eagle	*Harpia harpyja*
Green macaw	*Ara ambigua*
Scarlet macaw	*Ara macao*
Quetzal	*Pharomachrus mocinno*
REPTILES	
Central American caiman	*Caiman crocodilus*
American crocodile	*Crocodylus acutus*

SOURCES: Scientific names for birds (Stiles and Skutch 1989), reptiles (Dowling and Duellman 1978), and mammals (Wilson and Reeder 1993).

Although most of the people interviewed stated that they no longer hunted (almost all the survey species have legal protection), many had rifles or other arms in their possession. Approximately 3,400 sightings were located on the 1:200,000 topographic series for Costa Rica by the staff at the Regional Wildlife Management Program for Mesoamerica and the Caribbean (PRMVS). The points on the maps were digitized into an ARC/INFO coverage utilizing the Lambert North projection for Costa Rica, with the single attribute indicating species type.

Once the maps were prepared and printed, all twenty-one maps were subjected to a final review. Species with questionable locations were reevaluated and errors in mapping were corrected. We were especially careful to correct errors associated with the use of common names since these vary from region to region of the country. Passing through an intermediate stage of map review allowed us to better evaluate the wildlife data prior to conducting the analyses; these errors would be easier to miss if the data were in database format only.

Converting Data Points to Polygons

The gap analysis model is based upon the GIS overlay of three types of polygon map layers. The habitat and protected area data types were already stored in polygonal format, but it was necessary to convert the 3,400 wildlife data points into a set of polygons which characterized the twenty-one species distributions. Converting the wildlife data points into a meaningful measure of presence within a given habitat was based upon the methodology described in Scott et al. (1993). A point-in-polygon procedure was utilized to convert the wildlife sightings data to polygons more closely corresponding to the wildlife range. First, the wildlife data were overlaid on the habitat map. Then, every resultant habitat polygon that contained a point of a certain species was tagged as having that species present. According to this logic, a given polygon could have as many as twenty-one species present. There was not a mechanism employed to tabulate the frequency of any given species per polygon. Each polygon in the wildlife polygon map indicates the presence or absence of each of the twenty-one species in the polygon.

It was necessary to refine this system by limiting the size of the polygons in the habitat map before overlaying it with the wildlife data points. Without a spatially imposed limitation, a point representing a wildlife sighting in a pasture on the edge of a forest would be characterized as having a range as expansive as all of the connected pasture land in that portion of Costa Rica, perhaps tens of thousands of square kilometers. Likewise, a bird species sighted flying over a farm could result in marking an entire agricultural zone of the country as the habitat for that species. Although limiting the size of the habitat polygons did not eliminate the problem, the process reduced the extent of the phenomenon.

In order to define polygonal boundaries of wildlife data, it is recommended that political boundaries, such as counties, be used in combination with habitat data (Scott et al. 1993). However, the political units in Costa Rica are too large to serve this purpose. Another alternative is to use watershed boundaries. The methodology selected for this study divided the forest, agriculture, and pasture polygons into seven different types according to the life zone methodology described in Holdridge (1971). The life zone system indicates potential forest types based upon latitude, altitude, precipitation, and evapotranspiration potential. Several hundred life zone polygons provided a more meaningful technique for dividing the large polygons than did arbitrary political units, and the predicted life zone made for a natural combination with actual land cover. Life zones also are more biologically meaningful than political units or small watersheds. Twenty-four classes of potential forest types were mapped for Costa Rica (Bolaños and Watson 1993) and were available in a 1:200,000 map series. These data were digitized, and the twenty-four classes were grouped into seven altitudinal categories (plate 2). The seven life zone categories were then overlaid with the habitat map. This map was then overlaid with the wildlife data points to derive wildlife habitat polygons.

An example of the process of converting point data to polygonal data is provided in order to visualize the quality of wildlife data. An example of the original point data collected for the white-faced capuchin (*Cebus capucinus*) is presented in figure 13.2. The 313 data points for the white-face capuchin were overlaid with the habitat map, and all polygons containing data points were "filled." The resultant data file presented in figure 13.3 is the GIS file used in the gap analysis for the white-faced capuchin discussed in detail in the next chapter.

An overlay of all four primate species is presented in figure 13.4. Since the geographic range of the squirrel monkey (*Saimiri oerstedii*) is limited to the southern region of Costa Rica, all four species are present only in that area. By overlaying all four primate distributions, it is possible to identify numerous areas utilized by one or two species. Likewise, one can see the few areas utilized by three or more of the primate species.

The same procedure was employed for all twenty-one species distributions (plate 3). Note the large area of the country where there were no species sighted. These white polygons are either developed areas where wildlife is seldom seen or remote areas where the humans who were interviewed had seldom been. No

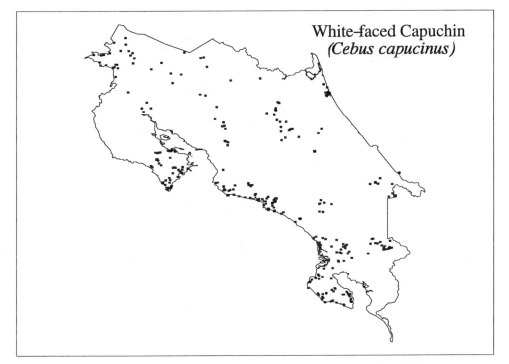

FIG. 13.2 Original point data collected for the white-faced capuchin (*Cebus capucinus*)

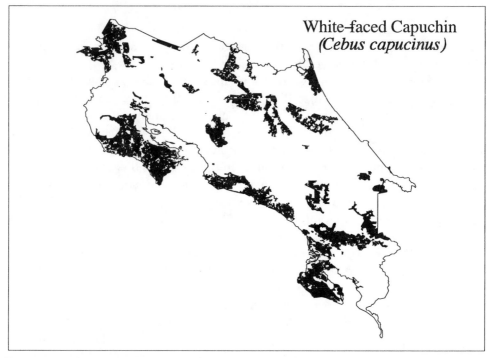

FIG. 13.3 Polygonal habitat data for the white-faced capuchin (*Cebus capucinus*)

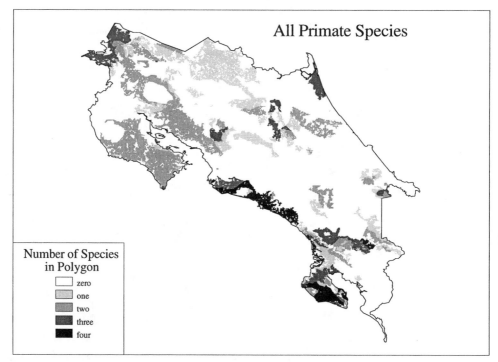

Number of Species
in Polygon

zero
one
two
three
four

FIG. 13.4 Overlay map of all four primate species

polygons were identified as being utilized by more than eighteen of the twenty-one species. Those areas having the highest species overlay intensity (fifteen to eighteen species; pink shading) included Osa, Guanacaste, and Tortuguero (figure 2.2), which was expected as they are some of the most biologically diverse areas in Costa Rica. Most of the other polygons indicating presence of eleven or more species (pink and brown shading) were within or adjacent to protected areas. Some of the polygons indicating the presence of seven to ten species (green shading) and three to six species (dark blue shading) are forested areas, but most are agriculture or pasture areas.

References

Bolaños, R. A. and V. C. Watson. 1993. *Mapa de Zonas de Vida de Costa Rica: Hojas Liberia y Nicoya. Escala 1:200.000* (Ecological map of life zones in Costa Rica: [According to the system of classification of life zones of the world by L. R. Holdridge; nine map sheets at] 1:200,000 scale). San José, C.R.: Centro Científico Tropical (Tropical Science Center).

Dowling, H. G. and W. E. Duellman. 1978. *Systematic herpetology: A synopsis of families and higher categories.* New York: Hiss.

Holdridge, L. R. 1967. *Life zone ecology.* San José, C.R.: Tropical Science Center.

———. 1971. *Forest environments in tropical life zones.* Oxford: Pergamon.

Instituto Geográfico Nacional de Costa Rica (IGN). 1984. Unpublished preliminary land use map of Costa Rica (nine maps at 1:200,000 scale). San José, C.R.: IGN.

Jenkins, R. E. Jr. 1988. Information management for the conservation of biodiversity. In E. O. Wilson, ed., *Biodiversity*, 231–39. Washington, D.C.: National Academy Press.

McCoy, M. B., C. S. Vaughan, M. A. Rodríguez, and D. Kitchen. 1990. Seasonal movement, home range, activity and diet of collared peccaries (*Tayassu tajacu*) in Costa Rican dry forest. *Vida Silvestre Neotropical* 2(2): 6–20.

Scott J. M., F. Davis, B. Csuti, R. Noss, B. Butterfield, C. Groves, H. Anderson, S. Caicco, F. D'Erchia, T. C. Edwards, Jr., J. Ulliman, and R. G. Wright. 1993. Gap analysis: a geographical approach to protection of biological diversity. *Wildlife Monograph No. 123*, The Wildlife Society.

Stiles, F. G. and A. F. Skutch. 1989. *A guide to the birds of Costa Rica.* Ithaca, N.Y.: Comstock.

Vaughan, C. 1983. *A report on dense forest habitat for endangered wildlife species in Costa Rica.* Heredia: Universidad Nacional Antonoma de Costa Rica.

Vaughan, C., M. McCoy, and J. Liske. 1991. Scarlet macaw (*Ara macao*) ecology and management perspectives in Carara Biological Reserve, Costa Rica. *Proceedings, First Mesoamerican workshop on conservation management of macaws of the genus Ara.* Tegucigalpa, Honduras.

Wilson, D. E. and D. M. Reeder. 1993. *Mammal species of the world.* 2d ed. Washington, D.C.: Smithsonian Institution Press.

14

Error and the Gap Analysis Model

Jennifer N. Morgan and Basil G. Savitsky

ERROR is a concept of growing concern to the geographic community as GIS usage and products rapidly are becoming more widespread. An understanding of the limitations of ecological modeling should serve to further the appropriate application of the gap analysis model.

Three functions have been identified that biological models perform to varying degrees of quality (Levins 1966). Any given model can maximize realism, precision, or generality, but no model can maximize all three qualities. Realism indicates the ability of the model to define reality. Precision is the accuracy associated with the measurements used in the model. Generality is the ability to apply the model in a variety of settings. A model that is highly realistic to the wildlife and habitat characteristics of the western United States probably would have low generality to the study of wildlife in Central America. A model that also requires high precision is difficult to apply in other settings which cannot meet the high precision standards. Gap analysis is a model that has great generality—it can be applied in a variety of geographic settings and at a variety of geographic scales. However, there are precision and realism limitations associated with the gap analysis model as a result of its generality. The constraints associated with precision will be discussed in the context of geographic error. The constraints associated with realism will be discussed in the context of biological error.

Geographic Error

Cartographic and thematic error are two major categories of geographic error (Veregin 1989). The cartographic errors introduced in the Costa Rica project were associated with a variety of point and line data. The positional accuracy of the digitization of the original wildlife data indicated on the map sheet was on the order of 100 meters. The positional accuracy of the lines transferred from the 1:200,000 map sheets is similar. The line work includes the protected area boundaries and the life zone data. The positional accuracy of the habitat data is approximately 200 meters for two reasons. First, the habitat data were based upon an unpublished 1984 land cover map. The copies obtained for digitization were not able to be registered to the original 1:200,000 sheets with greater accuracy than 200 meters. Second, the 1984 data were updated with TM imagery. The geographic registration of the imagery to 1:50,000 topographic maps was performed to within one pixel width or 28.5 meters. However, the final habitat map was generated by the aggregation program (discussed in chapter 13) in which forty-nine pixels were grouped, resulting in pixels that were 200 meters on each side.

The positional accuracy of the original wildlife data is difficult to assess. Since the 3,400 data points were collected through interviews, there is variation in the knowledge and degree of geographic specificity of each individual who was interviewed. It was estimated by the staff who performed the interviews that the wildlife sightings indicated on the 1:200,000 map sheets could vary by as much as 0.5 to 1.0 centimeters from the point intended to be indicated on the map by the respondent. This means that the point in the database may differ by one to two kilometers from where the individual actually saw the species.

The thematic error in the Costa Rica project is associated primarily with the habitat data. Inaccuracies in the wildlife data were observed and corrected in draft plots of species distribution maps. The error introduced in misclassifications of habitat categories can contribute extensively to erroneous conclusions. All classification maps derived from remotely sensed data contain errors. Jensen (1995) cites Anderson et al. (1976) in suggesting that 85 percent overall accuracy is an acceptable target for land use mapping.

An accuracy assessment of the habitat map indicated that it has an overall accuracy of 74 percent (table 14.1). The assessment was performed by UNA using data from a current IGN project. The IGN project will provide 1:200,000 land cover maps of Costa Rica. A stratified random sampling approach was utilized to collect 1,372 reference points. The stratification was performed geographically and by class. Geographic stratification involved selecting a uniform distribution of points from the nine 1:200,000 map sheets covering the country. Stratification by class was performed by seeking a sample of points for each habitat class present within a given map sheet. For example, effort was made to collect reference points for each of the nine classes within each of the nine map sheets. Such sampling was not always possible because some habitat classes (such as mangroves and subalpine scrub) are not present throughout the country. Individual reference points were randomly selected.

Information in the error matrix (table 14.1) is ordered by habitat classes

TABLE 14.1 *Error Matrix for Habitat Map*

Classification data	Reference Data[a]									Row Total
	P	F	A	W	M	B	W	U	S	
P	*644*	129	37	1	0	1	1	2	0	815
F	123	*220*	6	0	0	0	0	0	0	349
A	17	1	*85*	0	0	0	0	0	0	103
W	4	8	2	*29*	0	1	0	0	0	44
M	0	3	1	2	*23*	1	0	0	0	30
B	0	0	0	0	0	*6*	0	0	0	6
Wa	0	0	0	1	0	0	*6*	0	0	7
U	5	0	4	0	0	0	0	*2*	0	11
S	1	3	0	0	0	0	0	0	*3*	7
COLUMN TOTAL	794	364	135	33	23	9	7	4	3	1372

Overall Accuracy = 74%		Omission Error				Commission Error			
P	=	81%	P	=	150 / 794	=	19%	P	=	171 / 815	=	21%
F	=	60%	F	=	144 / 364	=	40%	F	=	129 / 349	=	37%
A	=	63%	A	=	50 / 135	=	37%	A	=	18 / 103	=	17%
W	=	88%	W	=	4 / 33	=	12%	W	=	15 / 44	=	34%
M	=	100%	M	=	0 / 23	=	0%	M	=	7 / 30	=	23%
B	=	67%	B	=	3 / 9	=	33%	B	=	0 / 6	=	0%
Wa	=	86%	Wa	=	1 / 7	=	14%	Wa	=	1 / 7	=	14%
U	=	50%	U	=	2 / 4	=	50%	U	=	9 / 11	=	82%
S	=	100%	S	=	0 / 3	=	0%	S	=	4 / 7	=	57%

NOTE: Accuracy assessment data were collected using stratified random sampling. Frequency of accurately classified pixels are indicated in italics.
[a]P = pasture, F = forest, A = agriculture, W = wetlands, M = mangroves, B = barren, Wa = water, U = urban, S = subalpine scrub.

according to the frequency of reference data points that were collected. Omission error occurs when a pixel is not assigned to its appropriate class, and commission error occurs when a pixel is assigned to a class to which it does not belong (Jensen 1995). For example, all the mangrove reference points were properly identified (omission error was zero percent), but seven other points were incorrectly classified as mangroves (commission error was 34 percent).

Eighteen percent of the error in the habitat map results from confusion between forest and pasture (table 14.1). The use of the forest habitat to define polygons as suitable habitat for wildlife in the gap analysis model contributes to error in the output from the model. There is additional error created by combining various data layers which are each positionally accurate to within 100 or 200 to 2,000 meters and a thematic data layer which is 74 percent accurate. The combinatorial error has not been measured but should be noted, especially in the context of planning for field verification of specific geographic areas identified in gap analysis.

Biological Error

Wildlife phenomena are problematic to measure and map. Difficulties include complexity of species behavior and temporal dynamics. For example, habitat preference of a given species changes during the day and over the year (for the scientific names of the following named species, see table 13.3). Scarlet macaws nest in forests, but may feed in mangroves, and can be sighted in flight over agricultural or pasture areas between their nesting and feeding habitat. The possibility of the misidentification of the species which are sighted must be considered in any database on wildlife.

Forest of some type is the primary habitat utilized by all twenty-one species. Variations in forest, such as those occurring in various life zones or according to an elevation gradient, were not addressed. Also, the extent to which habitat other than forest were utilized by the twenty-one species was not evaluated.

One component of potential biological error was introduced into the database by including all sightings within the last five years. The decision was made to obtain data over a five-year period in order to gain as much data as possible about each species. The gap analysis did not distinguish between the dates of the sightings, so the species distribution is biased toward being more broad than current conditions may support.

Scott et al. (1993) list ten limitations associated with gap analysis. One objective in identifying these limitations is that gap analysis is a coarse-filter and regional-planning tool. Thus, its output should be used accordingly and in conjunction with follow-up fieldwork. One of the limitations listed by Scott et al. (1993) is the minimum mapping unit. Patches of habitat smaller than the 200-meter cells (four hectares) utilized in the habitat data layer of this project are present in the landscape and are undoubtedly utilized by some of the species, but the level of scale of the species-habitat relationship can only be assessed at or above the scale of the minimum mapping unit.

An additional limitation listed by Scott et al. (1993) is the predictive quality of all species distribution maps. The occurrence of a given species in the past in a given area does not assure continued presence of that species. Likewise, a habitat patch identified in gap analysis may not be large enough to meet the variable needs of a given species. The identification of potential conservation areas at the landscape-planning level needs to be confirmed in a more detailed assessment.

Evaluation of Cartographic and Biological Error

An assessment of both cartographic and biological error was performed through an analysis of all the wildlife data points that were outside the predicted forested habitat. This criterion was met by 2,100 of the 3,400 data points. A database was created that listed each point, species type, and distance to the nearest forest polygon. The distances were evaluated cumulatively for all species and on a species-by-species basis in order to identify trends in the data which might separate cartographic error from edge behavior. It was anticipated that some of the species that had more narrow habitat cover requirements, such as the tapir (which is a very shy mammal) or the jaguar, would have lower distances than species that were more generalist in their habitat utilization—for example, white-faced capuchin and some of the small cats. It also was anticipated that the distances of the more generalist species might have a bimodal distribution, indicating one cluster of distance values associated with cartographic error and a second cluster associated with edge or roaming behavior. It was hypothesized that the cluster of distance values associated with cartographic error would have low values, representing points that should have been placed within forest boundaries. The cluster of distance values associated with biological error would have high values, indicating animal behavior well outside the forest habitat.

In order to specifically evaluate the occurrence of either edge behavior or anomalies in the 2,100 points, a GIS function was used to determine the closest occurring forest habitat. The function evaluates each point separately, finds the closest forest polygon, and measures the distance. The data from this function were stored by the program in a separate file containing three attributes: the wildlife point identification number, the type of species in question, and the calculated distance. The distances were then measured through a statistics program for occurrence of means and ranges. The average distance to the nearest forest boundary was 1,641 meters. This was within the range of cartographic error which had been estimated as potentially present in the original wildlife sightings by interview respondents. The average distances of each species are listed in rank order (table 14.2). Using behavioral information of each species concerning their normal range and edge requirements, it is evident that the means could be attributed either to normal or abnormal behavior patterns or to cartographic error.

Sixty-three percent of all animals observed in the USAID project occurred outside their primary habitat, the forest. For some of the species this could be expected. A cougar, for example, which is utilizing an edge species like deer for food, would be found outside the forest more often. The jaguarundi is noted by Mondolfi (1986) as "preferring" the edge habitat, rather than the internal forest, and is observed in a variety of habitats (Eisenberg 1989). Other broadly tolerant species include the squirrel monkey, found often in agricultural areas and close to human settlement (Vaughan 1983). The white-faced capuchin, as well, under no hunting pressure (Vaughan 1983), often occupies disturbed forests as well as mangrove and palm swamps (Timm et al. 1989). Birds, like the harpy eagle and the macaws, would likely be identified in the air over open land or feeding outside of forest (Vaughan 1983). Further, a crocodile or caiman would be well

TABLE 14.2 *Tabulation of Distances Between Wildlife Points Outside Forested Habitat and Nearest Forest Polygon*

Species	Number of Observations	Number of Observations Outside Forest	Percentage of Observations Outside Forest	Mean Distance from Forest (m)
Great curassow	210	117	56	1051
Tapir	129	45	35	1084
Jaguar	94	47	50	1167
White-lipped peccary	114	57	50	1219
Jaguarundi	134	87	65	1420
Quetzal	78	33	42	1439
Giant anteater	49	25	51	1440
Great green macaw	58	30	52	1478
Ocelot	134	83	62	1479
Mountain lion	91	51	56	1528
Paca	288	175	61	1601
Scarlet macaw	323	229	71	1630
White-faced capuchin	325	207	64	1666
Collared peccary	237	141	59	1669
Central American caiman	164	121	74	1699
Harpy eagle	40	16	40	1722
Margay	145	85	59	1795
Howler monkey	263	180	68	1836
Spider monkey	181	105	58	1917
American crocodile	230	168	73	1948
Squirrel monkey	118	98	83	2248
OVERALL SPECIES AVERAGE	162	100	62	1641

placed in delta habitat with few trees, its range more directly related to water than to forest (Vaughan 1983).

However, it is not expected that all the species would be found more often outside the forest. The white-lipped peccary is considered a wilderness species and is found in dense, primary forests (Emmons 1990). Distributions are inconsistent and often unpredictable due to exploitation and habitat destruction (Emmons 1990). The spider monkey is found chiefly in primary forest, almost exclusively in large undisturbed tracts (Timm et al. 1989). The habitat of the tapir, especially where heavily hunted, and of the quetzal is also tied to unaltered vegetation (Vaughan 1983; Timm et al. 1989; Emmons 1990). The percentage of quetzal and tapir observations occurring outside of forest was 42 percent and 35 percent of the observations, respectively, and were in fact two of the six lowest percentages of all species (table 14.1). However, 58 percent of all spider monkeys observed occurred outside forest habitat.

One possible explanation for nonforest observations is that the four-hectare size of the minimum mapping unit in the habitat database excluded smaller patches of forest habitat. These areas might be large enough to support small species like the paca, with small territories often associated with water (Emmons 1990; Eisenberg 1989), or those with lesser range requirements. Howler monkeys, for example, typically have small home ranges and can survive in small fragments of forest (Eisenberg 1989). They have been known to occupy stands of forest bordering water courses in areas heavily deforested (Vaughan 1983). In many instances these thin stands of trees are bordered on either side by light secondary growth, and then by developed or pasture land. The image analysis may not have classified these areas as forested. However, the size of the stands might be large enough to support the primates, or provide enough protective cover for other animals such as the jaguar or the paca.

Several of the animals studied, while primarily occurring in forest habitat, will utilize nonforested regions if they are available. Increased fragmentation, stemming from increased deforestation in Costa Rica, may cause such animals to come out of the forest habitat more often. Collared peccaries are noted by Leopold (1959) as very adaptable. Borrero (1967) says that the collared peccary is an animal of both the deserts and jungle in tropical and semitropical habitats. Larger felids, including the mountain lion and jaguar, will make use of the most available food source, which might be the cattle in the pasture land close to their forest habitat (Emmons 1990). While they may not be generalists, the cats may be utilizing a food source that is generalist. The jaguarundi, smallest of the wild felines, is also the most adaptive of the small cats (Timm et al. 1989). With its nonvaluable fur, and without hunting pressure, the jaguarundi may sometimes be found near villages (Vaughan 1983; Emmons 1990). Even the small margay, while preferring dense forest areas, will utilize altered habitats and semi-open areas, mangrove, and charral (Eisenberg 1989; Vaughan 1983).

One way to judge whether these points were reasonable occurrences would be to judge the size and type of stand of forest with which they are most closely associated. The NEAR function of ARC/INFO was used to find and measure the distance to the closest forest habitat for every point outside forest. However, it did not pinpoint exactly where or what type of forest it had identified. If it were to identify which forests it had judged as closest, it could be stated that each point was plausible or not. For example, a jaguar was noted as approximately 2,000 meters outside a forest polygon. If that polygon represents a large, dense forest sufficient in size to accommodate the large cat's home range, then the point could be judged plausible. If the forest polygon were an isolated, excessively small fragment, then the point would be unreasonable and due to some form of cartographic error.

The average distance outside of forest was 1,641 meters for all the species. All four primates had averages higher than this. The lowest averages were noted for the curassow (1,051 m) and the tapir (1,083 m). The curassow is a popular game species (Vaughan 1983), and the tapir, with the lowest average of nonforest point observations (35 percent), is an extremely shy animal found in undisturbed habitats. These lower distances, then, suggest that the ranges may not be unreasonable.

The majority of the points, 68 percent, were 2,000 meters or less outside of forest habitat. It may have been useful to add a 2000-meter buffer to the forest polygons in the habitat database to include these points within forest. However, this was not done because the relationship between the nonforest observations and the habitat is not fully understood. It is impossible to make a recommendation on this matter without a more qualitative analysis of the adjacency of these nonforest observations to forest. The fact remains that these are one-time sightings of animals and could have included animals dispersing between populations as well as animals foraging for cover or food.

As far as estimating anomalies or errors that might have occurred, less than one percent of all nonforest observations occurred at 9,000 meters or more outside the forest. The largest number of these sightings, three, were of squirrel monkeys. Again, the size of the primate is small enough to be able to occupy minimal stand size not identified by mapping. The rarity of these occurrences points toward aberration. However, further analysis of exact location of these points would be necessary to state conclusively whether or not they are examples of cartographic error or anomalies.

This analysis proved inconclusive in attributing the nonforest observations to behavior patterns of the species or to errors in the database. It was predicted that patterns in the mean distances of these points to forest would indicate behavior or error. Bimodal distributions of distances could have indicated that one group of observations for a species was due to behavior while the second was due to error. However, none of the species demonstrated bimodal distributions.

References

Anderson, J. R., E. Hardy, J. Roach, and R. Witmer. 1976. *A land use and land cover classification system for use with remote sensor data.* U.S. Geological Survey Professional Paper no. 964. Reston, Va.: USGS.

Borrero H., J. I. 1967. *Mamiferos Neotropicales.* Cali, Colombia: Universidad del Valle, Departamento de Biologia.

Eisenberg, J. 1989. *Mammals of the Neotropics.* Vol. 1, *The Northern Neotropics.* Chicago and London: University of Chicago Press.

Emmons, L. H. 1990. *Neotropical rainforest mammals: A field guide.* Chicago and London: University of Chicago Press.

Jensen, J. R. 1995. *Introductory digital image processing: A remote sensing perspective.* 2d ed. Englewood Cliffs, N.J.: Prentice-Hall.

Leopold, A. S. 1959. *Wildlife of Mexico: The game birds and mammals.* Berkeley and Los Angeles: University of California Press.

Levins, R. 1966. The strategy of model building in population biology. *American Scientist* 54: 421–31.

Mondolfi, E. 1986. Notes on the biology and status of the small wild cats in Venezuela. In S. D. Miller and D. D. Everett, eds., *Cats of the world: Biology, conservation, and management*, 125–46. Washington, D.C.: National Wildlife Federation.

Scott, J. M., F. Davis, B. Csuti, R. Noss, B. Butterfield, C. Groves, H. Anderson, S. Caicco, F. D'Erchia, T. C. Edwards Jr., J. Ulliman, and R. G. Wright. 1993. *Gap analysis: A geographical approach to protection of biological diversity.* Wildlife Monograph no. 123 (41 pp.). Bethesda, Md.: The Wildlife Society.

Timm, R. M., D. E. Wilson, B. L. Clauson, R. K. LaVal, C. S. Vaughan. 1989. *Mammals of La Selva–Braulio Carrillo Complex, Costa Rica.* North American Fauna no. 75: Washington, D.C.: U.S. Fish and Wildlife Service, Department of the Interior.

Vaughan, C. 1983. *A report on dense forest habitat for endangered wildlife species in Costa Rica.* Heredia: Universidad Nacional Antonoma de Costa Rica.

Veregin, H. 1989. Error modeling for the map overlay operation. In M. F. Goodchild and S. Gopal, eds., *Accuracy of spatial databases,* 3–18. London: Taylor and Francis.

15

A GIS Method for Conservation Decision Making

Basil G. Savitsky and Thomas E. Lacher Jr.

THE first objective of this chapter is to document the protected areas data used in the Costa Rica gap analysis. The second objective is to categorize the output from the gap analysis model in the context of the Habitat Conservation Decision Cube. The third objective is to interpret the gap analysis results and the utility of the Habitat Conservation Decision Cube in the Costa Rica project.

Protected Areas Data

Gap analysis requires a map layer of the existing protected areas in order to assess the gaps in the conservation network. The boundary data on national parks and other protected areas in Costa Rica was provided by the Paseo Pantera project (see chapter 11). The Paseo Pantera database includes protected area boundaries for the seven Central American countries south of Mexico (Carr, Lambert, and Zwick 1994). The data pertaining to Costa Rica were extracted from this database. The original source data were provided to Paseo Pantera staff by the National Parks Service of Costa Rica in the form of 1:200,000 map sheets indicating the boundaries of existing and proposed national parks, forest reserves, anthropological or tribal reserves, and private reserves. These data were digitized and stored in ARC/INFO format. Potential habitat linkage areas between parks were added by the Paseo Pantera staff but were utilized only nominally in this project.

A map of the protected areas is shown in figure 15.1 with the national parks indicated in black and the other protected areas indicated in gray. Although there

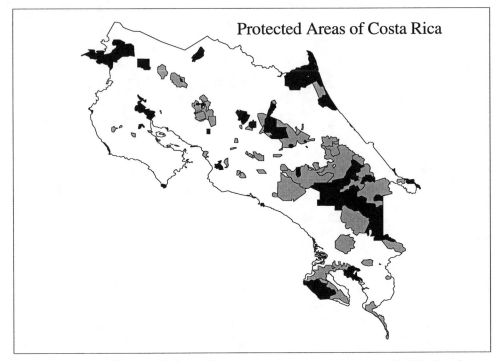

FIG. 15.1 Protected areas of Costa Rica (national parks are indicated in black, other protected areas in gray)

is variation in the ability of national parks, forest reserves, and anthropological reserves to provide protection for wildlife, in this study there was no distinction made between different types of protected areas. For the purpose of the Costa Rica gap analysis, all protected areas were treated as equal. The proposed linkage data were not used in the initial application of the gap analysis in this project. Although the gap analysis methodology did not address variation in types of protected areas or in the proposed linkage polygons, an assessment of the distribution of wildlife sightings within the various types of protected areas and proposed linkages was made and will be discussed in a later section of this chapter.

Habitat Conservation Decision Cube

The three decision vectors that form the Habitat Conservation Decision Cube are the three types of GIS layers utilized in gap analysis—species distributions, habitat type, and protected areas. The wildlife, habitat, and protection map layers and the resultant possible combinations of these three geographic vectors can best be understood in the context of the Habitat Conservation Decision Cube presented in figure 15.2 and described in table 15.1.

Gap analysis has focused attention on one of eight possible combinations in the cube (wildlife present, habitat available, unprotected area) in order to identify optimal strategies for additional wildlife protection areas. The other seven possible combinations of the decision vectors also provide meaningful spatial information but are commonly left as unused by-products in gap analysis.

Hypothetical examples of the eight options in the context of the type of information each one supplies for conservation policy follow. The utility of this policy framework as applied in Costa Rica will be covered in the next section of this chapter.

The *Wildlife protected* category (w+ h+ p+) exemplifies the ideal situation for wildlife conservation. From the point of view of wildlife conservation, these areas are the most effective and the highest priority areas in the park system. In terms of conservation management, it should be ensured that these areas continue to be managed according to the level of wildlife management standards currently employed. It might be useful for resource managers in the National Parks Service to assess further the *Wildlife protected* areas by comparing the percentage of that area in the national park system to the percentage of that area in forest and anthropological reserves. Such tabulation provides a mechanism for measuring how effective the park system is in meeting needs associated with wildlife management. It is possible either to highlight success in some areas for select species or to identify where additional management efforts could be allocated.

The *Conservation gap* category (w+ h+ p-) corresponds to the output from a typical gap analysis and identifies areas that should be added to the conservation system. For example, one review identifies several cases where gap analysis was used to recommend wildlife movement corridors for large mammalian species (Harris and Atkins 1991). The review examines potential habitat conservation areas of Florida panthers, grizzly bears in Yellowstone National Park, black bears in the eastern United States, and several African and Asian species. Although gap analysis serves as a tool to identify *Conservation gaps* potentially useful in corridor implementation, identified gaps must be assessed individually for their suitability to land acquisition strategies for the protection of wildlife. Variables that need to be evaluated include field verification of the number of species currently using the area, the population size of a species of concern, the relative status of each species (common, rare, endangered), and the suitability of the area for protection. A single map could be produced indicating areas most worthy of receiving additional protection or several maps might be produced for various species groups, i.e., birds, primates, and cats. These types of maps facilitate long-term strategic planning for corridors between parks or for additional buffer areas around parks. The relative priority of identified gaps is not addressed at this phase of analysis. Additional information needs to be collected before making

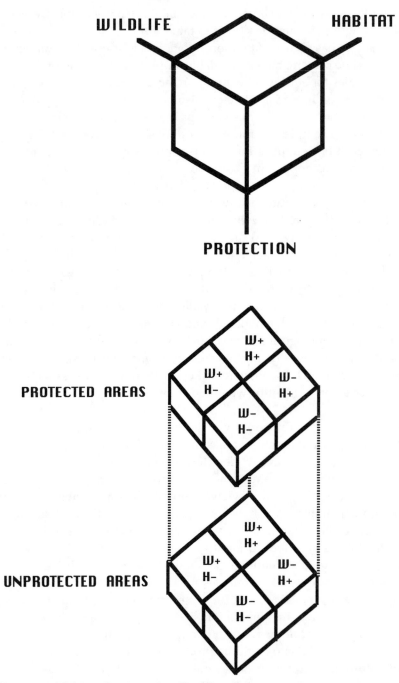

FIG. 15.2 Habitat Conservation Decision Cube

TABLE 15.1 *Eight Possible Policy Options in the Habitat Conservation Decision Cube Formed by the Presence and Absence of Wildlife, Habitat, and Protected Area*

Decision Cube Option Areas	Wildlife (w)	Habitat (h)	Protected (p)
Wildlife protected	+	+	+
Conservation gap	+	+	−
Potential habitat restoration	+	−	+
Further wildlife study	+	−	−
Protected area data gap	−	+	+
Unprotected area data gap	−	+	−
Negotiation area	−	−	+
Developed area	−	−	−

the economic and political decisions necessary to implement actions based upon the biological framework provided by the gap analysis.

The *Potential habitat restoration* category (w+ h- p+) indicates areas where a species has been observed in a protected area in habitat not normally associated with that species. These geographic areas provide useful information in the selection of habitat restoration projects because they are already in some form of protected status. Management actions may be required to ensure future use of that portion of the protected area by a given species or group of species. Habitat restoration is typically an expensive conservation practice, but Jackson (1992) cites the work of Janzen (1988) in Costa Rica where tropical dry forest is being regenerated in conjunction with cattle grazing and fire prevention as a type of assisted natural regeneration. The gap analysis model is useful in identifying geographic areas that have potential for habitat restoration. However, field verification of a proposed restoration area is required to determine whether the area is logical or whether the identified polygon was associated with species edge behavior. For example, variable interpretation is required for data resulting from the sighting of a primate species, such as the white-faced capuchin, which utilizes a wider variety of habitat than a feline species, such as the margay, which is more selective in its habitat requirements. (For the scientific names of these and the following named species, see table 13.3.) Thus, decisions about habitat restoration should be made in the context of an individual species or group of species as opposed to a general gap analysis performed on all species.

The *Further wildlife study* category (w+ h- p-) indicates areas which require further analysis by wildlife specialists in order to determine why a species was sighted outside its preferred habitat. The more detailed analysis should verify species presence in the unpredicted areas and assess edge behavior of the species. It may be necessary to relax the habitat requirements for a species. For example, if the number of sightings of a bird species is found to be equal in forested habitat and agricultural areas, then agricultural areas or at least a broad edge of agricultural areas should be included as the habitat for that species in future gap analyses. It may be found that the species is too much of a generalist to be used as an indicator species (Scott et al. 1990). Note that for both policy options where wildlife is present but habitat is not (*Potential habitat restoration* and *Further wildlife study*), it is possible that the species were sighted prior to changes in the habitat or that the species is utilizing small patches of habitat which cannot be resolved at the landscape level of analysis.

The *Protected area data gap* category (w- h+ p+) is one of two types of data gaps. Data gap polygons occur as a result of the presence of habitat data and the absence of wildlife data for a given polygon. It is not certain that the wildlife are absent from that area, only that wildlife data are not present. In a national survey, sightings cannot be expected in all suitable habitat areas, particularly where vast wilderness areas are concerned. *Protected area data gaps* also can represent areas where a species was extirpated prior to protection. For example, viable habitat for mountain lions still is present in the Great Smoky Mountains National Park, but the species is no longer present in the region. *Protected area data gaps* also may prove useful in the reintroduction of rare or endangered species, such as the red wolf program in the Great Smoky Mountains (Parker 1990). A map of *Protected area data gaps* is useful in developing strategies for further field research on population distributions.

The *Unprotected area data gap* category (w- h+ p-) indicates areas that are similar to *Protected area data gaps*, both in terms of their data-uncertainty status in the gap analysis model and in terms of their biological potential. However, the unprotected areas do not warrant as great a need for further research as *Protected area data gaps* because the latter are more likely to be associated with some form of conservation action. An exception to this occurs when an *Unprotected area data gap* is adjacent to a protected area.

The *Negotiation area* category (w- h- p+) indicates areas that are neutral in terms of wildlife conservation and that hold potential as a point of negotiation for access to extractive industry within a protected area. For example, if the wildlife concerns are considered in the process of identifying a site for an agro-forestry project, then these areas are much more attractive than sites having higher conservation status. It is possible that these areas may even be used to geographically trade for more desired corridor or buffers areas, either by altering management practices or by implementing legal changes in the park boundaries, thus generating enough revenues through sales to acquire more desirable lands. The *Negotiation area* category must be interpreted with caution. For example, an area identified in the center of a park is not as suitable as an area identified on the edge of a park. If *Negotiation areas* are utilized, it should be noted that maps only serve to define the negotiation process; numerous other forms of information will need to be considered before a trade is implemented. Trades or sales are advisable only to the extent that they do not compromise other goals of the park.

The *Developed area* category (w- h- p-) indicates areas that present another neutral case for wildlife conservation. Most of these areas are already developed or in agricultural use. Thus, these areas may be considered as the background in which wildlife conservation must operate. Mapping *Developed areas* in juxtaposition to protected areas is useful in the evaluation of proposed conservation areas because edge conditions of one proposed reserve may be superior to the edge conditions of another proposed reserve.

Interpretation of Results

Interpretation of the results in this project were performed at two different levels—the species level and combinations of species. Gap analyses were performed individually for each of the twenty-one species, for all the species in combination, and for five species in combination. The first part of this section covers findings from all the gap analyses. The second part addresses wildlife frequency analyses which were performed. The third part of this section examines the policy options arising from the analysis of one of the species, the white-faced capuchin. The fourth part of this section addresses the policy options arising from the analyses of five species and of all twenty-one species.

GENERAL FINDINGS

The two most important findings from reviewing all the gap analyses are as follows. First, there are few *Conservation gaps* identified for addition to the protected areas system in Costa Rica. The low incidence of *Conservation gaps* results from the percentage of the landscape already in the conservation system, and from the rapid deforestation of unprotected lands. This is reflected in the related facts of Costa Rica's strong commitment to conservation as expressed in its extensive park system, and in Costa Rica's 2.9 percent annual deforestation rate (Jones 1992). In short, if land is not currently protected, then it is probably already cleared or will be in the near future. Trends in population growth and economic development will undoubtedly place new pressure on resource managers to maintain the integrity of the current conservation system (Leonard 1987). As a result, attention should be given to strengthening the quality of the existing system of protected areas. Evaluation of the utility of various protection categories (park, forest reserve, and anthropological reserve) in serving wildlife needs should facilitate continuous enhancement of wildlife management standards on all types of protected lands.

The second finding is the geographic extent of data gaps within the park system. There are some remote mountainous areas within protected areas in eastern Costa Rica which remain poorly described with regard to the wildlife data. A priority for further research in Costa Rica is to perform a more focused gap analysis on La Amistad International International Park, which includes the major portion of the area under question. By combining the survey approach taken in this study with existing range data and with output from a predictive habitat model, it should be possible to develop a more robust wildlife data layer for use in the gap analysis model. It may be necessary to reduce the number of species of concern in order to achieve this objective.

Wildlife Frequency Analyses

Before performing the polygon overlay in the gap analyses that resulted in a series of maps, simple frequency tables were generated to assess the intersection of each set of species in the original wildlife point data with the protected area polygons (table 15.2). The national parks accounted for 718 (21 percent) of all the wildlife sightings. Fourteen percent of the sightings were on proposed linkages, 12 percent were on forest reserves, 5 percent were on anthropological reserves, and 1 percent were on private reserves. Almost half of the wildlife data points (47 percent) did not occur on any type of protected land or recommended linkage area. Concerning individual species, those species distributions that coincide most with the existing conservation network were the jaguar, mountain lion,

Table 15.2 *Intersection of Wildlife Points with Protected Area Polygons*

Species	Percent Protected	Frequency of Sightings by Protection Status[a]						Species Total
		P	F	A	L	PR	O	
Jaguar	65	39	15	5	5	2	28	94
Mountain lion	65	33	15	5	12	6	20	91
Tapir	64	53	24	6	13	0	33	129
Green macaw	64	16	16	1	5	1	19	58
White-lipped peccary	59	44	18	4	13	0	35	114
Great curassow	51	59	38	10	32	1	70	210
Harpy eagle	48	8	11	0	8	0	13	40
Ocelot	48	23	22	14	20	5	50	134
Collared peccary	47	52	20	16	41	24	84	237
Margay	42	32	14	10	16	5	68	145
Spider monkey	40	40	28	6	13	0	94	181
Giant anteater	39	14	4	1	7	0	23	49
Central American caiman	38	29	22	12	16	0	85	164
Paca	38	53	34	21	53	1	126	288
Jaguarundi	36	26	11	9	18	2	68	134
Quetzal	37	17	8	4	11	0	38	78
White-faced capuchin	31	61	28	13	53	2	168	325
American crocodile	31	22	38	11	40	0	119	230
Howler monkey	28	44	23	6	39	0	151	263
Scarlet macaw	19	40	19	1	51	0	212	323
Squirrel monkey	15	13	4	1	10	0	90	118
Category Total	—	718	412	156	476	49	1,594	3,405
Percentage of Grand Total	—	21	12	5	14	1	47	

[a]P = parks, F = forest reserves, A = anthropological reserves, L = proposed linkages, PR = private, O = outside reserves.

tapir, and white-lipped peccary, with each having between 64 and 67 percent of its sightings in the protected area network. The point distributions of species which coincide the least with the conservation network were the squirrel monkey (15 percent coincidence) and the scarlet macaw (19 percent). The howler monkey, the white-faced capuchin, and the American crocodile had 28 to 31 percent coincidence. The remainder of the species ranged from 36 to 59 percent coincidence.

The results from the intersection of the wildlife points with the habitat polygons are presented in Table 15.3. Forty-seven percent of the wildlife sightings were coincident with some form of developed land use (pasture, agriculture, and urban). Forty-four percent of the sighting were coincident with natural land cover (forest, wetlands, mangroves, and subalpine scrub). Eight percent of the sightings were coincident with the unknown / mixed / clear category.

SINGLE SPECIES GAP ANALYSIS

Each of the eight possible decision outcomes are reviewed using the example of the white-faced capuchin. The dark green polygons (plate 4) indicate *Wildlife protected* areas where white-faced capuchin are adequately protected. The red polygons indicate *Conservation gaps*. It is the relationship between these two categories that is significant in understanding the adequacy of the conservation system. The relationship between the *Wildlife protected* areas and the *Conservation gaps* needs to be interpreted visually and numerically. Visual inspection of the map allows interpretation of patterns such as relative proportion of one class to another and the proximity or isolation of the *Conservation gaps* in the context of the conservation system. Visual inspection also provides material for judgments about the general need for additional land acquisitions and the specific placement of those lands in a corridor pattern between protected areas or a buffer pattern around or adjacent to protected areas. There are twenty-three red poly-

TABLE 15.3 *Intersection of Wildlife Points with Habitat Polygons*

Habitat	Wildlife Sightings	Percentage
Natural Land Cover	1,492	43.8
Forest	1,238	36.4
Wetlands	133	3.9
Mangroves	111	3.3
Subalpine scrub	5	0.1
Water	5	0.1
Developed land use	1,642	48.2
Pasture	1,382	40.5
Agriculture	228	6.7
Barren	28	0.8
Urban	4	0.1
Unknown / mixed / cleared	271	8.0
TOTAL	3,405	100.0

gons—areas which serve as optimal land acquisition sites (plate 4). Compare the fourteen isolated *Conservation gaps* to the nine *Conservation gaps* adjacent to protected wildlife areas. Given the limited resources that can be employed for the conservation of a given species, such visual assessment is useful in efficient allocation of those resources to strengthen the existing network. Conservation biologists and politicians in Costa Rica need to decide whether it is more effective to add new buffer zones to existing reserves or to strengthen genetic diversity by supporting the continued survival of an isolated ecosystem. Having a visual geographic platform from which to build a framework to evaluate such issues is the type of contribution that can be expected from a national or landscape-level gap analysis.

A numerical ratio indicates the relationship between *Wildlife protected* polygons and the polygons indicating *Conservation gaps*. The geographic area of both categories was tabulated, and it was determined that there are 2,150 square kilometers of *Wildlife protected* areas and 251 square kilometers of *Conservation gap* areas identified in the gap analysis for the white-faced capuchin. The ratio of *Wildlife protected* areas to *Conservation gap* areas is 8.6 to 1. If the ratio were reversed, then the species would be in serious need of conservation action because there would be considerably more area in *Conservation gaps* than in the *Wildlife protected* category. However, the case appears to indicate that the white-faced capuchin has adequate conservation status in Costa Rica.

TABLE 15.4 *Ratio of the Geographic Area Associated with "Wildlife Protected" Areas to the Geographic Area in "Conservation Gaps"*

Species	Area (sq. km.)		Ratio
	Wildlife Protected	Conservation Gaps	
Tapir	2,168	67	32.4
Mountain lion	1,727	71	24.3
Jaguar	1,808	94	19.2
Harpy eagle	1,183	68	17.4
Quetzal	1,785	110	16.2
Jaguarundi	1,460	109	13.4
Paca	2,311	196	11.8
Ocelot	1,324	121	10.9
White-faced capuchin	2,150	251	8.6
Scarlet macaw	1,188	145	8.2
Central American caiman	954	126	7.6
Margay	1,580	216	7.3
Squirrel monkey	502	81	7.2
Collared peccary	2,185	410	5.3
Spider monkey	1,771	381	4.6
Great curassow	1,939	463	4.2
White-lipped peccary	1,424	427	3.3
Howler monkey	1,267	399	3.2
American crocodile	821	470	1.7
Green macaw	443	265	1.7
Giant anteater	617	375	1.6

The same type of ratios were calculated for all twenty-one species (table 15.4). Species with the highest ratios include the tapir, mountain lion, and jaguar. These species are either adequately protected or they utilize only a nominal amount of land outside the protected area system. Species having the lowest ratios included the American crocodile, the great green macaw, and the giant anteater, but in each case the geographic area of *Wildlife protected* areas exceeded the geographic area of identified *Conservation gaps.*

Potential habitat restoration areas for the white-faced capuchin are indicated in light green in plate 4. These are nonforested areas within parks which are being utilized by white-faced capuchins. In the case of Guanacaste, the large area indicated in northwest Costa Rica, much of the pasture is reverting to secondary growth forests on newly created park lands. An identification of similar types of areas strengthens the position of the resource manager in making recommendations for restoration. In the case of Tortuguero, the large restoration area indicated in northeastern Costa Rica, white-faced capuchins are utilizing forested wetlands. Although these areas are forested, a distinction was made between forest and wetlands in the habitat classification scheme, so these areas remain outside the defined habitat for white-faced capuchins. It is possible to relax habitat requirements and include wetlands with the forest as preferred habitat in future iterations of the model.

Areas requiring *Further wildlife study* are indicated in pink in plate 4. The relative proportion of pink areas in a species map was associated with the frequency of sightings outside forested habitat. Most species were similar to the white-faced capuchin in this category. Species having relatively few sightings, such as the harpy eagle and quetzal, occupied a small proportion of these areas. The tapir and three of the cats (the mountain lion, jaguar, and ocelot) also occupied a small proportion of these areas. The extent to which this is attributable to shy or nocturnal behavior or narrow habitat preference was not analyzed; however, some of the primate species appear to be more generalist in habitat requirements than the other species listed. It is probable that many of the areas for *Further wildlife study* were identified because the size of a patch of forest being utilized by the species was too small to map at the scale used in this study. For example, a squirrel monkey that was present in a very small patch of forest within a pasture would be interpreted as being present in the pasture and outside the forest habitat. It is also probable that many of the sightings occurred on the edge of a forested habitat and were inaccurately assessed as being outside the forest for reasons of geographic error (as discussed in chapter 14).

Shades of blue were used to indicate geographic distributions of the four policy options for which there were no species present. The greatest concentration of *Protected area data gaps* is in La Amistad International Park. *Protected area data gap* polygons are present in many of the forested regions of Costa Rica, but the remoteness of the large tract of land in eastern Costa Rica indicates that there is a need to develop a broader understanding of wildlife populations in the country.

Many of the large *Unprotected area data gaps* are adjacent to the northern border of La Amistad. Also, these are steep forested slopes and are undeveloped even though unprotected. There are numerous small forest patches that fall into the *Unprotected area data gap* category because they meet the habitat requirement. These areas are of lower priority than the *Protected area data gaps* in terms of designating additional wildlife data collection efforts because of the manner in which the single large tract of *Protected area data gap* overwhelms all of the other data gap polygons.

Two neutral categories for wildlife conservation are also indicated in plate 4. *Developed areas* provide the background for conservation management. The *Negotiation areas* are of interest to wildlife resource managers because they indicate protected areas that may be negotiable from the wildlife perspective (though possibly not negotiable from the perspective of other park management objectives). If an area between two parks has been identified as a *Conservation gap* that is desired for land acquisition, it may be useful to know which areas within the park could be leased for sustainable extractive activities as part of an exchange for the desired land acquisition.

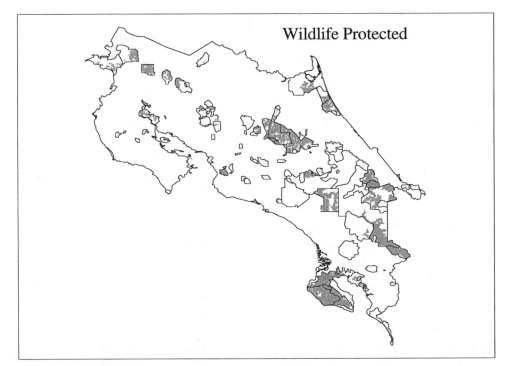

FIG. 15.3 Multiple species gap analysis: summary of *Wildlife protected* category (w + h + p+) for all twenty-one species. The protected wildlife category is indicated in gray and the protected area boundaries are outlined.

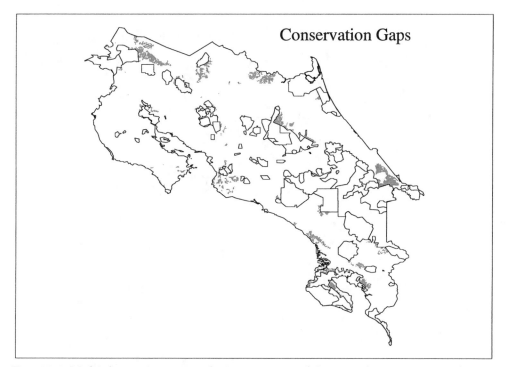

FIG. 15.4 Multiple species gap analysis: summary of *Conservation gap* category (w + h + p −) for all twenty-one species

MULTIPLE SPECIES GAP ANALYSIS

In many cases, it is advantageous to make conservation decisions on the basis of information supplied for an individual species. In other cases, it is informative to assess the distribution of the policy options in the Habitat Conservation Decision Cube for multiple species. This section addresses landscape patterns in Costa Rica when a group or all of the twenty-one species are considered concurrently. In each of the nine figures presented in this section, the boundaries of the protected areas are depicted for reference purposes. Place-names utilized in the following text were presented in figure 2.2.

The overlay of all the *Wildlife protected* areas for each of the twenty-one species indicates the extent to which the system of protected areas serves wildlife management purposes (figure 15.3). The protected areas for which *Wildlife protected* polygons are absent either contain nonforest habitat or are very remote or mountainous areas.

The total area of all of the *Conservation gaps* that were identified in the twenty-one different gap analyses is displayed in figure 15.4. Even when combining all the *Conservation gaps*, there are still not many tracts of land to evaluate at a more

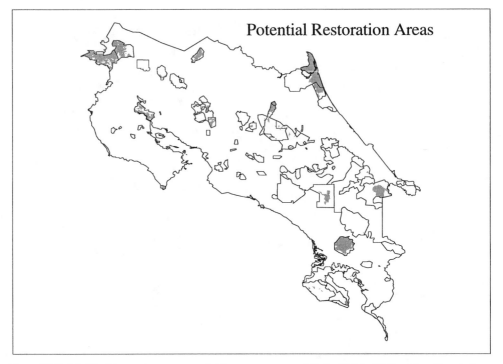

FIG. 15.5 Multiple species gap analysis: summary of *Potential habitat restoration* category (w + h − p +) for all twenty-one species

detailed scale. Most of the large *Conservation gaps* are adjacent to parks. Although a corridor pattern does not emerge, buffer areas are apparent. One noteworthy cluster for further evaluation occurs west of Tortuguero on the northern border of Costa Rica.

The areas in the *Potential habitat restoration* decision category are depicted in figure 15.5. Much of the area in Guanacaste is undergoing restoration from pasture to secondary growth forest. The polygon near Tortuguero is a result of wildlife sightings in the forested wetlands habitat and is not an area requiring restoration. One of the small polygons near La Amistad is subalpine scrub.

Areas identified in any of the gap analyses requiring *Further wildlife study* are shown in figure 15.6. These areas are primarily pasture and are associated with the large number of data points that were observed outside of forest. Because so much of the country is categorized as needing further study, this map indicates that not all maps are useful. The *Further wildlife study* decision category is most useful when applied to a specific species because a more manageable amount of information is generated.

When the two data gap categories were assessed in the multiple gap analysis, only those polygons without sightings were mapped. In contrast to the "or" logic used to create the maps where wildlife were present, maps of data gaps em-

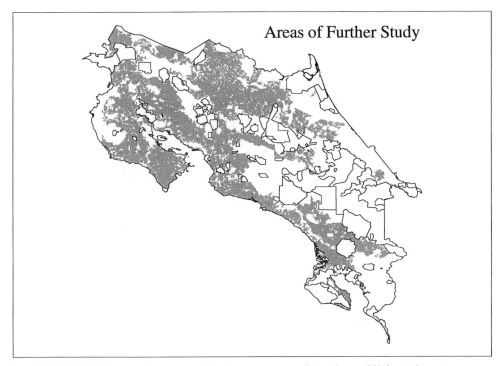

FIG. 15.6 Multiple species gap analysis: summary of *Further wildlife study* category
(w + h − p −) for all twenty-one species

ployed an "and" logic. For example, the data gaps for the harpy eagle are more extensive than the data gaps for the howler monkey because there were more howler monkey sightings. In the multiple species gap analysis, only the data gaps common to all species were mapped. *Protected area data gaps* are depicted in figure 15.7. Note the strong concentration of these areas within and near La Amistad.

Unprotected area data gaps are shown in figure 15.8. Note the broad distribution of these areas throughout Costa Rica. Most of these areas are relatively small parcels of isolated forest. The large *Unprotected area data gaps* that are adjacent to protected areas should be considered equally with *Protected area data gaps* in the identification of further wildlife data collection efforts.

The *Negotiation area* category is portrayed in figure 15.9. These areas need to be interpreted carefully and on an individual basis. If these areas have been compromised to some form of habitat degradation, then perhaps land use concessions may be employed to leverage acquisition of other lands. However, the areas may indicate unforested habitat that are protected (such as the large block of wetland areas near Tortuguero which are apparent in this map). The function that some of the areas within the park system may serve for species other than the wildlife that were examined requires evaluation. This study addressed only

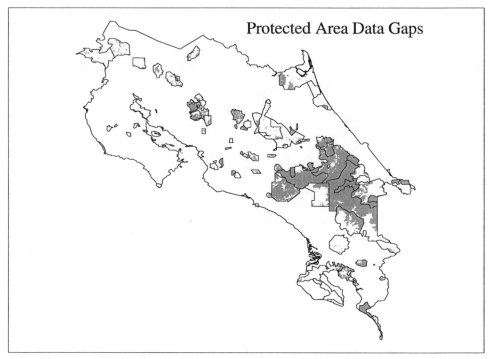

FIG. 15.7 Multiple species gap analysis: summary of *Protected area data gap* category (w- h+ p+) for all twenty-one species

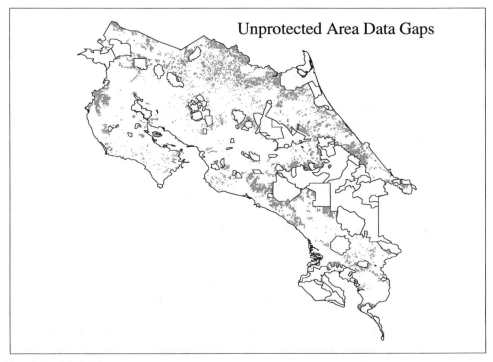

FIG. 15.8 Multiple species gap analysis: summary of *Unprotected area data gap* category (w− h+ p−) for all twenty-one species

FIG. 15.9 Multiple species gap analysis: summary of *Negotiation area* category (w − h − p +) for all twenty-one species

twenty-one of the hundreds of vertebrate species in Costa Rica. Likewise, these areas may be negotiable for wildlife conservation, but possibly not negotiable for other reasons for which parks are created.

Developed areas are indicated in figure 15.10. Note the extent to which the *Developed areas* and the park system border each other. This level of information is useful in identifying priorities for buffers to protect existing parks from the encroachment of human activity and in selecting additional park lands less likely to suffer from development pressures.

An additional multiple species gap analysis was performed for five of the twenty-one species. This process was performed to compare gap analysis results obtained from the examination of twenty-one species to a multiple species gap analysis using a smaller set of potential indicator species. The species that were selected were determined by patterns of habitat utilization, geographic distribution throughout the country, and frequency of observations (compared to species utilizing similar habitat). The collared peccary was selected as one of the five species in order to represent those species that utilize undisturbed forest habitat as well as habitat in the more fragmented landscape. The white-faced capuchin was selected as the species to represent the four primate species that utilize undisturbed forest. The crocodile was selected to represent those species associ-

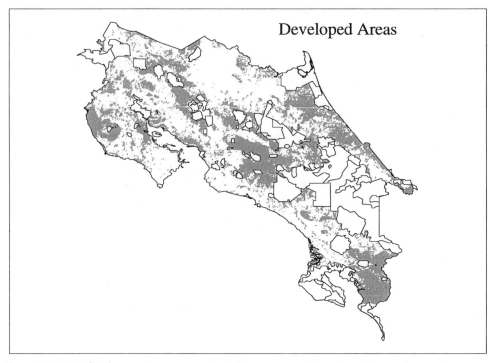

Fig. 15.10 Multiple species gap analysis: summary of *Developed area* category (w − h − p −) for all twenty-one species

ated with rivers, forested lowlands, and wetlands. The jaguar was selected to represent the species that utilize extensive interior forests. The quetzal was selected to represent the species found in montane forests.

The five-species gap analysis was performed by combining all polygons that had the collared peccary, white-faced capuchin, crocodile, jaguar, or quetzal present, either alone or in combination. This set of polygons was intersected with the habitat and protected area map layers to identify *Conservation gaps*. The results of the five-species gap analysis were compared visually and numerically to the multiple species gap analysis that utilized all twenty-one species. The visual comparison is presented in figure 15.11. The gray polygons indicate *Conservation gaps* identified by both of the multiple species gap analyses. The black polygons indicate *Conservation gaps* that were identified by the twenty-one species gap analysis, but were missed by the five-species analysis. Three of the five largest *Conservation gaps* were successfully identified by using only five species, but two of the largest *Conservation gaps* were missed. Of the two that were missed, one was used only by scarlet macaws and the other was used by margays, green macaws, great curassows, and giant anteaters. In general, the five-species gap analysis identified some, but not all, of the *Conservation gap* pattern in the landscape.

The numerical analysis measured the number of *Conservation gap* polygons that were identified by both multiple species gap analyses. The five-species gap

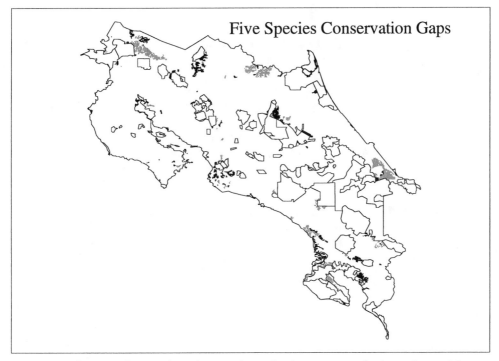

FIG. **15.11** *Conservation gap* (w + h + p −) results from gap analysis performed for five species compared to gap analysis performed for twenty-one species. Areas indicated in gray were identified by both analyses, and areas indicated in black were missed in the five-species analysis.

analysis was successful in identifying 57 percent of the *Conservation gaps* identified in the twenty-one species gap analysis. The ability to use the five species to identify the *Conservation gaps* associated only with the other sixteen species was lower, with 39 percent of those *Conservation gap* polygons identified. If this set of indicator species were to be used instead of the larger set of wildlife data, the benefits in reduced data collection would need to be offset by the cost of reduced information content ranging from 40 to 50 percent. In some countries or regions, such a level of reduced information content may be acceptable. This would particulary be the case in countries where there are few protected areas and where information to develop conservation strategies is needed rapidly.

References

Carr, M. H., J. D. Lambert, and P. D. Zwick. 1994. Mapping of biological corridor potential in Central America. In A. Vega, ed., *Conservation corridors in the Central American region*, 383–93. Gainesville, Fla.: Tropical Research and Development.

Harris, L. D. and K. Atkins. 1991. Faunal movement corridors in Florida. In W. E. Hudson, ed., *Landscape linkages and biodiversity*, 117–38. Washington, D.C.: Island Press.

Jackson, L. L. 1992. The role of ecological restoration in conservation biology. In P. L. Fiedler and S. K. Jain, eds., *Conservation biology*, 433–51. New York: Chapman and Hall.

Janzen, D. F. H. 1988. Tropical ecological and biocultural restoration. *Science* 239: 243–44.

Jones, J. R. 1992. Environmental issues and policies in Costa Rica: Control of deforestation. *Policy Studies Journal* 20: 679–94.

Leonard, H. J. 1987. *Natural resources and economic development in Central America: A regional environmental profile*. New Brunswick, N.J.: Transaction Books.

Parker, W. 1990. A proposal to reintroduce the red wolf to the Great Smoky Mountains National Park. In *Proceedings, First Annual Southern Appalachian Man and the Biosphere Conference*, 53. Norris, Tenn.: Tennessee Valley Authority.

Scott, J. M., F. Davis, B. Csuti, B. Butterfield, R. Noss, S. Caicco, H. Anderson, J. Ulliman, F. D'Erchia, and C. Groves. 1990. *Gap analysis: Protecting biodiversity using geographic information systems*. A handbook prepared for a workshop held at the University of Idaho, Moscow.

16

Using the Gap Analysis Model for Sustainable Development and Natural Resources Management in Developing Countries

Thomas E. Lacher Jr.

THE USAID-sponsored case study on gap analysis presented in this volume was conceived as a model for application toward conservation and development issues in other countries and regions. The likelihood that any collaborative, multidisciplinary, GIS-based research is conducted in a developing tropical country is contingent on many practical, logistical, intellectual, and philosophical factors. For each case, these factors need to de defined, understood, and resolved to the satisfaction of the collaborators. There will always be issues idiosyncratic to a special situation, but there are some common factors that can be presented and discussed.

Tools for the Effective Implementation of International Conservation Efforts

Conducting research requires access to the necessary tools. For application of GIS to international conservation efforts, these tools are hardware, software, data, and technicians (see figure 3.1). At present, costs are low enough for hardware purchases that most developing countries can maintain PC-based systems for running GIS software. For some less developed countries, costs for many software packages still remain high, but many corporations provide low-cost or free software to LDCs. The IDRISI software was created as part of a nonprofit research project at Clark University as a low-cost solution for the international implementation of GIS and image analysis research and project management. The Environmental Systems Research Institute, Inc. (ESRI), makers of ARC/INFO and Arc-View, also has a program for software distribution to government agencies and nongovernmental organizations in developing countries. Conservation International has developed a low-cost GIS package called CI-SIG that is available in Spanish and Portuguese. Hardware and software costs, once prohibitive, are now rarely an obstacle in most developing countries for conducting sophisticated GIS-based research.

Data costs were high in the past primarily because they were controlled by the governments and corporations of developed countries; therefore, few developing countries could gain access to the information even when the software and hardware were available. But these costs also have decreased (although the cost frequently depends on the type of sensor and the age of the data). Governments also often place restrictions on who can purchase the data at low cost. Currently, U.S. Government and Affiliate Users (USGAU) is the purchasing group with unrestricted rights to reproduce and distribute, within the USGAU, all unenhanced TM data purchased by USGAU for noncommercial uses, either from the National Satellite Land Remote Sensing Data Archive (NSLRSDA) or the Earth Observation Satellite Company (EOSAT). USGAU is broadly defined to include U.S. government agencies, U.S. government contractors, researchers involved with the U.S. Global Change Research Program or one of its international counterparts, and any other entities signing a cooperative agreement for the use of Landsat data for noncommercial purposes with the United States government.

Effective in April 1994, NSLRSDA adopted a new distribution policy for Landsat data and now distributes all Landsat Multispectral Scanner (MSS) data to all customers with no restrictions. EOSAT, the previous vendor for MSS, relinquished all rights to these data as of February 1993. The distribution policy effective October 1, 1995 (table 16.1) was slightly modified in October 1996, giving USGAU access to all unenhanced TM data purchased by USGAU. In addition, all TM data in the National Satellite Land Remote Sensing Data Archive are now available to USGAU at the cost of $425 per scene with an additional cost per scene ranging from $70 to $1,800 for the more recent data.

An institution in a developing country can presently acquire hardware, software, and data for even large-scale projects with a relatively small amount of money, if the appropriate cooperative agreements are in place. The highest costs remain those of personnel. The effective management of a GIS requires a highly trained and dedicated technician. Many developing countries have only a handful of trained technicians, and these are frequently severely overworked. The lack of sufficiently trained people is still the biggest problem in developing countries. Cooperative programs in education and training should provide the mechanism

TABLE 16.1 *Landsat MSS and TM Distribution Responsibilities, Effective October 1, 1995 (available TM data are unenhanced)*

Customer	MSS All data	TM		
		July 16, 1982 to 10 Years from Present	Sept. 27, 1985 to 1 Year from Present	1 Year from Present to Present
Public	NSLRSDA	NSLRSDA	EOSAT	EOSAT
USGAU	NSLRSDA	NSLRSDA	NSLRSDA	EOSAT

NOTE: Dates are on a sliding scale from Present. July 16, 1982, was the launch date of Landsat 4; September 27, 1985, was the signing date of the NOAA / EOSAT contract. (EOSAT = the Earth Observation Satellite Company; NSLRSDA = the National Satellite Land Remote Sensing Data Archive; and USGAU = the U.S. Government and Affiliated Users).

for addressing this need, although institutional support for salaries for full-time technicians, once trained, is critical. Finding—and keeping—competent staff requires a long-term commitment and is necessary if an agency or organization wishes to pursue GIS-based research and resource management.

Providing a decent salary is not the only obligation an organization must meet in order to conduct GIS research. The "brain drain" continues to be a problem in many developing countries. The quality of the work environment is frequently a more important reason than salary for emigration of professionals to developed countries. When an organization invests in training and hiring a GIS technician, it must also provide an unhurried and relaxed work environment that includes the freedom to pursue interests in research and publication. The lack of opportunities for professional development and the assignment of an excessive number of tasks will lead to dissatisfaction and, in many cases, burnout or loss of the technician. Therefore the total investment package must include training, salary, professional development, and a superior and competitive work environment. Once the hardware, software, data, and staff are in place, project planning and implementation begins.

Local, National, Regional, and Global Efforts

The feasibility of carrying out a project is strongly linked to the technical complexity inherent in the study. The technical complexity of conservation and development activities frequently is contingent upon scale. Larger-scale projects are also more logistically complex because they require more cooperation among agencies and organizations within a country, and eventually between or among countries. We define the scale of conservation and development projects as being either local, national, regional, or global.

LOCAL EFFORTS

These are small-scale projects often focused on a specific practical issue such as management of a watershed or planning of a development activity. Conservation activities related to the protection of small fragments of rare habitat or remnant populations of a rare or endangered species also are local in scale. These activities are frequently based in specific government agencies or are subcontracted to universities or consulting firms. The projects presented in chapters 7 to 10 are examples of local efforts. The hardware and technical requirements are such that many developing tropical countries are capable of doing high-quality GIS work at the local level.

NATIONAL EFFORTS

These are efforts that focus on some management or policy issue of national importance, such as the development of a national conservation plan, the management of threatened or endangered species, or the planning of demographic shifts or development activities at the national scale. National efforts are not necessarily border-to-border projects; in larger nations they more frequently cover large geographical areas such as the eastern seaboard of the United States or the Amazon Basin of Brazil. These projects usually are based in government agencies and frequently involve some level of international collaboration. International collaboration is frequently tied to the financing of these projects by an international aid agency. More affluent developing nations frequently have the capability to do independent work at this level. Among the major obstacles to conducting national efforts are data costs, storage capacity of the hardware, processing power, competent staff, and data collection. As hardware and data costs decline, developing countries are increasingly more able to conduct country-level studies. The gap analysis research presented in this book is an example of a national effort with international technical collaboration and the funding of a foreign aid agency (USAID). Another example of a national effort is the series of projects on priority areas for conservation carried out by Conservation International in collaboration with a variety of nongovernmental organizations (Tangley 1992). There have been two other national-level priority areas projects to date—Papua New Guinea and the northeastern Atlantic Forest of Brazil.

REGIONAL EFFORTS

Large management and conservation projects can span several countries in a relatively homogeneous region. The Paseo Pantera project in Central America is one example (Carr, Lambert, and Zwick 1994; also, see chapter 11 of the present volume). The project coordinated by Conservation International on conservation priorities for the Amazon Basin is another (Tangley 1992). These projects are international in scope, though frequently the cultures and/or languages are similar or shared. Often one nation tends to dominate because of superior technology and better access to funding, and collaboration is often strained because of this. International aid agencies will rarely disburse funds equally among all participating nations. The logistics of carrying out regional projects are complicated, and these efforts occasionally fail, often because of the participation of one key country is lacking.

Regional efforts will likely prove to be the most important in the future, as the emphasis of conservation activities shifts from the management of single species to the integrated management of landscapes (Lacher et al. 1995; Lacher and Calvo-Alvarado 1995; Noss and Cooperrider 1994). Few countries contain an entire ecosystem, and transboundary or multinational collaborations will become increasingly common. As difficult as regional efforts are, conservationists must begin to develop the infrastructure for these studies.

GLOBAL EFFORTS

Global projects address worldwide concerns such as modeling future climate in response to global warming or modeling the circulation of the world's oceans (Committee on Environment and Natural Resources Research of the National Science and Technology Council 1995; Sanderson 1994). The primary difficulty in these projects is handling and manipulating large and complex data sets rather than the collaboration of countries. For example, difficulty is encountered in reconciling disparate classification schemes or translating data acoss various spatial scales of measurement. Indeed, these analyses are so complex that the research effort is often dominated by one wealthy country. Global efforts often involve less international collaboration than much smaller-scale efforts, especially when the data are collected by remote sensors, as with much global change research.

Conservation and Development in the Tropics and the Role of International Cooperation

Most large-scale development activities in the tropics are driven either by developed countries, multilateral lending agencies, or multinational corporations. An example is the Tropical Forestry Action Plan (WRI 1985). Funding for the original plan was provided by the developed world and therefore the countries affected did not control the funds; the research priorities were criticized by some as reflecting a developed world bias (WRI 1990).

Most world leaders agree that future development should be sustainable and that conservation of the world's biodiversity is a priority (New Partners Working Group 1994), but few clear mechanisms have been established for the transfer of technology to guarantee inclusion of informed scientific decisions in the political process. Environmental impact assessments are required by law for most large development projects in the tropics. To be effective, developing countries must have access to sufficient technology and scientific expertise to be able to model large-scale impacts on complex ecosystems. Many large projects also have transborder impacts. Development often has international political implications, as evidenced by the large number of environmental concerns expressed during the negotiations of the North American Free Trade Agreement (NAFTA). Tropical conservation is international conservation and supersedes political boundaries (WRI/IUCN/UNEP 1992).

A series of issues and concerns must be addressed to guarantee the coexistence of development and conservation in the tropics. Because tropical conservation is both regional and multinational by definition, effective, long-term conservation will involve significant international collaboration.

SURVEYS AND BIODIVERSITY ASSESSMENTS

Conservationists must know what they have in order to protect or utilize it. This simple and fundamental premise is often the most contentious, acrimonious, and difficult step to achieve in a comprehensive conservation program. Most taxa that occur in the tropics are poorly known, and rarely are keys or field guides available for identification. In addition, many groups of organisms (insects, plants, and even mammals) are difficult to identify in the field even in well-studied temperate areas with access to abundant taxonomic keys and field guides. Researchers must therefore collect representative specimens which are subsequently identified by an expert on that particular taxon. In most cases the expert is connected with a natural history museum in a developed country, so specimens must be sent there, along with previously acquired, appropriate documentation and permits. The taxonomic expert must catalog the specimens and compare them to existing collections to determine if the species had been previously described or is new to science. If the area being surveyed is large, and numerous taxa are being sampled, there can be thousands of specimens (insects, other invertebrates, plants, vertebrates) to identify. As a consequence, researchers of the developed country and their staff and students must be compensated, research and materials costs reimbursed, and often an agreement is reached to leave part of the collection with the expert to enhance the museum's holdings and facilitate future identification. Many of the benefits of the systematics component remain in the developed countries, leaving developing countries without the expertise to classify their own flora and fauna. Finally, the experts are often accused of scientific imperialism for retaining specimens in their own collections.

Biodiversity surveys are the foundation for all future conservation, and natural history museums are the repositories of the biodiversity of our planet (Mares 1995). At a time when we most need their services, museums are under fire, and many conservationists feel that "quick and dirty" surveys will be sufficient (Roberts 1988). Embarking on the development of comprehensive, long-term conservation programs without sufficient data on the composition of the biological communities and the basic ecological roles of the species involved will likely result in failure (Ojeda 1994). Examples like that of INBIO in Costa Rica (Gámez 1994) are correct in placing a priority on surveys and assessment, assisted by international collaboration in funding, research, and technology transfer. Surveys and assessments are an indispensable first step, and efforts must be made for the equitable distribution of resources, specimens, and education.

ESTABLISHMENT OF CONSERVATION PRIORITIES

Once the distributions of species and ecosystems have been defined, a list of priorities for conservation must be developed. The most common method is based upon ecological triage: the most threatened and endangered receive highest priority. An unfortunate consequence of this approach is that an inordinate amount of time, effort, and money can be spent on protecting very small populations or very small fragments of habitat (Franklin 1993). If resources are limited (they almost always are), then the triage approach compromises the effective conservation of landscapes, ecosystems, and large reserves.

Careful thought must go into the planning of conservation priorities to avoid the error of saving a tree but losing the forest. The development of conservation priorities must strike a balance between creating very high-cost programs for saving single, rare species and developing integrated, large-scale landscape management plans. Single-species plans for developing countries must focus on lower-cost options. An example is the contrast between the expensive captive-breeding programs for the endangered Puerto Rican parrot (*Amazona vittata*) and low-cost, but effective, environmental education-based programs for the endangered Amazons of the Lesser Antilles, such as Dominica (Christian et al. 1996).

Conservation must also address nontraditional areas, such as buffer zones and private lands. The total area currently under some category of formal protection in the tropics is unlikely to increase dramatically. Even a doubling of size is improbable. Increasing attention is being paid to development of conservation corridors in Latin America to augment the protection afforded to wildlife by parks and reserves (Vega 1994). Most of the thinking behind corridors implies public ownership of the corridors. Public ownership is not necessary to preserve biodiversity however. Fonseca (1985) demonstrated that private reserves in the Brazilian Atlantic rain forest were more effective in protecting endangered species of primates than public parks and reserves, largely because of more effective monitoring of poachers and squatters. Mosaics of federal, state, and private lands in the eastern United States protect a substantial proportion of the original biodiversity of the region, even though the entire area was at one time deforested. The future of conservation will rest with the integrated management of public and private mosaics, much like the research being done on buffer zones in Costa Rica and Panama (Lacher et al. 1995).

LOCAL, REGIONAL, AND NATIONAL DEVELOPMENT PLANS

Any resident of the United States can relate to the shocking contrast that exists between a planned commercial development that takes into consideration the landscape and local architecture and an unplanned, sprawling strip mall. Both types of development make money, but planned, aesthetically pleasing projects are more willingly accepted by the community and will more easily garner long-term support than a garish mix of fast-food restaurants and used car lots. Increased public awareness of environmental issues and the belief that natural areas merit protection has resulted in greater pressure on the agencies that finance large-scale development in the tropics to avoid the "strip-mall" mentality of unplanned, uncoordinated development (Francis 1994). The World Bank recently instituted a number of environmental reforms in response to public pressure (Walsh 1986; Holden 1987).

Informed, strategic planning is a powerful tool when done correctly. Developing and developed nations together share responsibility for incorporating environmental issues, and in particular conservation planning, into local, regional, and national development plans. The concept of appropriate development requires planned change. The desire for change indicates a commitment to the future; planned change will require the application of the appropriate tools applied with the discipline of the planning process. Developing nations must supply the grassroots needs and local expertise. The developed countries can contribute greatly by providing technological assistance and the accumulated wisdom of past errors of development activities in the First World. Development plans must involve close coordination among government officials, project financiers, environmental engineers, economists, ecologists, wildlife biologists, and the local communities. Few tropical countries can afford either the failure of expensive investments or increased environmental degradation. Both lead inexorably to more poverty and an accelerated decline in the country's standard of living.

DEFINITION OF SUSTAINABLE DEVELOPMENT

The phrase "sustainable development" was first used in *World Conservation Strategy,* published in 1980 (IUCN/UNEP/WWF 1980). Standard definitions include "improving the quality of human life while living within the carrying capacity of supporting ecosystems" (IUCN/UNEP/WWF 1991:10), "development that meets the needs of the present without compromising the ability of future generations to meet their own needs" (World Commission on Environment and Development 1987:8), or "management practices that will not degrade the exploited systems or any adjacent systems" (Lubchenco et al. 1991:394). All definitions leave a great deal of room for interpretation. They also list few quantifiable criteria for evaluation although several publications provide detailed prose on what is meant by "sustainable development" (IUCN/UNEP/WWF 1991) or "excessively altered natural systems" (Lubchenco et al. 1991).

The goal of sustainable development is laudable and should be incorporated in all national and international development projects. It is imperative, however, that the sustainable development goals and objectives be clearly defined prior to the initiation of projects. These goals and objectives should be realistic, meaningful, measurable, and quantifiable. More importantly, they should be defined with local input, at the country, state, and community levels, even (and especially) when the projects are internationally financed. Much criticism of large-scale development projects in the tropics relates to the lack of community involvement in the planning process (Schwartzman 1986). Development will never be sustainable without the grassroots participation and support of the communities where the development will take place. The people that live and work at a project site have the greatest stake in sustainablility because they cannot simply walk away if the project falters; they must live with the long-term consequences. International and multilateral funding agencies must be sensitive to the needs and requirements of the local communities; further, it is imperative that they bring these communities into the project development phase, beginning with the earliest conceptual stages.

Conservation and development are essentially social issues that require economic and scientific inputs. The use of biological surveys and ecological research to develop conservation priorities will provide the scientific basis for sustainable development. The creation of synthetic national development plans will provide the economic framework for growth that will meet societal needs. When all of the above inputs are integrated with the grassroots interests of local communities, the elusive goal of sustainable development will be far easier to acheive. The use of digitial mapping tools to provide visual output to assist in the decision-making process will be an extremely valuable means for merging many layers of complex quantitative information into clearly identifiable patterns.

References

Carr, M. H., J. D. Lambert, and P. D. Zwick. 1994. Mapping of biological corridor potential in Central America. In A. Vega, ed., *Conservation corridors in the Central American region*, 383–93. Gainesville, Fla.: Tropical Research and Development.

Christian, C. S., T. E. Lacher Jr., M. P. Zamore, T. D. Potts, and G. W. Burnett. 1996. Parrot (Psittacidae) conservation in the Lesser Antilles with some comparisons to the Puerto Rican efforts. *Biological Conservation* 77: 159–67.

Committee on Environment and Natural Resources Research of the National Science and Technology Council. 1995. *Our changing planet: The FY 1995 U.S. Global Change Research Program.* Washington, D.C.: National Science and Technology Council.

Fonseca, G. A. B. da. 1985. The vanishing Brazilian Atlantic forest. *Biological Conservation* 34: 17–34.

Francis, D. R. 1994. IMF and World Bank 50th birthday bash: Critics crash party. *Christian Science Monitor,* October 3, 1994, 4.

Franklin, J. F. 1993. Preserving biodiversity: Species, ecosystems, or landscapes? *Ecological Applications* 3: 202–205.

Gámez, R. 1994. Wild biodiversity as a resource for intellectual and economic development: INBio's pilot project in Costa Rica. In A. Vega, ed., *Conservation corridors in the Central American region,* 33–42. Gainesville, Fla.: Tropical Research and Development.

Holden, C. 1987. World Bank launches new environment policy. *Science* 238: 769.

World Conservation Union (IUCN), United Nations Environment Programme (UNEP), World Wildlife Fund (WWF). 1980. *World conservation strategy: Living resource conservation for sustainable development.* Gland, Switzerland: International Union for Conservation of Nature and Natural Resources (IUCN), UNEP, and WWF.

World Conservation Union (IUCN), United Nations Environment Programme (UNEP), World Wildlife Fund. 1991. *Caring for the earth: A strategy for sustainable living.* Gland, Switzerland: International Union for Conservation of Nature and Natural Resources (IUCN), UNEP, and WWF.

Lacher, T. E. Jr. and J. Calvo-Alvarado. 1995. The AMISCONDE initiative: Restoration, conservation, and development in the La Amistad buffer zone. In J. A. Bissonette and P. R. Krausman, eds., *Integrating people and wildlife for a sustainable future: Proceedings of the first international wildlife management congress,* 440–43. Bethesda, Md.: The Wildlife Society.

Lacher, T. E. Jr., J. Calvo-Alvarado, M. Ramirez Umaña, and J. D. Maldonado Dammert. 1995. Incentivos económicos y de conservación para el manejo de las zonas de amortiguamiento: La iniciativa AMISCONDE. In G. A. B. da Fonseca, M. Schmink, L. P. S. Pinto, and F. Brito, eds., *Abordagens Interdisciplinares para a Conservaçao da Biodiversidade e Dinâmica do Uso da Terra no Novo Mundo: Anais da Conferência International,* 315–34. Belo Horizonte, Brazil: Conservation International.

Lubchenco, J., A. M. Olson, L. B. Brubaker, S. R. Carpenter, M. M. Holland, S. P. Hubbell, S. A. Levin, J. A. MacMahon, P. A. Matson, J. M. Melillo, H. A. Mooney, C. H. Peterson, H. R. Pulliam, L. A. Real, P. J. Regal, and P. G. Risser. 1991. The sustainable biosphere initiative: An ecological research agenda. *Ecology* 72: 371–412.

Mares, M. A. 1995. Natural history museums: Bridging the past and future. In C. L. Rose, S. L. Williams, and J. Gisbert, eds., *Current issues, initiatives, and future directions for the preservation and conservation of natural history collections,* 367–404. Madrid: Consejería de Educación y Cultura, Comunidad de Madrid, y Dirección General de Bellas Artes y Archivos, Ministerio de Cultura.

New Partners Working Group. 1994. *New partnerships in the Americas: The spirit of Rio.* Washington, D.C.: USAID and the World Resources Institute.

Noss, R. F. and A. Y. Cooperrider. 1994. *Saving nature's legacy: Protecting and restoring biodiversity.* Washington, D.C.: Island Press.

Ojeda, R. A. 1994. On biodiversity and quick and dirty surveys. *Mastozoologia Neotropical* 1: 164–65.

Roberts, L. 1988. Hard choices ahead on biodiversity. *Science* 241: 1759–61.

Sanderson, J. G. 1994. Global climate change and its effect on biodiversity: What can numerical models do today? In A. Vega, ed., *Conservation corridors in the Central American region,* 402–406. Gainesville, Fla.: Tropical Research and Development.

Schwartzman, S. 1986. *Bankrolling disasters.* Washington, D.C.: Sierra Club.

Tangley, L. 1992. *Computers and conservation priorities: Mapping biodiversity.* Washington, D.C.: Conservation International.

Vega, A., ed. 1994. *Conservation corridors in the Central American region.* Gainesville, Fla: Tropical Research and Development.

Walsh, J. 1986. World Bank pressed on environmental reforms. *Science* 234: 813–15.

World Commission on Environment and Development. 1987. *Our common future.* Oxford: Oxford University Press.

World Resources Institute (WRI). 1985. *Tropical forests: A call to action.* Vols. 1–3. Washington, D.C.: WRI.

———. 1990. *Taking stock: The Tropical Forestry Action Plan after five years.* Washington, D.C.: WRI.

World Resources Institute (WRI), the World Conservation Union (IUCN), and the United Nations Environment Program (UNEP). 1992. *Global biodiversity strategy: Guidelines for action to save, study, and use Earth's biotic wealth sustainably and equitably.* Washington, D.C.: WRI.

17

Application of the Gap Analysis Model in Regional and International Programs in the Tropics

Thomas E. Lacher Jr., G. Wesley Burnett,
Basil G. Savitsky, and Christopher Vaughan

Application of Gap Analysis in Other Tropical Developing Countries

One of the objectives of this research was to identify the minimum data requirements for the international application of the gap analysis model. Much research needs to be performed before specific data requirements can be listed; however, there are several findings and recommendations.

Costa Rica is a data-rich tropical country. Both the habitat map and the wildlife data were updates of previous mapping efforts. There are numerous countries that have neither the quality of land cover mapping nor a similar wildlife database upon which to build. Since wildlife data collection is expensive and habitat mapping requires both extensive time and competent staff who are trained in image analysis, alternative types of mapping efforts for data-poor countries follow.

HABITAT DATA FOR TROPICAL DEVELOPING COUNTRIES

If some form of land cover map already exists, it can be updated in similar fashion to this project, and probably with much less image analysis effort. Since the TM data were used to identify only four classes, and since the data were aggregated from 28.5 to 200 meters, the authors postulate that a sensor system which collects data at a coarser spatial resolution would be as effective for gap analysis as the TM data. Landsat MSS data are collected at a spatial resolution of eighty meters. This provides a database that is considerably simpler and smaller in data volume than TM imagery.

The Advanced Very High Resolution Radiometer (AVHRR) scanner has a spatial resolution of one kilometer and provides data useful for general vegetation monitoring. The effectiveness of vegetation mapping at one-kilometer scale for a national gap analysis remains to be evaluated. One problem with AVHRR data is that it is difficult to obtain cloud-free coverage in the tropics. Most mapping programs based upon AVHRR data require multitemporal data analysis, a complicated process. It may be advisable to utilize an AVHRR classification map, if one has been produced for the country or region, rather than processing new satellite data to create a habitat map. If no previous land cover map can be updated using remotely sensed data, then MSS or MODIS (Moderate-Resolution Imaging Spectrometer: see chapter 5) should be considered before relying upon an AVHRR-derived map because of the additional detail provided with the finer resolution scanners.

Wildlife Data for Tropical Developing Countries

There is great benefit in utilizing indicator species in data-poor countries. A focus on one given species at the top of the food chain may be all that can be obtained in some countries. The regional mapping approach performed by Carr et al. (1994) for the jaguar in Central America is a prime example of this level of conservation mapping. (For the scientific names of many of the species named in this chapter, see table 13.3.) The objective of the project was to identify a corridor for jaguars that could be utilized by and provide protection for a variety of other species as well.

More than one indicator species may be developed by many countries. By defining a smaller set of indicator species than the set of twenty-one species utilized in Costa Rica, effort may be directed to collecting similar high-quality survey data at a lower cost. The five-species gap analysis was performed in order to develop a reasonable understanding of the minimum number of species that could be considered in an international gap analysis program. The species of choice will vary from one country to another, but a certain amount of consistency should be expected within geographically contiguous international regions. Detailed projects, such as this project, serve to inform managers of other projects in the Central American region on the minimum wildlife data collection requirements for the region.

Gap Analysis Potential in Africa

The transference of a technology such as gap analysis between regions of the less developed world may present as much difficulty as the transfer of technology from the developed to the less developed world. The Afrotropical Realm (Udvardy 1975) and the Central American portion of the Neotropical Realm differ significantly in ways that suggest that a gap analysis technique developed in Costa Rica would not readily transfer to Africa without major modifications.

First, the megafauna of Africa is far more diverse than in the Neotropics (Haltenorth and Diller 1980). This increases proportionately the problems associated with identifying a useful group of indicator species upon which to base a gap analysis. Second, the areas of African nations are generally far larger than those in Central America. Only Rwanda, Burundi, Swaziland, Lesotho, and Gambia are smaller than Costa Rica while Zimbabwe is eight times as large, Kenya eleven times, Zambia fifteen times, Tanzania nineteen times, Zaire forty-six times, and Sudan forty-nine times as large. The increased size increases the difficulty and expense of gathering data, and it implies (all things being equal) an increased number of habitats requiring data gathering. In any event, wildlife biologists in Central America tend to limit their definition of wildlife habitat almost exclusively to forests. While the approach seems useful and appropriate in Central America, where forest is by far the most extensive type of natural vegetation, it is unsuited to Africa where wildlife of significance to management occupies a wider array of habitats—including savannas, semideserts, and deserts of various sorts.

The third major difference between the Afrotropics and Central America is one of relative wealth and poverty. It would be unkind to call Central Americans wealthy; however, their poverty stands in dramatic contrast relative to Africa's economic situation. The gross national product of such African wildlife giants as Tanzania and Zambia with their larger area and often strikingly larger populations barely match that of Costa Rica. A small gross national product usually translates into low personal incomes. The gross national product per capita in sub-Saharan Africa exclusive of South Africa is less than a third that of Central America's. The result is grinding, oppressive poverty for most Africans and no money for the most obvious, basic wildlife conservation such as law enforcement, much less advanced digital technologies. Gap analysis, seemingly most suitable for putting the finishing touches on an extensive system of reserves, would certainly seem an unheard-of extravagance to wildlife conservation officers who consider petrol for a vehicle to be a luxury.

A plethora of wildlife species in a large number of habitats over large but very poor nations make gap analysis a dubious tool for national conservation planning in Africa anytime in the foreseeable future. This is not, however, to say that there are no potential applications of gap analysis at other levels. At the supranational scale, international agencies would benefit from applying gap analysis at the level of Africa's biological provinces (Udvardy 1975). These regions, indifferent to political boundaries and generally larger than nations, represent, at least for Africa, important international planning units (Burnett and Harrington 1994). Gap analysis seems well suited to answer many of the questions which arise about conservation at the level of the biological province, from those centering on the sufficiency of protected areas to those concerned with the relationship between protected areas and mappable types of land use and social change. Gap analysis at the level of the biological province would undoubtedly require new definitions for needed data and considerable originality in generating that data; however, gap analyses of this type promise to assist considerably in identifying both protected areas and nations where international conservation assistance can achieve the greatest consequence for the least cost.

At an entirely different scale, there is the problem presented by the protected areas themselves. If a protected area's boundaries are straight lines meeting at right angles, one becomes suspicious that the protected area was created in an office far removed from the reality of the field. These kinds of protected areas present many problems. They include portions that need not and should not be protected in order to achieve conservation goals while critical and important adjacent areas are too often left out. Human and wildlife space and activity are often mixed in ways that are inconvenient, irritating, and dangerous for both humans and wildlife. Arbitrary boundaries increase local hostility toward protected areas and decrease popular support for conservation (Akama, Lant, and Burnett 1995), and Africa is full of arbitrarily bounded protected areas. There is a terrible need to adjust the boundaries of many of Africa's protected areas, but African nations attempting this run a gamut of criticism to the effect that they are abandoning their commitment to conservation, an accusation that can adversely affect other areas of international relations with the developed world (Burnett and Conover 1989).

Gap analysis offers a unique methodology for putting the study of boundary adequacy on something like a scientific footing. Once critical species are agreed on, critical habitat can be identified and adjustments to the land ownership pattern executed. The danger in this is that gap analysis is so far a technique for evaluating wildlife carried out by those who assume that protected areas are created to protect wildlife. In truth, protected areas are generally intended to protect a great deal more. Evaluating the adequacy of park boundaries is politically dangerous work, and the application of gap analysis to that process will require rethinking of the actual thing being conserved.

Ecosystem Management and Political Boundaries: A Protocol for the Management of Tropical Ecosystems

The unit of critical concern in conservation biology is the ecosystem. The protection of species is fundamentally dependent on the protection of their habitat, contingent upon the preservation of substantial areas of the ecosystems of the world. Ecosystems tend to be regional in distribution and almost always are

TABLE 17.1 *The Eight Steps of the Protocol for the Management of Tropical Ecosystems*

1. Conduct floral and faunal inventories
2. Generate a current map of land use activities
3. Develop five, ten, and twenty-five-year development plans
4. Develop corresponding five, ten, and twenty-five-year conservation goals
5. Generate GIS-based maps integrating the information in steps 1 through 4
6. Conduct a decision cube analysis for the five, ten, and twenty-five-year plans
7. Use the step 6 output to conduct conflict-resolution workshops
8. Present the final short- and long-term integrated plans

international; this is precisely the unit most difficult to study. Most applications of gap analysis have been at the level of a political unit, such as a state (Scott et al. 1993; Mann 1995) or country (Powell et al. 1995; USAID case study in this book). They therefore focus on fragments of many ecosystems rather than on a complete analysis of one ecosystem. If ecosystem management for more effective conservation is a goal of gap analysis, then future efforts should focus on the regional study of a focal ecosystem. We propose an eight-step protocol for this process (see table 17.1 and figure 17.1).

1. FLORAL AND FAUNAL INVENTORIES

Conservation priorities cannot be determined without scientific information on the patterns of biological diversity that are present. In many cases, basic ecological information relevant to conservation will also be required, such as important predator-prey, plant-pollinator, or seed-seed disperser interactions. Countries must realize that decreases in funding for basic biological and ecological research are not a viable shortcut to conservation.

2. CURRENT MAP OF LAND USE ACTIVITIES

Maps of recent (within five years) patterns of land use activities need to be produced for the region of interest. Maps can be produced using a combination of existing land cover maps, maps of potential vegetation, and remote sensing. The combination of maps of potential vegetation with recent remote sensing data provides critical information on the current status of habitat and the degree of disturbance.

3. FIVE, TEN, AND TWENTY-FIVE-YEAR DEVELOPMENT PLANS

Government agencies involved in economic development, natural resources management, and rural and urban planning generally develop five-year plans. These agencies must begin to think in longer terms. Ten and twenty-five-year plans need not be as detailed as five-year plans, but major trends in international financing and development should be identified and areas under consideration

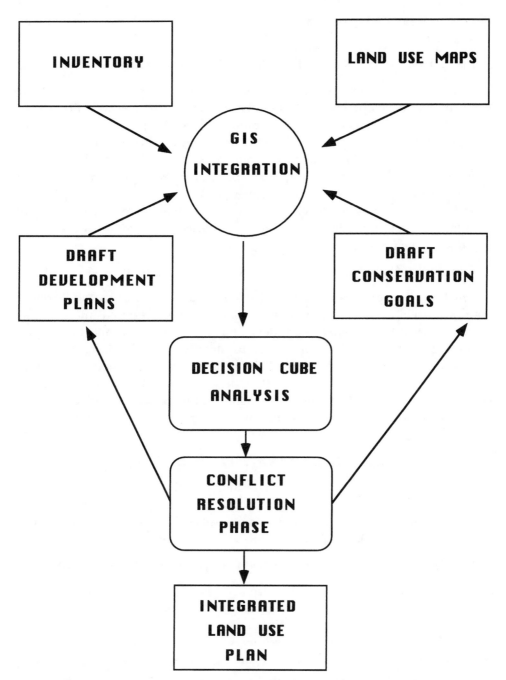

FIG. 17.1 Flow chart for the protocol for the application of the gap analysis model in developing tropical countries

for development need to be defined. Community input should be solicited for all three scenarios.

4. Five, Ten, and Twenty-Five-Year Conservation Goals

The same suite of government agencies and community groups involved in the formulation of development plans should also consider the creation of conservation goals. How much total area is to be protected? Which species and ecosystems have priority? Which areas currently are underprotected? Which areas have been so intensively disturbed that they will require restoration? Framing conservation goals in tandem with development goals will reveal potential areas of conflict well in advance. This will also allow governments to be aware of the potential environmental impacts of development activities; they then can more easily consider and project possible financing for conservation activities as part of the total development package.

5. Generate GIS-Based Maps by Integrating Steps 1–4

Information on species distributions, current land use, and five, ten, and twenty-five-year development and conservation plans can be integrated into a GIS so that maps of all three scenarios for development and conservation can be produced. GIS gives researchers the ability to identify spatial patterns of conflict between conservation and development. Researchers can then modify results by changing the weights associated with individual map layers, giving higher weights to conservation activities or development as priorities dictate. The GIS databases can be modified as more information is gathered or as any layer of the map is altered.

6. Conduct Decision Cube Analysis for Development Plans

Use the maps generated in the previous section to run the decision cube analysis for the five, ten, and twenty-five-year scenarios. Generate the eight-outcome matrices for any species or combinations of species of interest. Maps of regions of conflict can be developed and distributed to decision-makers.

7. Use Output to Conduct Conflict Resolution Workshops

Bring together representatives of government, industry, conservation organizations, academia, and the local communities to view the output of the decision cube analysis. Use the conflict resolution workshops to develop compromises regarding all areas of conflict. Workshops will allow all parties to express the perceptions of the relative priorities regarding conservation and development. This will help to eliminate the perception of hidden agendas in national economic development plans. It will also create a sense of national sovereignty with regard to internationally financed development and enhance the level of trust between developed and developing countries.

8. PRESENT FINAL SHORT-RANGE AND LONG-RANGE PLANS

Based upon the workshops, develop a consensus document on integrated natural resources management for the next twenty-five years. The document should be made available to public and university libraries and disseminated via the national media.

Teaching, Training, and Technology Transfer: Moving Beyond Scientific Imperialism

It is far more costly to treat the sick than to prevent disease. It is far more costly to incarcerate the criminal than to educate the child. Environmental cleanup efforts like the Superfund certainly cost more than effective environmental and technological planning would have cost (Miller 1990). It is difficult to conceive what the price will be for the reconstruction of our lakes, rivers, and forests. Environmental issues are economic issues, and planning and prevention will save billions of dollars of future expenditures. Most of these costs will have to be assumed by local, state, and federal governments; taxes will have to be raised and economic expansion will be stifled. Planning will be most effective when it involves grassroots participation in preventing future problems and resolving current ones.

The strategic importance of technology transfer is in the avoidance of future international crises that will incur financial or political costs. The transfer of technology can also bring direct economic benefits when the technology is leading edge and its introduction into the market will stimulate future sales. The United States and several other developing countries currently are among the global leaders in environmental technology. The judicious transfer of this technology to the developing world meets all the above criteria. It is currently in vogue to confer economic value to the conservation of biodiversity based upon future, unknown commercial benefits (Gámez 1991). These efforts are laudable but do not convince many conservative economists. The political and economic benefits of the transfer of environmental technologies are more obvious and direct.

Only through the transfer of the necessary capability for scientific decision making can the developed world assure that conservation and sustainable development will occur. This transfer concerns both the willingness of the developed world to share as well as the openness of developing countries to international collaboration (Mares 1991). These are issues that must be decided first locally, then regionally, and then globally. Development of global conservation protocols, such as *Agenda 21*, lends assurance that global resolutions are possible. The goal should be the elimination of political, economic, and scientific dependency. When these are eliminated and in-country expertise exists, the global goal of sustainable development can be achieved at much lower long-term cost.

Humans conserve natural environments ultimately because they believe that it is ethically correct to do so. Economic concerns can influence the details of conservation but will not change the perspectives of those who either support or oppose conservation on ethical grounds. A mixed approach of scientifically informed planning, assisted by digital mapping technologies and buttressed by the grassroots input and support of local communities, will yield the best long-term solutions to sustainable development. Sustainable development must be a wise economic decision; true commitment to the process will be guaranteed if it is a moral decision as well.

References

Akama, J. S., C. L. Lant, and G. W. Burnett. 1995. Conflicting attitudes toward state wildlife conservation programs in Kenya. *Society and Natural Resources* 8: 133–44.

Burnett, G. W. and L. M. B. Harrington. 1994. Early national park adoption in sub-Saharan Africa. *Society and Natural Resources* 7: 155–68.

Burnett, G. W. and R. Conover. 1989. The efficacy of Africa's national parks: An evaluation of Julius Nyeree's Arusha Manifesto of 1961. *Society and Natural Resources* 2: 251–60.

Carr, M. H., J. D. Lambert, and P. D. Zwick. 1994. Mapping of biological corridor potential in Central America. In A. Vega, ed., *Conservation corridors in the Central American region*, 383–93. Gainesville, Fla.: Tropical Research and Development.

Gámez, R. 1991. Biodiversity conservation through facilitation of its sustainable use: Costa Rica's National Biodiversity Institute. *Trends in Ecology and Evolution* 6: 377–78.

Haltenorth, T. and H. Diller. 1980. *A field guide to the mammals of Africa including Madagascar.* Translated by R. W. Hayman. London: Collins.

Mann, C. C. 1995. Filling in Florida's gaps: Species protection done right? *Science* 269: 318–20.

Mares, M. A. 1991. How scientists can impede the development of their discipline: Egocentrism, small pool size, and the evolution of "Sapismo." In M. A. Mares and D. J. Schmidly, eds., *Latin American mammalogy: History, biodiversity, and conservation,* 57–75. Norman: University of Oklahoma Press.

Miller, G. T. Jr. 1990. *Resource conservation and management.* Belmont, Calif.: Wadsworth.

Powell, G. V. N., R. D. Bjork, M. Rodríguez, and J. Barborak. 1995. Life zones at risk. *Wild Earth* 5: 46–51.

Scott, J. M., F. Davis, B. Csuti, R. Noss, B. Butterfield, C. Groves, H. Anderson, S. Caicco, F. D'Erchia, T. C. Edwards Jr., J. Ulliman, and R. G. Wright. 1993. *Gap analysis: A geographical approach to protection of biological diversity.* Wildlife Monograph no. 123 (41 pp.). Bethesda, Md.: The Wildlife Society.

Udvardy, M. D. F. 1975. *A classification of the biogeographical provinces of the world.* IUCN Occasional Paper no. 18. Morges, Switzerland: IUCN.

Appendix 1
GPS Receivers with GIS Capability*

Manufacturer	Model	Max. no. satellites tracked	List Price in U.S.$ (war./mo.)
Ashtec, Inc.	G-12	12	inquire (12)
	Reliance	12	inquire (12)
	Super C/A-12 Sensor	12	$5,000 (12)
	Super C/A-12 Surveyor	12	$9,000 (12)
Canadian Marconi Co.	CMT-1200 ALLSTAR GPS	12	$295 (12)
	CMT-8700 GPS Sensor	12	$995 (24)
	CMT-8900 DGPS Sensor	12	$1,895 (24)
Centennial Technologies	SATNAV PCMCIA Card	9	$595 (12)
Communication Navigation	GEO-Base	8	inquire (6–12)
	GEO-Tracker	8	inquire (6–12)
	Target-GPS	8	inquire (6–12)
Corvallis Microtechnology	MC-GPS	6	$3,950 (3)
	MC-GPS-CM	6	$5,950 (3)
	PC5L-GPS (MS-DOS 5.0)	6	$4,950 (3)
	PC5L-GPSCM (MS-DOS 5.0)	6	$6,950 (3)
	PC5L-GP-9000	12	$9,850 (3)

*All information in this appendix was condensed from *GPS World* (editors), "*GPS World* receiver survey" (1996), *GPS World* 7(1): 32–50.

Manufacturer	Model	Max. no. satellites tracked	List Price in U.S.$ (war./mo.)
Furuno Electric Co., Ltd.	GN-74	8	inquire (12)
GARMIN International	CPS 20	8	quantity pricing (12)
	GPS 25	12	quantity pricing (12)
	GPS 30 TracPak	8	quantity pricing (12)
	GPS 35 TracPak	12	quantity pricing (12)
Geotronics AB	Geotracer 2102	12	$9,950 (12)
Leica AG	SR 260	6	$9,750 (12) complete field operations
Leica Navigation and Positioning Division	MBS-1	12	$4,970 (12)
	MX 300	6	$4,695 (12)
	MX 4200 upgrade	12	$2,795 (12)
	MX 8601	6	$3,950 (12)
	MX 8602	6	$4,150 (12)
	MX 8604	6	$4,550 (12)
	MX 8612	6	$5,950 (12)
	MX 8614	6	$6,350 (12)
	MX 8650	12	nr (12)
	MX 9012 R	12	$8,000 (12)
	MX 9112	12	$9,900 (12)
	MX 9212	12	$4,970 (12)
	MX 9400N	12	$6,490 (12
Magellan Systems	FieldPro V	12	$1,395 (12)
	GPS Commander (PPS)	12	inquire (12)
	GPS Commander (SPS)	12	inquire (12)
	GPS Hawk Arabic	12	inquire (12)
	MBS-1	12	$5,995–$9,995 with options
	NAV 1000M5	12	inquire (12)
	Promark X	12	$2,895 (12)
	Promark X-CP	12	$4,495 (12)
Motorola AIEG	Basic Oncore	8	quantity pricing (12
	VP Oncore	8	quantity pricing (12
	XT Oncore Shielded Case	8	quantity pricing (12
Navstar Systems/ NavSymm	Kernel 12	12	$2,795 (12)
	Kernel 6	8	$995 (12)
	XR5.M (12)	12	$5,095 (12)
	XR5.M (6)	8	$2,595 (12)

Manufacturer	Model	Max. no. satellites tracked	List Price in U.S.$ (war./mo.)
Northstar Technologies	8500 Beacon Receiver Board	NA	$675 (24)
	8700 GPS Sensor	12	$995 (24)
	8800 Beacon Receiver	NA	$1,095 (24)
	8900 DGPS Receiver	12	$2,780 (24)
	941 Series GPS Navigator	12	$2,295–$3,295 (24)
	951 Series Electronic Chart	12	$2,895–$3,795 (24)
NovAtel Communications	GISMO	12	$9,950–$13,450 (24)
	GPSCard OEM Performance Series	12	$3,495–$5,990 (12)
	GPSCard OEM Standard Series	12	$2,495–$3,990 (12)
	GPSCard PC Performance Series	12	$3,495–$5,990 (12)
	GPSCard PC Standard Series	12	$2,495–$3,990 (12)
	Hydrographic Surveyor	12	$6,995–$7,995 (12)
	RT-20	12	$9,995 (12)
Omnistar	6300A Plus	8	$6,200 (12)
Premier GPS Inc.	Newton Surveyor Jr.	8	$4,499 (12)
	Smartbase-12	all in view	$9,398 (12)
	Smartbase-8	8	$7,998 (12)
Rockwell Semiconductor Systems	Zodiac/Jupiter	12	$70 (18)
Sercel	NR 108	10	$9,980 (12)
Sokkia Corporation	GSR 1000 (North and South America only)	12	$9,000 (12)
	GSR 1100 (North and South America only)	12	$6,900 (12)
	S100	6	$1,995 (12)
	S200	12	NA (12)
Starlink Inc.	DNAV-212	12	$5,000 (12)
Trimble Navigation	GeoExplorer	8	$2,995 (3)
	Mobile GPS Locator	8	$495 (12)
	Mobile GPS PC Card 110	8	$595 (12)
	Mobile GPS PC Card 115	8	$1,295 (12)
	Site Surveyor SS	9 (12 optional)	inquire (3)
	SVeeSix 104	8	OEM pricing (12)
II Morrow Inc.	Apollo Gis 940	6	$2,995 (12)

Appendix 2
Ordering Information for Map of the Habitats of Costa Rica

A poster sized (26 x 30 inches) and more detailed version of the map shown in color plate 1 is available. The map includes information on obtaining data sets used in the USAID project that are currently available on the Internet. To place a map order contact:

Kathy Skinner
Strom Thurmond Institute
PO Box 345130
Clemson University
Clemson, SC 29634–5130
telephone (864) 656–4700; fax (864) 656–4780

Shipping and handling costs for the map tube mailing are $5.00 for U.S. requests and $8.00 for international requests (prices subject to change). Make checks payable to Clemson University.

Appendix 3
Description of the Twenty-one Wildlife Species

Information on the bird species is from Perrins (1990) and Stiles and Skutch (1989). Information on mammals is from Nowak (1991) and Timm et al. (1989). Information on reptiles is from Burton and Burton (1975) and Ross and Magnusson (1989). Data on the status of species is from the World Conservation Union (1988) and MINAREM/MNCR/INBIO (1992).

Mammal Species

Primates

Alouatta palliata (mantled howler monkey, Mono congo). The howler monkey is among the largest of the New World primates, with a head and body length of 56 to 92 centimeters and a tail length of 59 to 92 centimeters. It has a preference for primary forest but occurs in disturbed habitats as well and can be found between southern Mexico and Ecuador. It is the most abundant nonhuman primate in Costa Rica. The howler monkey is not listed by the IUCN.

Ateles geoffroyi (black-handed spider monkey, Mono colorado). The spider monkey is an agile primate measuring 38 to 64 centimeters in head and body length and 51 to 89 centimeters in tail length. The black-handed spider monkey inhabits rain and montane forests between northeastern and western Mexico and western Panama. The spider monkey is listed as vulnerable by the IUCN.

Cebus capucinus (white-faced capuchin, Mono carablanca). The white-faced capuchin inhabits a variety of types of forest types and can be seen in mangroves and sparsely forested areas. The white-faced capuchin is found from Belize and Honduras to western Colombia and Ecuador. It measures 31 to 57 centimeters in head and body length and 30 to 56 centimeters in tail length. The white-faced capuchin is not listed by the IUCN.

Saimiri oerstedii (Central American squirrel monkey, Mono ardilla). This squirrel monkey is only found in a small area on the Pacific coast of Costa Rica and Panama. It utilizes primary and secondary forests as well as cultivated areas. The squirrel monkey has a head and body length of 26 to 36 centimeters and a tail length of 35 to 43 centimeters. The squirrel monkey is listed as endangered globally by the IUCN and vulnerable in Costa Rica.

CATS

Herpailurus yagouaroundi (jaguarundi, Leon Breñero). The jaguarundi is a small cat that inhabits lowland forests and thickets between southern Texas and northern Argentina. It has two color phases, gray to black and red. The jaguarundi has a head and body length of 55 to 77 centimeters, a tail length of 33 to 60 centimeters, and weighs 4.5 to 9 kilograms. The jaguarundi is listed as indeterminate by the IUCN.

Leopardus pardalis (ocelot, Manigordo). The ocelot is also a small cat. It can be found in humid tropical forests and fairly dry scrub between Texas and northern Argentina. The ocelot has a background color of yellow to gray with dark streaks and spots. It has a head and body length of 55 to 100 centimeters, a tail length of 30 to 45 centimeters, and weighs 11.3 to 15.8 kilograms. The ocelot is listed as vulnerable by the IUCN and endangered in Costa Rica.

Leopardus wiedii (margay, Caucél). The margay resembles the ocelot but is smaller and has a longer tail. It is mainly a forest dweller and can be found between northern Mexico and northern Argentina. The margay is yellowish brown with rows of dark brown spots. It has a head and body length of 46 to 79 centimeters and a tail length of 33 to 51 centimeters. The margay is listed as vulnerable by the IUCN.

Panthera onca (jaguar, Jaguar). The jaguar has been exterminated in the United States, in much of Central America, and in most of Mexico, Argentina, and eastern Brazil. It is a spotted cat that is found in forests and savannas. The jaguar has a head and body length of 112 to 185 centimeters, a tail length of 45 to 75 centimeters, and weighs 36 to 158 kilograms. The jaguar is listed as vulnerable by the IUCN and endangered in Costa Rica.

Puma concolor (mountain lion or cougar, Puma). The mountain lion is also known as cougar, panther, and puma. It has the greatest natural distribution of any mammal in the western hemisphere other than man. It can be found at elevations from sea level to 4,500 meters and in grasslands, swamps, and all types of forest. The mountain lion can be found wherever cover and prey are available. It has two color phases, cinnamon and gray. The male has a head and body length of 105 to 196 centimeters, a tail length of 66 to 78 centimeters, and weighs 67 to 103 kilograms. The cougar is listed as vulnerable in Costa Rica.

OTHER MAMMALS

Agouti paca (paca, Tepezcuintle). The paca is a nocturnal rodent that inhabits forested areas near water. It is found between central Mexico and Paraguay. The paca is brown to black with four rows of white spots on each side, and it has a white underpart. It has a head and body length of 60 to 80 centimeters, a tail length of 2 to 3 centimeters, and weighs 6.3 to 12 kilograms. The paca is not listed by IUCN.

Myrmecophaga tridactyla (giant anteater, Oso caballo). The giant anteater is distinguished by its long narrow snout and its bushy tail. It is found in humid forests, swamps, grasslands, and savannas between Belize and northern Argentina. The giant anteater is gray with a black diagonal stripe with white borders. It has a head and body length of 100 to 120 centimeters, a tail length of 65 to 90 centimeters, and weighs 18 to 39 kilograms. The giant anteater is listed as vulnerable by the IUCN and endangered in Costa Rica, and might already be extinct in the country.

Tapirus bairdii (Baird's tapir, Danta). The tapir is a shy, solitary animal. It is dark or reddish brown and has thick skin and bristly hair. The tapir inhabits woody or grassy habitat where water is available. It can be found between southern Mexico and Colombia and Ecuador. It has a head and body length of 180 to 250 centimeters, a tail length of 5 to 13 centimeters, and weighs 180 to 320 kilograms. The tapir is listed as vulnerable by the IUCN.

Tayassu pecari (white-lipped peccary, Chancho de Monte) and *Pecari tajacu* (collared peccary, Saíno). The peccary is similar to the wild hog and grubs for food with its snout. The species are found between southern Mexico and northeastern Argentina. Peccaries utilize a variety of habitat from forest to desert scrub. They are mostly herbivorous but will also consume snakes or small vertebrates. Peccaries have a head and body length of 75 to 100 centimeters, a tail length of 1.5 to 5.5 centimeters, and weigh 14 to 30 kilograms. The white-lipped peccary is larger than the collared peccary. The white-lipped peccary is dark brown to black and is white on the sides of its jaws. The collared peccary is dark gray with a white collar on its neck. The white-lipped peccary is listed as vulnerable in Costa Rica; neither species is listed by IUCN.

Bird Species

Ara ambigua (great green macaw, Guacamayo verde maior). The green macaw inhabits humid lowland forests between eastern Honduras and northwest Colombia and western Ecuador. It grows to 79 centimeters in height. In Costa Rica it specializes on the fruit of *Dipteryx panamensis* and is largely restricted to the Caribbean lowlands. The great green macaw is not listed by the IUCN. In Costa Rica it is threatened.

Ara macao (scarlet macaw, Guacamayo rojo). The scarlet macaw is a multicolored parrot which inhabits lowland forests up to elevations of 400 meters. The scarlet macaw is an adaptable bird which thrives in a variety of habitats. Its populations appear to be limited by the availability of trees having suitable nesting cavities. Scarlet macaws are generally seen in pairs, grow to 85 centimeters, and can be found from southern Mexico to northern Bolivia and central Brazil. Currently restricted in Costa Rica to isolated areas and reserves on the Pacific slope. The scarlet macaw is not listed by the IUCN, but is considered vulnerable in Costa Rica.

Crax rubra (great curassow, Pavón grande). The great curassow is one of the first birds to disappear after the forest is exploited by humans. It is similar in body shape to a pheasant and is approximately 97 centimeters in length. The great curassow inhabits undisturbed mature forest and scrub between Mexico and western Ecuador and western Colombia. In Costa Rica it persists in some of the larger national parks. The great curassow is not listed by the IUCN; it is vulnerable in Costa Rica.

Harpia harpyja (harpy eagle, Aguila arpía). The harpy eagle is one of the most powerful birds of prey in the world, capable of taking large monkeys, sloths, and porcupines. It is 91 to 110 centimeters in height. The harpy eagle can be found from southern Mexico to northern Argentina, typically in lowland tropical forest. Nearly extinct in Costa Rica, with a few perhaps surviving in the Osa Peninsula, the Talamanca Mountains, and near the Nicaraguan border. The harpy eagle is listed by the IUCN as rare globally. It is considered threatened in Costa Rica.

Pharomachrus mocinno (resplendent quetzal, quetzal). The quetzal lives in humid cloud forests, usually between elevations of 1,200 and 3,000 meters. It has a size of 35 to 38 centimeters and can be found between southern Mexico and western Panama. It can be found in deforested areas if sufficient feeding and nesting trees remain. The resplendent quetzal is listed by the IUCN as vulnerable.

Reptile Species

Caiman crocodilus (common caiman, Guajipal). The common caiman is indeed one of the most common species of crocodilians and occurs in a variety of fresh water habitats. Caimans feed primarily on insects, other invertebrates, crabs, and fish. The caiman can be found from southern Mexico through the Amazon to northern Argentina. The common caiman is listed by IUCN as threatened.

Crocodylus acutus (American crocodile, Cocodrilo). The American crocodile is among the largest of reptiles and can attain lengths of greater than six meters. It can be found in rivers and shallow waters such as swamps and marshes as well as in estuarine and coastal areas. The crocodile can be found in Florida and the Caribbean Basin and from southern Mexico to northern South America. It occurs on both coasts of Costa Rica. The American crocodile is listed by IUCN as endangered.

References

Burton, M. and R. Burton. 1975. *Encyclopedia of reptiles, amphibians, and other cold-blooded animals.* New York: Crescent.

MINAREM/MNCR/INBIO. 1992. *Estudio Nacional de Biodiversidad.* San José, C.R.: Ministerio de Recursos Naturales, Energía, y Minas, Museo Nacional de Costa Rica, Instituto Nacional de Biodiversidad.

Nowak, R. M. 1991. *Walker's mammals of the world.* 5th ed. Baltimore: Johns Hopkins University Press.

Perrins, C. M. 1990. *The illustrated encyclopedia of birds: The definitive reference to birds of the world.* Englewood Cliffs, N.J.: Prentice-Hall.

Ross, C. A. and W. E. Magnusson. 1989. Living crocodilians. In C. A. Ross, ed., *Crocodiles and alligators,* 58–73. New York: Facts on File.

Stiles, F. G. and A. F. Skutch. 1989. *A guide to the birds of Costa Rica.* Ithaca, N.Y.: Comstock.

Timm, R. M., D. E. Wilson, B. L. Clauson, R. K. LaVal, C. S. Vaughan. 1989. *Mammals of La Selva–Braulio Carrillo Complex, Costa Rica.* North American Fauna no. 75. Washington, D.C.: U.S. Fish and Wildlife Service, Department of the Interior.

World Conservation Union (IUCN). 1988. *1988 IUCN red list of threatened animals.* Gland, Switzerland: International Union for Conservation of Nature and Natural Resources.

Appendix 4
Summary of Wildlife Survey

Category	Occupation	Number
Researcher	Parataxonomy	7
	Wildlife	1
	Conservation	13
	Biology	5
	Archaeology	1
	Subtotal	*27*
Security	Park Guard	59
	Wildlife Inspector	11
	Rural Guard	27
	Police	3
	Subtotal	*100*
Education	Environmental Education	3
	Teacher	2
	Student	2
	Retired	3
	Subtotal	*10*
Domestic	Housewives	5
	Subtotal	*5*

Category	Occupation	Number
Service Industry	Forest Fire Fighters	2
	Municipal Government	2
	Office Worker	2
	Construction	7
	Mason	1
	Forestry Technician	2
	Tanner	1
	Maintenance	2
	Waiter	2
	Administrator	8
	Miscellaneous	6
	Drover	6
	Photographer	2
	Tourism Worker	5
	Tour Guide	2
	Subtotal	*50*
Fishing	Fisherman	11
	Subtotal	*11*
Agriculture	Farmers	172
	Ranchers	6
	Day Laborer	8
	Migrant Worker	6
	Field Boss	5
	Farm Owner	3
	Equipment Operator	3
	Subtotal	*203*
	TOTAL	*406*

Breakdown by Time of Residence

Range	Number of People
0 to 5 years	55
6 to 10 years	46
11 to 15 years	28
16 to 25 years	64
More than 20 years	213
TOTAL	*406*

Appendix 5
List of Participants at UNA/USAID GIS Workshop (March 6–8, 1995)

Institution	Name
Acueductos y Alcantarillados	Gerardo Ramirez Villegas Roy Valverde Villalobos Ovares
Area de Conservación La Amistad	Nelson Mora Mora Adrian Arias N. Fernando Quirós B. Boris Gamboa Valladares
Area de Conservación Tortuguero	Carlos Manuel Calvo Gutiérrez Eduardo Rodríguez Herrera
Area de Conservación Pacifico Central	Miguel Madrigal
Area de Conservación Volcanica Central	Rodolfo Tenorio Jiménez
CATIE, Turrialba	Grégoire Leclerc
Centro Científico Tropical	Patricia Barrantes Padilla Carlos Rodríguez Rodríguez

Institution	Name
Clemson University	Thomas E. Lacher Jr. Basil G. Savitsky
Comisión de la Sociedad Civil, MIRENEM	Victor Villalobos Rodríguez
Comisión de Ordenamiento Territorial, SINADES (Sistema Nacional de Desarrollo Sostenible)	Jorge Cotera Mira Oscar Luke Sánchez
Consultora Cuatro	Estaban Dorries B.
Dirección General Forestal	Vera Violeta Montero Castro
DRIP (Desarrollo Rural Integral Peninsula), Peninsula de Nicoya	Tiny Luiten
Fundación ACCESO	Maria Sáenz Gómez
FUNDECOR	Johnny Rodriguez Chacón
INBIO	Marco Castro Campos Verónica Sancho Solls
Instituto Costarricense de Electricidad	Johnny Molina Garcia Javier Saborio Bejarano
Instituto Costarricense de Turismo	Francisco Aragón Solórzano
Instituto Metereologico Nacional	Jorge Arturo Barrantes
Instituto Desarrollo Agrario	Jorge Campos Salas
Instituto Geográfico Nacional	Fernando Quirós Christian Asch Quirós Carlos Elizondo Solls
Ministerio de Agricultura y Ganadería	Oscar Gómez Carlos León

Institution	Name
Ministerio de Ciencia y Tecnologia	Teresita Quesada Granados
MIRENEM	Walter Quirós González
OET	Jenny Juárez Porras
Parques Nacionales	Jorge Cerdas Aguilar
SENARA	Sandra Arradondo Li Germán Matamoros Blanco
SISVAH	Melvin Molina Herra
UCR, Escuela de Geografía	Francisco Solano Mata
UCR, CIGEFI	Javier Soley Alfaro
UNA-ECG	Timothy Robinson
UNA-TELESIG	Jorge Fallas Gamboa Wilfredo Segura López Carlos Madriz Vargas Henry Chaves Klel

Contributors

Jeffery S. Allen is the Research Coordinator at the Strom Thurmond Institute of Government and Public Affairs at Clemson University, Clemson, South Carolina.

Joseph A. Bishop is a Ph.D. candidate in ecology at Pennsylvania State University, State College, Pennsylvania.

G. Wesley Burnett is a professor at Clemson University, Clemson, South Carolina, in the Department of History/Geography and the Department of Parks, Recreation, and Tourism Management.

Margaret H. Carr is an assistant professor in the Department of Landscape Architecture at the University of Florida, Gainesville.

Jorge Fallas is a professor in the Regional Wildlife Management Program for Mesoamerica and the Caribbean (PRMVS) at Universidad Nacional, Heredia, Costa Rica.

Thomas E. Lacher Jr. is Professor and Caesar Kleberg Chair in Wildlife Ecology and Fisheries Sciences at Texas A&M University, College Station, Texas.

J. David Lambert is a Research Manager at the University of Florida Geoplan Center and is a Ph.D. candidate in Urban and Regional Planning at the University of Florida, Gainesville.

Grégoire Leclerc has a Master of Science degree in Radiobiology and a Ph.D. in Physics from Sherbrooke University, Canada. He completed a postdoctoral fellowship with the Centre d'Applications et de Recherches en Télédétection (CARTEL) in the Centro Agronómico Tropical de Investigación y Enseñanza (CATIE) in Costa Rica. He is now Senior Research Fellow working in the GIS facility of the International Center for Tropical Agriculture (CIAT) in Cali, Colombia.

Wilfredo Segura López received his Master of Science degree at the Regional Wildlife Management Program for Mesoamerica and the Caribbean (PRMVS) at Universidad Nacional, Heredia, Costa Rica.

Michael McCoy is a professor in the Regional Wildlife Management Program for Mesoamerica and the Caribbean (PRMVS) at Universidad Nacional, Heredia, Costa Rica.

Jennifer N. Morgan received a Bachelor of Science degree in Aquaculture, Fisheries, and Wildlife at Clemson University, Clemson, South Carolina, and is currently working toward a Master of Science degree in Forest Resources at the University of Georgia, Athens.

Johnny Rodriguez Chacón has a Bachelor of Engineering degree in Tropical Forestry from Universidad Nacional, Heredia, Costa Rica. He has been in charge of the GIS facility of the Fundación para el Desarrollo de la Cordillera Volcanica Central (FUNDECOR) since 1993.

G. Arturo Sánchez-Azofeifa is an associate research professor at the Research Center on Sustainable Development (CIEDES) at the University of Costa Rica, San José.

Basil G. Savitsky is an assistant professor in the Graduate School of Geography at Clark University in Worcester, Massachusetts, and Coordinator of the Master's Program in GIS and International Development.

Christopher Vaughan is a professor in the Regional Wildlife Management Program for Mesoamerica and the Caribbean (PRMVS) at Universidad Nacional, Heredia, Costa Rica.

Elizabeth A. Wentz is an assistant professor in geography at Arizona State University in Tempe.

Index